17.00

V
8

COMMUNITY
NORMALITY
& DIFFERENCE
MEETING SPECIAL NEEDS

AUP Titles of Related Interest

ANXIETY AND THE DYNAMICS OF COLLABORATION
Paul Pengelly and Douglas Woodhouse

CONSULTATION IN RESIDENTIAL CARE
Children in Residential Establishments
edited by W R Silveira

CHILDREN NEED GROUPS
R Silveira and G Trafford

CARE OF THE ELDERLY
D J Hunter, N McKeganey and I MacPherson

DEPRIVATION AND HEALTH IN SCOTLAND
V Carstairs and R Morris

COMMUNITY NORMALITY & DIFFERENCE

MEETING SPECIAL NEEDS

EDITED BY

S R Baron & J D Haldane

ABERDEEN UNIVERSITY PRESS
Member of Maxwell Macmillan Publishing Corporation

First published 1992
Aberdeen University Press
© S R Baron and J D Haldane 1992

British Library Cataloguing in Publication Data
A catalogue record for this book
is available from the British Library

ISBN 0 08 041400 1

Typeset by Hewer Text Composition Services
Printed by Athenaeum Press Ltd

Contents

List of Contributors

Stephen Baron is a Lecturer in Sociology and Social Policy and Warden of Murray Hall at the University of Stirling.

Judith Brearley is a Senior Lecturer in Social Work at the University of Edinburgh.

Nils Christie is Professor of Criminology at the University of Oslo.

Chris Cullen is Professor of Learning Difficulties at the University of St. Andrews.

Graeme Farquharson is Director of Peper Harow, Godalming.

W. I. Fraser is Professor of Mental Handicap at the University of Wales Medical School, Ely Hospital, Cardiff.

Mike Hailey is a co-worker at The Mount Community, Wadhurst.

Douglas Haldane is a Psychotherapist and Consultant in St. Andrews.

Andrew Jahoda is a Psychologist with Solihull Health Authority.

Ivana Markova is Professor of Psychology at the University of Stirling.

D. W. Millard is a Lecturer in Applied Social Studies and Fellow of Green College, University of Oxford.

Stephen Sands is a co-worker at Heimsonderschule Föhrenbühl, Heiligenberg-Steigen, Germany.

Stuart Whiteley is a Consultant Psychotherapist, Organisational Analyst and Secretary of the International Association of Group Psychotherapy.

James Whyte is Emeritus Professor of Practical Theology and Christian Ethics at the University of St. Andrews and former Moderator of the General Assembly of the Church of Scotland.

Preface

Stephen Baron and Douglas Haldane

This book is a record of work occasioned by the fiftieth anniversary of the founding, in 1940 in Aberdeenshire, Scotland, of the Camphill Movement. In the United Kingdom this is one of the largest groups of communities caring for children, young people, adults and the elderly who have special needs: some 1550 persons in 32 different communities. Internationally, the network of Camphill Communities now extends to 17 countries.

Several years before this anniversary was due, a small group consisting of Camphill co-workers and persons like ourselves who were in some way associated with the work of the Communities, thought of two ways of celebrating this event: a Festschrift in the form of critical evaluations of the work of Camphill, written by professional personnel such as psychologists, social workers, psychiatrists, who had sought the help of Camphill in the continuing care of their pupils, clients, patients; and a conference, bringing together such professionals and Camphill co-workers. We saw such activities as celebrating an achievement, assessing the Camphill experience in the context of other kinds of therapeutic community and in the wider context of other forms of care. They offered an opportunity for reflection and review of the past, together with the challenge of anticipating needs to be met in the development of services.

Our discussions took place in the context of major, indeed revolutionary, changes in the administration, financing, organisation and monitoring, of all services for those with special needs. At the same time, at least in the Camphill Communities in Scotland (which were those of which we had most direct experience) significant changes were taking place, some accompanied by evident turbulence. There had been an expansion of provisions and resources; some of the Communities had radically re-organised their relationships to each other in terms of funding and financial resources; the governance of the Schools in Aberdeen had undergone a change, moving away from a paternalistic authority dynamic to a more collegiate functioning; the doctors serving the Schools and other

Communities near them were reviewing the nature, aims and organisation of their work.

Recurring themes in our discussions were the nature and meaning of community, the relevance of this for therapy, how best to make provisions for those with special needs, taking account of individuals, not only of groups or categories. A particular debate was about the place of residential institutions within a nationally organised scheme based on new legislation, central government regulation and local authority control, which seeks to give priority to 'care in the community'.

Eventually we decided to organise a residential working conference on the concepts of *Community, Therapy* and *the Individual with Special Needs* which would be hosted by, but not be primarily concerned with, the Camphill Communities. All participants would be staff from a range of agencies and disciplines, including co-workers from a number of Camphill Communities, but none would be 'representing' their agencies and disciplines. They would be asked to share preparation for the conference by studying a series of working papers which we planned to commission.

Our own contribution to the organisation of the conference and preparation of this book arises out of a long-term association with the Camphill Movement. One of us is a sociologist with an interest in the common, often conflicting ground between the State and voluntary provision for those with special needs; the other is a psychiatrist, in practice as a psychotherapist, concerned about provision of services and development of organisations. During the past decade, we have been increasingly active 'participant observers' involved in a consultant capacity to several of the Camphill Communities in Scotland; engaged with them in a range of discussions and negotiations with other agencies and authorities; active in seeking to promote transactions between Camphill and other systems, while having our homes and main professional work elsewhere.

The Scottish Neighbourhood of the Camphill Movement at an early stage agreed to fund the whole process of planning, conference organisation and preparation of a book for publication; and the Camphill Schools offered to host the conference. It will therefore be not surprising that, apart from the chapters by Sands and Hailey which specifically describe Camphill philosophy and experience, we should choose in several chapters to use the experience of Camphill Communities to exemplify current debates, arguments and conflicts in relation to the care, education and treatment of those with special needs. We believe that these Communities, characterised by particular philosophies and practices, nevertheless are sufficiently similar to many other residential institutions and to other voluntary agencies to be used to illustrate problems which apply to others and which are of acute and *general* contemporary concern. So while this book is not, after all, a Festschrift for the work of the Camphill Communities, it is one product of their generosity of spirit in allowing critical commentary on their experience to form a significant part of a wider exploration.

Part 1

Introduction to Part 1

The chapters which constitute Part 1 of this book were prepared with several aims in mind: they were to be working papers for a conference, the preparatory material, the stimulus for discussion which would be available to all participants; they were to be position papers, in which the authors would be invited critically to explore and comment on aspects of what had been identified as the central themes; they were to be raw material for the commentaries presented at the conference (Part 2 of this book); and they were, we hoped, the chapters of a book.

All the authors were sent an outline of the proposed book and of each working paper and each was given a brief for their particular contribution. While a fairly tight editorial policy was intimated, and some negotiation was undertaken, decisions about structure and content were primarily the responsibility of the authors and their versions of the working papers were what were circulated for the participants before the conference.

Once an agreement was reached about publishing, it was apparent that a number of the working papers would need to be reduced in length. It is these modified versions which constitute Part 1 of the book.

CHAPTER 1

Community, Therapy and the Individual with Special Needs: A Framework

Stephen Baron and Douglas Haldane

The passing of the *National Health Service and Community Care Act* 1990 heralds changes in the care of those with special needs potentially as epoch-making as those of the Great Confinement of two centuries' ago which initiated the incarceration of large populations into 'institutions'. So comes to a fruition a process of de-institutionalisation which has been in train for at least 30 years since Enoch Powell, as Minister of Health, announced the intention to transfer psychiatric services from their base in mental hospitals into 'the community' – a term not defined and capable of a variety of interpretations. Since 1963 this model has spread from the psychiatric services to virtually all forms of welfare provision. Today we are in a period of striking certainties about the value of community care, still strangely combined with silences and absences about the details of what care in the community means, and how it is to operate for the benefit of those with special needs. In the political and administrative turbulence which characterises the preparation for instituting the new system by April 1993 the debate has, understandably, and in many senses properly, revolved around questions of timetables and resources. In this chapter, and in commissioning the other chapters of the book, we have stepped back from these immediate issues in order to ask some of the prior questions about care and the community. In doing this we have been influenced by shared personal interpretations of the field: that the move to care in the community is being undertaken without the requisite groundwork in the critical scrutiny of the theories, the proposed models of care in the community, and of their posited efficacy; and that there has been an overhasty rejection of *all* forms of 'not-Community Care'.

A clue to this lack of clarity is given by the tortured and torturous state of our language for talking about those who, to step outside contemporary uncertainties and return to an older, more forthright, Lancastrian common-

3

sense, are 'not quite right'. These linguistic issues are the main focus of the chapters by Markova and Jahoda and by Christie, as well as providing a continuo for other chapters. Writing about the area of 'special needs' currently is to steer between the Scylla of using terms with derogatory implications and the Charybdis of tortured grammar and euphemism. In order to capture something of this linguistic flux, and the social realities to which it relates, we asked the authors all to address three key concepts: *community*, *therapy* and *the individual with special needs*. These three concepts allow us to bring together:

◦persons who are defined as being cognitively deficient in some respect, a difference which is held to affect wider aspects of their being;

◦those persons in therapeutic types of relationship which aim to transform them towards the normal, the ordinary, the healthy;

◦those persons and those relationships as embedded in a wider field of social relations which may foster, block or transform therapeutic intentions and actions.

Questions of community, the formation of communities, changes in communities, the loss of community, have provided an increasing staple for Western intellectual life for at least two centuries, yet there is little agreement over the meaning of the term. Hillery's classic paper, now over 30 years old, found 94 then extant definitions of the term in the sociological literature (Hillery, 1955). While this diversity could simply be an index to a lack of conceptual clarity (amongst sociologists if not others) it would be difficult to account for the effectivity of the word if this were the case; such potent social effects as the use of the word 'community' creates are based on more than confusion.

A more fruitful approach to definition perhaps is that of Raymond Williams, who analyses the history of the term 'community' as one of the "Keywords" in the development of 'culture and society'. For Williams 'community' is unique amongst terms for social organisation in that it has no positively evaluated opposite; it is a "warmly persuasive word" (Williams, 1976, p.66) which seems never to be used unfavourably. This remarkable quality is further defined by Williams in his *The Country and The City* where he traces, through the imagery of the urban and the rural, the perpetual leitmotif of the experienced, ever recent, loss of an organic, whole way of life. The continuity of this theme in literature Williams traces from Hardy's novels back to Hesiod's *Work and Days* in the ninth century BC (Williams, 1975). 'Community' is a central part of this Golden Age myth which Williams so brilliantly demolishes in *The Country and The City*: the continuous construction of an idyllic past of plenty and social harmony which acts as an immanent critique of contemporary social relations. Central to this imagery is the contrast which Tönnies formalised in the late nineteenth century between 'community' (Gemeinschaft) and 'association' (Gesell-schaft), the former being characterised by integrative and expressive relationships, the latter by fragmentary and instrumental relationships

(Tönnies, 1955). The chapter by Whyte takes the definition of a healthy 'community' as its central theme while Sands focuses on the re-creation of 'community' with and through those with special needs.

'Community' is not simply mythical; indeed it derives much of its persuasive power from having real referents in social experience, in empirical social groups. When care is being attributed to 'the community' to whom does this refer? On this point current policy is remarkably silent. We can learn a little about the role of the family from documents such as the Audit Commission's Report, *Making a Reality of Community Care* (Audit Commission, 1986) and the White Paper, *Caring for People* (HMSO, 1989a), how this has, apart from the aberrant period of the Great Confinement, been the historical locus of care of those in need and how this is being restored as *a*, if not *the*, major site of care for those with special needs. We can learn little from such sources about the social contexts in which these families are expected to operate except that those with special needs will be integrated into 'the community'.

The 'integration' of those with special needs into 'the community' is one of the key themes of the policy of decarceration, a theme heavily redolent of the crisis of educational policies towards ethnic minorities in the late 1960s and early 1970s when hopes of 'assimilation' (the elimination of difference) turned to hopes for 'integration', the (grudging) pluralist acceptance of difference and hope for social peace. The parallels between the two discourses are striking: both blacks and those with special needs look different (from . . .), have communication systems which are different (from . . .), behave in ways which are different (from . . .) and challenging (to . . .); both appear to fail (in . . .) and are subjected to routine denigration. The consequences of both deliberate State policy and of informal popular culture towards blacks in this period (and beyond) in the creation of circumscribed areas of residence ('ghettos'); in offering 'opportunities' which were, in reality, closed (structural social mobility); in treating minority culture as pathology (-linguistic deprivation and the black family form); in marginalising minority groups from sources of social power (in the 'institutions') and, thereby, in fostering militant resistance (Black Power), have been dramatically demonstrated in the 1980s. Despite these parallels key questions remain unaddressed: should policies towards those with special needs be assimilationist or integrationist; are our assumptions of 'difference' an active component of the problem; do policies of formal equality actually reproduce inequality; do policies of integration actually marginalise; is militant resistance by those with special needs to be expected; if not, why not? Christie's chapter begins to pose some of these currently unspeakable questions by arguing in defence of the *self-made* ghetto.

Residential location is a fundamental process of social differentiation in our current society and depressingly repetitive media reports, as well as judicial decisions, suggest that the unitary inflection of 'the community' is quite false. Given a proposal to locate people with special needs in 'the community', the community rapidly fragments into hostile groups, each defending their own location from invasion. With the class-based nature of the housing markets, care in 'the community' can thus become care in those locations with least power to resist; a form of *enforced* ghettoisation.

'Community' has developed a specifically policy-related application in the past two decades. Many existing State institutions and practices have had 'community' added to their titles, 'community schools' and 'community policing' being two major examples. Further, new State practices have been developed which carry the 'community' label, particularly 'community development'. While at one level this may seem no more than the addition of a warm persuasive glow to possibly unpopular institutions, the specific location of such practices suggests more. In this period community schools developed in areas where hostility to State education was at its strongest, community policing where racial tensions were at their highest, community development where the restructuring of capital was at its most destructive. In this usage 'community' was something of a metaphor for areas of perceived social crisis.

This metaphor was, and is, powerfully consequential in allowing new forms of State organisation to develop which are altogether more intrusive in their detailed surveillance and control of everyday lives in such areas of 'crisis' (Cockburn, 1977; Baron, 1988, 1989). Community schools sought to intervene in family lives and childrearing practices on an expanded scale; community policing heralded more intensive intelligence gathering and collation systems; community development the detailed management of redevelopment on a mass scale. The logic of 'care in the community' in terms of its development of increased State intervention into previously relatively 'private' areas of social life, is explored in the chapter by Baron.

A further usage of the term 'community' for current purposes is its delimitation of specific small social groups with a primary purpose of care for those with special needs, the therapeutic communities. Developing largely during and after the 1939–1945 War, these may be distinguished from other forms of collective care by the emphasis on the community as a therapeutic process in itself rather than simply as the site of some other process of therapy (Hinshelwood & Manning, 1979; Kennard & Roberts, 1983; Manning, 1989). The nature of such communities is outlined in the chapter by Whiteley while the nature of the Camphill Communities is explored by Hailey in his chapter.

Such separated communities are currently facing fundamental challenges on a number of fronts. One internal dynamic is that of generational change, as the people who helped preach the original crusade retire, with leadership passing to second or third generation staff; these are the processes of charisma and routinisation which Manning analyses (Manning, 1989). Closely allied with this process in some cases are the dynamics of expansion. The provision pioneered in therapeutic communities has often identified previously unmet needs/potentials resulting in a rapid increase in 'demand'

and the consequent, often problematic, dynamics of expansion and identity maintenance, of innovation and stability, and even of unity and schism. Such dynamics are explored in the chapters by Brearley and Farquharson.

The move to 'community care' poses fundamental challenges for therapeutic communities (and vice versa) in the positing, by others, of such separateness as provision only of the last resort. This is threatening the continued existence of some communities. It is also likely to amplify current changes in referral practices for many communities whereby admissions, previously of people with a broad cross section of difficulties, are increasingly of people with a narrow range of difficulties, usually those for whom no other placement can be found. How therapeutic communities can operate in this changed political and organisational context is discussed in the chapter by Millard.

The juxtaposition of 'community' with 'therapy' raises important issues for the programme of community care. Whereas in therapeutic communities there are clear conceptions of how the 'community' is to operate in a 'therapeutic' manner, the same cannot be said of the move to community care. It is clear that 'the community' is to be more than simply the *site* of care, that it is, in itself, to provide a dynamic for care and therapy. What is not clear in the thinking are questions of the preconditions in 'the community' for therapy to be possible and the processes by which 'the community' is to operate therapeutically. Such issues are addressed in the chapters by Whyte and Sands.

A final usage of 'community' for current purposes is its denotation of communality, of shared life situations, irrespective of geographic location. In the move to care in 'the community' the communality of those with special needs has been little considered and, in this, the policy of community care is no different from most other fields of thought. Two major poles may be defined in this context: an often religious concept of a community of suffering, and a materialist concept of a community of interest. In between these poles there are various positions which define the sharedness of handicap. The policy of community care is radically atomistic, revolving around an increased 'clientness', e.g. the assessment of individual needs, the provision of individual care 'packages'. Whether, and how, a communality of special needs should be maintained in the new context are issues addressed by Christie in his chapter.

Whereas 'community' is a term which has always been fraught with difficulties, 'therapy' is a term which has become significantly more problematic in recent years; indeed some now argue that it should be replaced by 'healing' to signify a more spontaneous, natural and self-originating process of self modification. 'Therapy' as a concept, on the other hand, signifies a sharper definition of pathology and an active, external intervention to negate this, both overwhelmingly under the control of another, the therapist. Both of these components of 'therapy' are being increasingly challenged. Fraser's chapter analyses the current state of the training of 'professionals' and, finding it wanting, outlines striking proposals for improvement.

The attempts to change our language of special needs to less negative forms, to emphasise the 'rights' of those with special needs, especially the right to be 'normal', and to stress a social model of handicap, all contain the perhaps irresoluble tension between emphasising the existing dignity-normality-completeness of the individual *with* their special needs, and the requirements of 'social role valorisation' for a super-conformity to norms. Such super-conformity is to be achieved through the systematic reform of precisely those 'special' characteristics. Cullen's chapter contains a radical vision of how this project can be achieved.

While therapy was dominated by a mechanistic medical model it was relatively straightforward to define the principles of diagnosis and treatment and to evaluate the outcomes of therapy. 'Normalisation' with this contradictory core makes the establishment of such process and outcome criteria very difficult, perhaps arbitrary. With an increased emphasis on 'quality of care', and on tight cost accounting, the relationship, in terms of evaluation, between different models of care, operating according to different principles and aiming for different outcomes, is of vital importance. These issues are explored in the chapter by Baron and in the final chapter while Christie further considers his conception of those with special needs as being *extra*ordinary (Christie, 1989).

Professional roles have been thrown into some confusion by these changes in theory, policy and practice. At one level this is signified by the decline in the dominance of the doctor in dealing with those with special needs (as in wider areas of social life) and the rise, perhaps to dominance, of the social worker. More fundamentally the very status of being a 'professional' has recently been under attack both from a free market position (as a sophisticated restrictive practice) and from radical democratic positions (as constituting a major means of authoritarian social control). The meaning of being a 'professional' was a constant reference theme in the Conference and is discussed in the penultimate chapter by Haldane and Baron.

The third of our terms, the individual with special needs, we have adopted, in all its ambiguity, as the current dominant term in the field(s). It is a premise of such widely different traditions of social research as phenomenological attribution theory, structuralist Marxism and post-structuralist discourse analysis that the way in which we construe, label and thereby approach the individual is consequential. Such consequences lie not only in terms of our perceptions of the individual but also in terms of that person's self concept and the real social relations which they are able to form. How to identify and name those with special needs, how to describe them as special and therefore different, without using names which are demeaning and negatively discriminatory in a real way, has been a matter of concern for over 30 years.

'Mental deficiency' gave way to 'mental handicap' and eventually to the use of the term 'special needs', a term which puts emphasis on the average or normal or better endowed to take responsibility for providing responses to those special needs, which of course require to be defined and categorised if these responses are to be specific and particular, not vague and global.

But there are still those who think that any kind of categorisation is of itself a process of inappropriate labelling, not defining or classifying someone's state, or functioning, or needs, but confining them in ways which are constrictive to freedom, dignity and development. For many, great efforts must be made to find definitive terms which are in some way neutral, unattached to particular constructs about difficulties or needs. Those who work in any way with persons who have special needs, physical, emotional or cognitive, must work delicately, so as not to risk offence and real denigration.

While the care and welfare of the mentally and physically handicapped was undertaken primarily within hospitals, and within the framework of a range of medical models, such people were called patients. Within residential communities they may variously be described as pupils, trainees, students, which emphasises their role as learners; or as villagers, which equates them with those who live in what might be called villages in the community. As care has become more the responsibility of local authority social services they have become clients. To an increasing extent they are becoming customers – people like everyone else, with a right to ask for or expect services and to pay for them, for whom 'products' are supplied and costed. While the suppliers of commercial products must pay adequate attention to what the customer wants, as well as what they might need, scant attention has been paid to the views of those thought to have special needs by those now charged with providing services in the community. One must be careful and tentative in the use of descriptive terms and constantly alert to ensure the rights of those who have handicaps; but many who have responsibility for developing the provision of care in the community are assertive about the terms which ought to be used and confident about what those with handicaps must be *given* to ensure that their needs are met. Informed consent is a principle increasingly appreciated as central in the provision of medical care and treatment: its application to the world and lives of the handicapped, those in some way comparatively restricted in their potential, has so far been minimal. The unilateral nature of this model is taken up in the chapters by Baron, by Sands and by Haldane and Baron, where arguments are developed about more reciprocal possibilities in which those with special needs are seen to offer as much as they are to receive, both in terms of inter-personal relations and in terms of the development of societies as a whole.

So far we have discussed the issues of construing persons with special needs in terms of those professionally involved in their care. There is however a further, and in many sense more important, arena of labelling, the community itself. If the aspiration of policy is the integration (or, perhaps, the assimilation) of those with special needs into communities, then their construction in popular culture is absolutely critical. Apart from the posited creation of those with special needs as super-normal through a process of normalisation, the policy of community care is silent on this matter; how those with special needs are to become valued members of the community, even matters of 'public education', are not addressed, and examples of practice suggest little thought and even less success. Markova and Jahoda in their chapter address the conditions necessary for such changes.

Questions of popular culture are matters not of free-floating perceptions but of defining the meanings of people in their everyday social relations. The unilateral emphasis of the normalisation model in which the person with special needs is construed as an essentially passive consumer, of services, of rights, inhibits the development of the other major component of a full social role, the person as producer, as the bearer of duties. How a fully reciprocal social role for those with special needs may be fostered, and thereby perceptions altered, are questions which it is most appropriate to raise in the context of the fiftieth anniversary celebrations of the Camphill Communities as, in these communities, such models have been consistently developed.

The path of developing these models has not been easy. The unorthodox philosophy and the community approach of the Camphill Movement to the care of those with special needs has constantly raised the immensely practical question of how to maintain the identity and integrity of the project while conducting transactions with more mainstream agencies and meeting the demands of State regulation. In the past ten years these issues have been posed in sharply different ways as the tempo of reform and the extension of State regulation have increased. How to balance the demands of the emerging contractor-client model of care, and of the increasingly detailed focus of State regulation, with the essentials of therapy conducted according to quite different logics, are questions not restricted to the Camphill Communities and are delineated in the chapter by Baron.

The past decade, the period of our closest engagement with the Camphill Communities, has been a period of some expansion and development but also one of consolidation. It has also been characterised by the constant need to adapt to changing expectations, opportunities and constraints. In the internal dynamics of generational change the Camphill Communities share much with other therapeutic communities in their trajectories. How theories can be reformulated, organisational changes negotiated, and therapeutic roles recast, while maintaining essential continuity, are issues addressed by Brearley in her chapter. How such groups as the Camphill Communities can enter into productive dialogue with forms of provision different from their own, and with regulatory authorities, while maintaining necessary boundaries and integrity is explored in the final chapter.

One vital feature of these communities is that the learning and training of co-workers, what in other settings might be called their professional development, as well as the kind of persons-in-relationship they become, takes place almost exclusively within the institutions, ethos, discipline and fellowship of the Camphill Movement. Such a process contributes to the feeling of community and to a sense of strength and confidence. All such communities however are in danger of becoming self-perpetuating, closed systems, at risk of becoming too distanced from, or even irrelevant to the needs of the wider society of which they are part. As social care becomes increasingly professionalised the competing demands of standardisation and of training appropriate to a diversity of provision remain to be resolved, despite the advent of training consortia, the Diploma in Social Work, N.C.V.Q and SCOTVEC qualifications and the publication of the Parker proposals. Here Fraser's chapter contains important proposals about the place of the work of communities such as the Camphill Communities in the training system as a whole, while the strategies available to organisations such as Camphill for dealing with such external demands are explored in the final chapter.

The recent expansion of the Camphill Movement is often seen as discordant with current policies of a move from residential institution to life in the community for those with special needs. The same agencies, sometimes the same individuals, who enthusiastically seek placements for their clients in Camphill can be vehement in their view that the Camphill Communities should be disbanded and their residents dispersed to houses in 'the community'. In these criticisms there appears sometimes a conflict of attitude that Camphill residents are both inappropriately privileged yet denied their rights to normality. The contradictory structural pressures within the State which lead to such incompatible judgments are explored in the chapter by Baron.

One particular response to these issues by some Communities in Scotland is to have imported into their settings consultants who share common ground in their long-term knowledge of and interest in the work of the Camphill Movement, but otherwise are different in profession, experience, training and the organisational contexts in which they have worked. While not all co-workers have approved of their presence or of what they do, they have been encouraged to be involved in a wide range of activities: administration and organisation, the training and practice of co-workers, work with children, adolescents and young adults. Some of this work has involved direct teaching, or regular supervision, or offering advice, or making recommendations. More important in the development of work over time has been a collaborative effort between consultants and co-workers (individually or in small groups) to identify and clarify problems being encountered, to find ways to their resolution and to learn from this process. It was in this spirit of the full exchange of cognate but different experiences that the Conference was organised, the participants invited and this book produced.

CHAPTER 2

The Language of Special Needs

Ivana Markova and Andrew Jahoda

Why is the Earth called 'Earth'?

Individuals are born into the world of language, a collective product of people passed on from generation to generation. Just as with other human activities, once language is acquired by an individual it becomes more or less automatised in daily discourse and used without constant mental monitoring. In unreflective naming and labelling of events and people, one becomes desensitised to the actual meaning of what one says and to the impact of that meaning on those who have been so labelled. As Goffman (1963) points out, words such as 'cripple', 'bastard' or 'moron' are used in daily discourse as metaphors or imagery without much thought as to how they may affect those to whom they refer.

Moreover, there appears, in daily discourse, to be a childlike belief in a causal relationship between words and the properties of the objects they identify. As Vygotsky (1986) pointed out, preschool children explain the names of objects by their properties. For example, experiments have shown that, according to the logic of a preschool child, "a cow is called 'cow' because it has horns". However, even in the popular culture of the adult world a similar logic applies. Vygotsky referred to an anecdote according to which a layperson, having heard a conversation between the students of astronomy, expressed his difficulty in comprehending one problem as follows: "I understand that by means of different instruments it has been possible to measure the distance from the Earth to the most remote stars and to describe their position and motion. But I do not understand how it has been possible to discover the names of stars". According to this way of thinking there appears to be a deep rooted assumption of a direct relationship between the properties of an object – or of a person – and its name or a label attached to it. By calling something or someone by a certain word one defines that object's or that person's identity and therefore its place in the world. Being called or labelled in a particular way means that the

12

labelled object or person evokes certain types of responses from those of others. The association between names and objects is so strong in popular cultures that calling something by a particular name can determine the very fate of that thing. In her *Purity and Danger* Douglas (1966) maintains that certain kinds of images are never spelled out in language for people's fear that the very words might bring about the calamity to which they refer. Similarly, Sontag (1979) refers to the names of diseases as having a magic power over people:

> In Stendhal's *Armance* (1827), the hero's mother refuses to say 'tuberculosis', for fear that pronouncing the word will hasten the course of her son's malady. And Karl Menninger has observed (in *The Vital Balance*) that 'the very word "cancer" is said to kill some patients who would not have succumbed (so quickly) to the malignancy from which they suffer'. (Sontag, 1979, p.10)

By token of the same logic there is a wide-spread belief that by naming a thing or person differently, the assumed properties of that thing or person will also be changed. In the field of the language of special needs we have recently witnessed considerable efforts to move away from such terms as 'idiot', 'imbecile', 'mongol', 'mental retardation', 'retardates', 'mental handicap', and to substitute for them such terms as 'learning difficulties' and 'special needs'. Following the way of thinking in popular logic, to say that a person is 'mentally handicapped' suggests that the person displays definite or obvious characteristics which allow others to distinguish him or her from the non-handicapped. In other words, to label someone as 'mentally handicapped' implies that mental handicap lies simply within the individual.

The assumption that mental handicap lies within the individual has recently been severely criticised by many (cf. e.g. Mercer, 1973). It has been argued, instead, that the individual is handicapped in so far as he or she lacks the intellectual capacities to meet the demands which society places on him or her. As Serpell (1982) comments, "an intellectual handicap can only be understood in relation to a set of cultural norms" (Serpell, 1982, p.1). The attempts to change the terminology concerning mental handicap, therefore, clearly reflect the awareness of the cultural boundedness of labelling and the effort to dissociate people with special needs from the denigrating characteristics that had been built into the meanings of discarded terms through societal values, attitudes and representations. But such changes in terminology would be fruitless if they were not accompanied by implicit and explicit changes in societal values and representations of mental handicap. The changes in labels and names would only be temporary because the new terms would quickly acquire the meaning of the discarded terms and the re-naming could start all over again.

In this chapter we want to draw particular attention to the relationship between the language of special needs and the underlying social attitudes, values and representations. It is not labelling as such that is damaging to the labelled but the underlying attitudes and behaviours, whether expressed explicitly or implicitly, of those who use such labels. The main problem with these underlying social attitudes and representations is that they are rarely verbalised, indeed their owners are often unaware of their existence. It is because they are implicit and difficult to identify that they are immune to change. Yet it is mainly through these implicit social attitudes and representations that people with special needs are treated as inferior citizens. Since these implicit meanings are so difficult to identify one can say that they live a life of their own and that the less aware people are of them the greater their influence (Moscovici, 1984).

The Labelling and Categorisation of People with Special Needs in an Historical Context

The term 'idiot' came originally from the Greek words 'idiotas', i.e. a private person, and 'idios', i.e. peculiar. These terms therefore did not simply refer to a person who had a lack of understanding, but they also meant that such a person was set apart from others because he or she was unable to participate in communication. Thus, these terms also reflected the social consequences of the person's handicap. From antiquity those labelled as 'idiots' were despised, persecuted and even killed (Barr, 1904). Even Calvin and Luther denounced them as devil's changelings and recommended killing them (Haffter, 1968). It was thought that idiocy of children was a punishment for the parents' sin. However, information concerning the position of people with special needs before the nineteenth century is a patchy and confused affair (Ryan & Thomas, 1987).

Educational reform

The specialist services for people with special needs which arose in the last two centuries took the form of institutions. The common threads which led to the growth of institutions for people with special needs cannot be understood by sole reference to this group. The institutional movement reflected the enormous upheaval of society caused by the industrial revolution. It is not accidental that institutions were built, not only for people with learning difficulties, but also for the old, the sick, the poor, law-breakers and people who were mentally ill, and sometimes a combination of these (Foucault, 1977; Ryan & Thomas, 1987; Scull, 1977). However, the humanitarian endeavours of these early institutions in the nineteenth century for people with special needs were unique in their aims to be educational establishments. The pioneering work of Itard and his fellow Frenchman Sequin, in the educational sphere, gave credence to the possibility of reducing the handicaps of people previously considered ineducable before returning them to society. To these ends the educationalists of the nineteenth century pioneered a range of educational techniques and philosophies which might be considered progressive by today's standards. These services in turn brought new terminology and classifications of people with special needs, expressing and defining not only the status of the individual in terms of grades of mental defect, but also indicating methods of training and future possibilities for such an individual. As the purpose was to train people to live in the community (Lazerson, 1975), the education was also moral. People should be good citizens.

At the beginning of the twentieth century Barr (1904, p.90) identified five main classes of people with special needs: idiots and idio-imbeciles, requiring asylum care; moral imbeciles, requiring custodial life and permanent guardianship; imbeciles, requiring long apprenticeship and colony life under protection; and the backward or mentally feeble, who could be trained for a place in the world. Moral imbeciles and imbeciles were further subdivided into low grade, middle grade and high grade and these subdivisions are still used by hospital staff today.

Moral degeneracy

The concern with morality set the stage for a change of emphasis from the protection of people with a mental handicap to the protection of society from those with mental handicap. Despite the fact that the benevolence of many of the early institutions was prompted by Christian principles, others believed that the behaviour of people with mental handicap represented a regression back to a more 'primitive' state of a human being as a result of divine punishment for their parents' immoral behaviour (Ryan & Thomas, 1987). Thus, in a popular culture, the concept of mental handicap as a form of moral degeneracy had already been mooted. The category of 'moral imbecile' was introduced in Barr's above (1904) classification. The term 'moral imbecile' included those ranging from "low grade: . . . temperament bestial . . . [to] high grade: . . . with a genius for evil" (Barr, 1904, p.90). Towards the end of the nineteenth century, the application of simplistic theories of inheritance reinforced fears that people with mental handicap represented a throwback to a more primitive state. An illustration of these beliefs was calling people with Down's Syndrome 'mongols'. This was because their distinctive features were thought to represent a regression to a mongolian race.

The alarmist projections of the eugenics movement led to a fear that people with a mild mental handicap would undermine the fabric of society because they were thought to be the most morally degenerate. As Barr wrote of a physician in charge of a large mental handicap hospital early this century:

> The recognition of the moral imbecile [people with mild mental handicaps], and the absolute necessity of a life long guardianship, protection against temptation and all the horrors of criminal procedure, were long and strenuously insisted

upon by Dr. Kerlin in the name of science, of sociology, as a matter of political economy, of the protection of homes, and all that man holds dear. (Barr, 1904, p.68)

Begab (1975) commented that people with a more severe mental handicap continued to be perceived as pitiful for longer than those with a mild mental handicap. However, by the turn of the century people with more severe mental handicap were considered as part of the same wider social evil. As Barr commented:

> The protection which society demands and needs to be advised of is, first from the burden of the untrainable idiot both in the homes and training schools and also in the schools for the other kind of defectives, i.e. those for the blind and deaf and mute; second from the disadvantage resulting from those intermingling in the schools of normal with backward children; third from mischief which whether trained or untrained the irresponsible imbecile is likely to perpetrate if unguarded; still more from the tragedies certain to be enacted by the moral imbecile, and above all else, protection from an increase of an evil growth which if unchecked is inevitable. (Barr, 1904, p.89)

I.Q. tests

The early twentieth century also marked the development of I.Q. tests, designed to separate those requiring special schooling from those who were to enter mainstream education. Unlike the innovative nineteenth-century educational developments for people with severe mental handicap, there was apparently little that was 'special' about education for people with mild mental handicaps. The aim was to provide a vocational training for people with mild mental handicaps and prevent ordinary children from being held back (Lazerson, 1975; Ryan & Thomas, 1987). This original aim was characterised by Binet's (1905) attempt to identify the employment status of a group of ex-special school pupils. Studies carried out using I.Q. tests in the first three decades of this century bolstered the views expounded by the eugenics movement. People from ethnic minorities, the deprived and the poor, all performed badly on I.Q. tests (Begab, 1975; Lazerson, 1975; Ryan & Thomas, 1987). The belief grew that I.Q. tests measured a genetically endowed level of intelligence which could not be improved.

On the whole, such simple hereditary theories have since been discounted, along with the view that people with mental handicap are immoral or a threat to society. I.Q. tests are now regarded as culture-bound measures and intelligence is not viewed as a fixed trait (Mittler, 1979). However, there is still a range of attitudes and myths which are held by the public and by professionals which derive from fears widely held at the turn of the century. For instance, fears of promiscuity and sexual deviance of people with a mental handicap, which still exist in some quarters today, derive from the alarmist days of the eugenics movement (Ellwood, 1981).

The use of tests of intelligence and their particular interpretation leads to yet another misleading view of people with a mental handicap. Since psychological tests assign a particular mental age to people with mental handicap there is a widely held belief that people with mental handicaps are childlike. The image of a 25-year-old man or woman as having the mental age of an 8 or 9 year old is extremely powerful and carries with it a range of connotations about the person far wider than the intellectual capacities measured by the test. For example, men or women with mental handicap might be prevented from having a relationship with someone of the opposite sex because they are presumed innocent of such matters. Greengross (1976) pointed out that many parents take it for granted that their son or daughter will never marry or lead an ordinary adult life, due to their handicap. Therefore the thought of sexual relations never crosses these parents' minds. The idea of a mental as distinct from a chronological age is not merely a scientific one but is interwoven with much older beliefs about the childlike innocence of people with mental handicap. Just as the origins of many currently held attitudes can only be understood by reference to the past, equally the genesis of new ideas concerning mental handicap can only be understood in an historical context.

The Labelling and Categorisation of People with Special Needs in a Contemporary Context

Today, attitudes held towards people with mental handicap are complex and often ambivalent. Many people who have little or no contact with people with mental handicap may talk with concern about 'them' and treat 'them' kindly. Pittock and Potts (1988) found that their respondents, overall, showed favourable attitudes towards people with learning difficulties, but they viewed them as needing supervision. Jahoda (1988) discussed the case of local residents who mounted a protest campaign when it was proposed to establish a staffed group home in a 'conscrvation area' of Stirling. As Eayrs and Ellis (1990) point out, public impressions are composed of a mixture of 'positive', 'negative' and sympathetic attitudes. A 'sympathetic' attitude itself can have both positive and negative associations:

> It is positive, perhaps, in terms of promoting charitable donations from the public, but negative in that it reflects the patronising, distancing and marginalisation of one group of individuals by another. (Eayrs & Ellis, 1990, p.350)

Attitudes towards people with learning difficulties are thus wide ranging and their categorisations are deep rooted in historical and social contexts. In this section we shall consider some consequences of the labelling and categorisation of people with learning difficulties in present society.

Living in a world apart

While families know and love their sons and daughters as individuals, this does not mean that they are immunised from negative attitudes towards handicap. For example, parents sometimes hold very protective attitudes towards a son or daughter with a mental handicap, however mild it may be. Card and Horton (1982) surveyed the views of parents of people with mental handicap over the age of 16 living in the Eastbourne area. They found that over 90 per cent of the parents wished their son or daughter to remain at home until they were too old or infirm to look after their offspring any more. Moreover, if and when their son or daughter moved on from the family home, the majority wanted him or her to live in a residential facility as protective as the family home.

In recent research in Scotland it was found that some mothers of people with mental handicap held the view that their sons and daughters were 'essentially different' from other people (Jahoda et al., 1988) The very fact of having a mental handicap was considered by these mothers to mean that their sons and daughters were cut off from the wider social world, and that they were 'happy in their own wee world'. The notion that people with a mental handicap remain in a childlike state was put forward as an explanation by several mothers participating in this research. One mother had told her daughter that she had to go to a special school in the following words: "you're handicapped, you're special, you're different from other people".

The representation of the mentally handicapped as living in a world apart reminds one of the title of a French monograph by Chombart de Lauwe (1971), Un Monde Autre. This monograph is concerned with the social representations of childhood, and Chombart de Lauwe argued and demonstrated how the world of the child can be understood only by contrast with the world of the adult (Farr, 1984). Our own study, too, has demonstrated that, for some parents and staff in Adult Training Centres, people with a mental handicap somehow never grow up from their childhood (Jahoda et al. 1988, 1989). Such views are reinforced, as already pointed out, by the image, perpetuated by tests of intelligence, that adult people with learning difficulties have the mental age of children.

This permanent world apart is also apparent in the way non-handicapped people talk to and communicate with the mentally handicapped. Leudar (1981) suggests that the social position of people with a mental handicap, even in the relatively non-institutional environment of an Adult Training Centre, is such that their experience of communication is one of being placed in a non-reversible role. In particular, they are not given equal opportunities to initiate and perpetuate discourse, to put forward questions, to make statements, explanations or justifications, to express their attitudes and feelings openly, to regulate behaviour by giving commands or permissions, or by opposing commands.

What is common in all stigmatised treatments of people with learning difficulties, be it be travelling on a bus of a particular colour to a special school, being rejected and called names by their peers in the neighbourhood, or being over-protected by parents, is that such people are set apart from others and given an inferior social status.

A recent study into the quality of care of people with moderate to severe learning difficulties (Jahoda & Markova, 1990) has shown that in spite of the emphasis on community care and community services, such people, whether they live in hospitals or in hostels, have virtually no interactions with people outside the establishment in which they live. Only 3 per cent of all interactions in hostels and 1 per cent of all interactions in hospitals of people with learning difficulties were with outsiders. Moreover, it was found that the majority of interpersonal interactions in hospitals are only functional, and not social in the proper sense of the word 'social'. This means that they are concerned with the participants' physical needs and their behaviour, with routines and rules, rather than with conversations and interactions expressing an interest in the participants as human and social beings. The vast majority of interactions are very brief in duration and it is most unlikely for a participant to be involved in an interaction for longer than 10 minutes. It was found that 87 per cent of interactions between hospital staff and residents are shorter than one minute. These results suggest that residents' interactions with staff are mostly of a superficial nature because they do not allow a topic to be developed.

In the hostel settings staff are more likely to initiate interactions with residents lasting over a minute. Similarly, when hostel participants initiate an interaction with staff, it is far more likely to last over one minute than is the case in hospital wards. In general, however, most interactions are of a fleeting nature and do not give a resident time to express his or her wishes and feelings.

This study has also revealed that in hospital wards the interactions initiated by a person with moderate to severe learning difficulties are mostly ignored by the staff, while in hostels staff react to them mostly with a friendly attitude. In hospital wards participants are rarely encouraged by staff to initiate communication. Impersonal attitudes by hospital staff most often occur in combination with interactions about the participants' physical needs. In hostels, interactions about physical needs are most likely to be accompanied by a helping or directing attitude.

Adopting a social categorisation approach, St. Claire (1986) explored representations of mental handicap by the general lay public and by professional and other groups. She found that beliefs about people with a mental handicap by the general lay public are closely related to their personal experience. With more personal contact the general lay public had more positive beliefs about mental handicap. For example, while unacquainted lay persons rated people with special needs as 'nasty to live with', 'depressing', 'friendless', 'unwanted' and 'hard done by', acquainted persons rated them as 'nice to live with', 'cheering', 'popular', 'wanted' and 'well treated'.

Moreover, the data showed that psychologists had far more negative expectations about people with special needs – probably due to their training. In their ratings there were categories referring to abnormality and intelligence, dependency and inability to cope, which evidently reflected professionalised attitudes that people with a mental handicap are patients and not people (St.Claire, 1986, p.241). These findings clearly have implications for policies concerning people with special needs and the role of professionals in services. If the training of professionals works against a change of social representations of handicap one has to think carefully about what training should and what it should not include.

Numerous research studies have shown that once a person is labelled it is very difficult for him or her to shed the label (Jahoda, 1988). Edgerton (1986) carried out a case study of an individual who was 'delabelled' when he was found to have an I.Q. well above the level which denotes an intellectual deficit. In his conclusion Edgerton made it clear that the individual cannot simply discard the label of being 'mentally handicapped' by showing that the label is not applicable to him or her as a person. Rather, the label has to be eliminated through some kind of professional 'delabelling'. It was thus shown that the most direct effect of the label was not on the labelled person but on the people in his or her social world, such as parents, teachers and the providers of services, among others. Thus, if one is not taken seriously as a person one may not have the power to alter one's circumstances, and one may be shaped into a 'handicapped' individual whether the label is applicable or not.

Normalisation

The programme of 'normalisation' is perhaps the most important single attempt to delabel people with special needs and to reconstruct the categories into which they have been placed by society. Originally a Scandinavian concept, normalisation is concerned with the right of people with mental handicap to live as normal a life as possible. It is defined as "making normal mentally retarded people's housing, education, working and leisure conditions. It means bringing them the legal and human rights of all other citizens" (Bank-Mikkelsen, 1976, p.56).

Wolfensberger (1972, 1980a, 1980b), the first American exponent of this philosophy, was primarily concerned with public education about mental handicap. He shifted the emphasis of normalisation to a consideration of the ways in which people with special needs could overcome their 'devalued' status. He argued that symbols, whether consciously or unconsciously maintained, such as language and images, play an important role in positive and negative evaluations of people and objects. Such images are reflected in how people with a mental handicap are talked about by others, and how others behave towards them, collectively in the form of services, and individually within and outside services. From these attitudes comes self-fulfilling prophesy, which means that if people are expected to behave in a particular manner then the likelihood is that they will behave in that fashion. Wolfensberger (1972) proposed that, to overcome the devalued images of people with a mental handicap, it is necessary to give them culturally valued social positions, and this, in turn, would lead to more enhanced social images of such individuals and to their greater competence. As part of this process behavioural techniques and positive interventions would be used to attempt to make people with a mental handicap more socially competent and their handicap less apparent. Thus to compensate for their handicap, people with mental handicap would need to ensure that they appeared as ordinary as possible, or were seen to be conservative as opposed to unconventional. Moreover, Wolfensberger (1972, 1980a, 1980b) and Wolfensberger and Thomas (1981) propose that all actions towards, or associations made with, people with a mental handicap have to be carefully analysed in case they are consciously or unconsciously demeaning. Obviously the most subtle of such images are the most difficult to identify and eradicate. To interpret the underlying intentions of even the most basic of actions towards another in the social world can be problematic, let alone any attempt to do this with grey areas. For example, a picture from a fairy story hanging on the wall in a hostel for adult people with a mental handicap might signify that the residents are seen as childlike or, in contrast, in a different adult context the picture might be admired as a work of art. If the residents of a hostel go out wearing clothes whose colours are badly matched, does this devalue people or, on the other hand could it be untrue that most people really wear matching or complementary colours? The danger of using such criteria against which to judge and interpret the actions of people with mental handicap, and the behaviour of others towards them, is that it is likely to reinforce the status of people with mental handicap as an extraordinary group. It could also make professionals self-conscious in their dealing with people with mental handicap and create barriers between the two parties. Moreover, is individual dignity, spontaneity and choice made secondary to good appearances? The two are not always compatible.

The Rejection of Labelling and Categorisation by People with Special Needs

Studies into the effect of labelling and categorisation consistently show that people with special needs are acutely aware of the denigrating nature of the labels attached to them and that they consistently reject the labels and categorisation imposed on them by society. Participants in such studies know that the stigma is associated with their status as 'handicapped' persons. For them, the stigma of a label is a social representation with which they have to cope in their everyday lives. For many people such a stigma is not passively accepted but actively resisted, and they have developed strategies of coping with it (Edgerton, 1967; Edgerton & Berkovici, 1976; Cheston, 1988). About two-thirds of adolescent participants in Cheston's (1988) study had experienced labelling and being called names by their peers, bullying, or came home covered in spittle. While for some of them incidents of such informal labelling originated outside the home, for others it actually originated at home (Cheston, 1988; Jahoda et al., 1988). Participants who resided in a mental handicap hospital felt that they were subject to rules and to a life style that characterised them as having different needs from 'outsiders' and as lacking in human dignity. Most of them rejected the view that they were 'patients'. Instead, they felt that it was their isolation in the hospital that led others, outside the hospital, to stigmatise them. One hospital resident in the study expressed his feelings as follows:

> When I came in at first, I didn't ken I was called a patient. I was always wondering what a patient was. I know now I'm a patient. In this hospital you're classed as patients, residents, high grades, low grades and all this. I never kenned I was a patient. I thought how you was to get treated just the same as anybody else outside. It should all be stopped, classed as patients. We're no dogs or animals or that. We're just the same as anybody else. They should stop all this, they should call them the same as the rest, just call you by your name. (Cattermole et al., 1988, p.139)

The majority of the participants in this study rejected the view that they were 'essentially different' from people without a handicap. While they accepted that they had specific difficulties in learning, they condemned the attitude that they were, thereby, any less worthy as persons. They were aware that their role of being globally handicapped was imposed on them as a result of social prejudice.

Towards a Change of Social Attitudes, Representations and Categories

It was pointed out at the beginning of this chapter that language is not a neutral set of labels. Rather, words have diagnoses and prognoses, reflecting societal beliefs, attitudes and representations, built into their meanings. Therefore, it is not a change of labels and categories as such that is required for people with mental handicap to become citizens with equal rights and duties, but a change in the social representations of handicap underlying such labels. In particular, it is fundamental that it is the implicit and unreflective representations that must be changed for genuine progress to occur.

Recently, ingenious research has been started, asking the question as to what kinds of images and messages are conveyed by posters produced by the various voluntary agencies which work on behalf of people with handicaps (Stockdale & Farr, 1987). The authors have analysed the messages in these posters and what they communicate to the public. While some are designed to evoke pity, others ask for money and yet others inform the public about various aspects of handicaps. The most sophisticated are those that address the viewer directly and make him or her responsible not only for the existing labelling of people with special needs but also for initiating changes and for creating new social representations: "You say Mongol. We say Down's Syndrome. His mates call him David". Or: "Sarah's just learnt to say hello. Can you learn to stop saying Mongol?" Following this work, Eayrs and Ellis (1990) explored the relationships between the viewers' perceptions of posters representing mental handicap and willingness to give money to a charity supporting people with a mental handicap. It was found that if the posters elicited feelings of guilt, sympathy and pity, the viewers were more prepared to give money than if the images on posters presented those with a mental handicap as having the same rights and value as the non handicapped. The authors suggest that charity campaigns should rethink their aims along the following lines: first, they should aim, rather than at the donation of money, at promoting acceptance and active involvement with people with learning difficulties by the general public; secondly, they should aim to change attitudes towards handicap rather than attempt to arouse guilt.

Participants in the study into training for independent living (Jahoda *et al.*, 1990) made it very clear that their priority was to be integrated into the local community rather than to live on the margins of society and in isolation from the 'non-handicapped'. As one who attended an Adult Training Centre commented:

> I didn't ask to be the way I am, it's just one of those things you've got to live with. If you try and talk to someone and tell them where you work, they've got no time for you. Makes me feel that size (the participant made a gesture towards the ground indicating how small he felt) as though I could just crawl into a hole and curl up. (Jahoda & Markova, 1990, p.139)

Thus staff working in residential and daily services should be encouraged to create opportunities for people with learning difficulties to develop friendships and to experience a wide range of social encounters. The focus of social activities of people with learning difficulties should be geared towards integration rather than segregation.

To change attitudes towards people with special needs and the language referring to them requires public and professional re-education. For example, one cannot expect dramatic changes in the attitudes and role perceptions of hospital staff merely by choosing the place where they work, i.e. in staffed houses for people with learning difficulties rather than in hospital. Such changes in the work settings must be accompanied by appropriate staff training which would induce staff to adopt new work habits and attitudes. For instance, staff should have experience of working in more 'homely' settings where they do not wear uniforms, where they use the same cutlery as residents and where they are not in the habit of referring to residents as 'low-grades'. Training could perhaps be augmented by job swaps with community-based services outside hospital, which might demonstrate that other approaches are practically possible.

Replacement of residential staff's controlling role must begin with a reassessment of the notion of the 'training' of residents. Of course, teaching and sustaining skills are important elements of staff's work. Given their disability, people with moderate to severe learning difficulties are always likely to require some support in the management of their daily living tasks. However, if staff see their main role as that of training, their focus of attention will remain on the disability rather than on the potential of residents. This blurs staff's sensitivity to individuals and maintains social distance. This particular issue was raised by a member of staff in a local authority hostel at a feedback meeting of the study's findings for staff members. The staff member explained how a woman had recently moved from a long-stay hospital to the hostel where he worked. Before she arrived he was sent a computer printout about her which contained a long list of her problems and weaknesses. This section was followed by one that should have listed her strengths, but in this section it was simply stated 'zero' (Jahoda & Markova, 1990).

In order to shed pejorative meanings of words concerning people with special needs, change of categories and labels must be accompanied by change of underlying public images, attitudes and representations of mental handicap. Language is a cultural and societal product which is forged by speaking, and it cannot be dissociated from the social contexts in which it has been created. If the general public forges words by negative attitudes, negative attitudes will become part of the meaning potential of these words. In contrast, if the general public forges language with positive attitudes encouraging integration and with attribution of agency to people with special needs, such attitudes and attributions will, in turn, impregnate the meaning potentials of words. This also means that when people with special needs become genuinely integrated into the community, 'the language of special needs' will become a redundant term without a referent. This is the aim towards which we should strive.

CHAPTER 3

The Professions, Knowledge and Practice

W. I. Fraser

Introduction

When I first stayed in the Camphill Schools at the Thirtieth Anniversary, I wondered what were the common denominators in the high quality of life for people with learning difficulties there? Since that time, quality of life issues have assumed a new and proper importance, and checklists and assessment schedules of the environment have proliferated (e.g. Donaldson *et al.*, 1988). For the individual with a learning difficulty, the quality of life in a particular environment needs to be spelt out in outcomes consensually agreed in everyday lay terms, and can be measured in terms of *health maintenance and gain*; *skill acquisition*; and *engagement with others*.

Of these, the last seems to be the best indicator of quality of life, in that a person will not engage in the world if he or she is depressed, unhappy or unwell, and engagement in the world is a prerequisite for learning. Rather than list the many and increasing number of professionals who look after those with learning difficulties, this chapter will focus on the knowledge, skills and attitudes required to engage those with learning difficulties in the world, in work and in family life, and, looking beyond current legislation, at the principal professionals, viz. the doctor, the 'teacher/ therapist' and the manager of handicap services irrespective of professional background.

This chapter will also raise concern about future professional relationships. What is often no more than lip service continues to be paid to multidisciplinary education, and the implementation of the *National Health Service and Community Care Act* (HMSO 1989a) has been sadly delayed. This will allow time to reflect on the dismantling of current joint planning and its replacement by parallel planning and training, and to examine points where professionals can share training and to consider whether concepts such as a School of Learning Difficulty might be useful.

The Unifying Professional Skill: Engagement

One of the best examples of the professional-handicapped person disjunction is in the film "The Rainman": After Raymond, the young man with Autism, had been abducted by his brother, Charlie, the crucial meeting to decide on Raymond's return to the institution takes place – this multiparty 'interview' illustrates professionals' interviewing failures. The interview consists of Raymond, Charlie (his brother), the second opinion doctor – all three sitting at a table, and Dr Bruner, the Director of the Institution, standing in the background at the window.

Second opinion specialist:	Raymond, I'm not a judge and jury, just a doctor making a recommendation to a court (sic) . . . Walbrook is one of the finest institutions in the country . . .
Charlie:	Raymond improved further in a week than in 20 years in the institution.
(turns to address Bruner)	. . . I can tell you anything, I can tell you nothing, you still wouldn't know the difference!
(Dr Bruner moves over to sit down)	
Dr Bruner:	He's not capable of making a relationship with you.
Charlie: (challenges)	Did you spend 24 hours a day with him?
Dr Bruner:	You can't look after him without professional help.
Charlie:	When we started out he was only my brother in name and this morning we had pancakes – when Charlie Babbett made a joke, I made a connection.
Dr Bruner:	Raymond is unable to make these kinds of decisions.
Raymond excitedly finger-flips.	
Second opinion doctor:	Do you want to stay with your brother? "Yes"
(across the table)	
(repeats x 3)	Do you want to go back to Walbrook? "Yes" Can you make a distinction between Walbrook and Charlie? "Mm."
Charlie:	You made your point. You don't have to humiliate him.
Second opinion doctor:	Dr Bruner, can I have a word with you for a minute, please?
(Doctors flee the room)	
Raymond:	I like having you for my brother. I'm an excellent driver.

(brothers rub heads)   I like having you for my brother.
(Entire interview on Raymond's future lasts 5 minutes.)

This illustrates that these professionals had neither the knowledge of Raymond's central problem (which is one of a poorly developed Theory of Mind – see below), nor the skills to communicate with developmentally disabled people, to understand the latters' problems with the conventions of language and read their intentions. It illustrates also the mutual needs to save face and the widespread ignorance of what are the rules of 'multi-party interviewing'.

In a recent study, Duckworth *et al.*, (in press) have shown that medical practitioners who profess to be specialists in Mental Handicap have no superior skills in interviewing those with learning difficulties. An inexperienced junior doctor is just as good; in fact, the strongest correlation was with age – the younger the staff are, the better they relate to people with learning difficulties. Both in our study and in a separate study by Burford (1988), which involved medical students at the beginning and at the end of their training, those just starting out were better at engaging with profoundly mentally handicapped people. It is as if one gets de-trained in medical school and further de-trained with age! Some medical schools in some disciplines, e.g. psychiatry, attempt to redress this at postgraduate level, but nowhere to my knowledge is there a curriculum where doctors can learn the skills of interacting with people with learning difficulties.

Recently I received a letter from a young man who had once been in Camphill. There is obvious frustration and confusion over inability to communicate his emotional needs and understand other people's mental states:

> I have never in my life made friends since I left Camphill and I never will in my life until I am a very very old person be able to make friends because of the fact that people just take and don't give or pay back by reciprocating because they are too anti-social, inflexible, unsociable, bone selfish, bone idle, bone lazy, unwilling and unprepared to talk to me when I talk to them. My second point is the troubles all in my life are people who depress and irritate me by being foul, unpleasant, unco-operative, unhelpful, unreasonable, because they are so anti-social, pigheaded, piggish, inflexible and unsociably ruthless, arrogant and consendingly (sic) very rude and vulgar to me in the past.

Anyone who works with those with learning difficulties ought to have training in the skills of engagement, communicating with, and appreciation of social and language impairment and its underlying causes including developmental delay in the 'Theory of Mind'.

People with learning difficulties have problems with their communication. It singles them out. Whatever their differences (and a more heterogenous group is hard to find), those with learning difficulties are all united in being recognised as unusual by 'ordinary' people through their communicative interactions. They do not design adequately-extended discourse, providing information piecemeal, omitting necessary information, including irrelevant details and incomplete thoughts, and running unconnected thoughts together (Kernan & Sabsay, 1989). It is difficult to understand their intentions. Of course, they may 'get by' if they have an understanding caregiver. The real problems start when they have to conduct conversations with people who are not familiar with them, particularly in unusual situations, when they may become nervous and even agitated and disturbed. The ordinary public do not have the time or the patience to listen to rambling inappropriate discourse. Leudar (1989) has pointed out that those with learning difficulties are more likely to violate maxims of conversations: these are ordinary communicative conventions which listeners assume that speakers are abiding by. Such maxims are quality (the convention that we expect people to speak the truth, and not to say things for which they lack adequate evidence); quantity (that the person speaks as informatively as is required); manner (that they avoid obscurity of expression and ambiguity); and most of all, relevance.

One of the greatest problems faced by those with mild learning difficulties, is their limited repertoire of conversational topics, and sadly, not only are they limited in the topics they can call upon, they often do not display reciprocal interest in the general topics introduced by others. The result is that the person with learning difficulties is an unrewarding, self-centred and uninteresting conversational partner. The professional often cheerfully ignores these deficiencies, but, through the lack of adequate feedback in early childhood (which is when these violations of conventions and unclarity of intentions are ironed out in normal children, often cruelly, by other children), the person with learning difficulties faces rejection, and friendlessness in adult life.

The person (although puzzled as to why he or she is getting it wrong) usually has insight that he or she is disturbing to be with, and he or she takes steps to avoid being judged as incompetent. This varies from loudly boasting false claims of accomplishments, swearing and cursing, displaying great knowledge of curious or irrelevant topics, and boasting about transparently false sexual conquests to save face and to protect his or her fragile self-esteem. So often, as in "The Rainman" script, we as professionals do little to save the esteem of the person with learning difficulties: when we are not clear about what they have said, we turn immediately to another person for verification; we do not give them time to answer; we do not listen; we do not adequately teach them interactional skills.

People with severe learning difficulties will commonly have problems with first order representation, i.e. knowing that a word e.g. 'banana' represents a yellow curved edible. The notion that autistic people have a poorly developed Theory of Mind (see Bishop & Adams, 1989; Frith, 1989) suggests that in Autism there is a neurodevelopmental delay or damage to links in the brain which allow metarepresentational capacity, i.e. second order representation.

The child giggling at his or her mother pretending a banana is a telephone, has to 'decouple' the connection between the banana representing food and the banana as representing the telephone. Children with Down's Syndrome can do this easily and play the pretence. These children usually have a well-developed sense of humour; people with Autism do not. It was indeed a breakthrough when Charlie reported that Raymond had laughed at his joke. Many people with learning difficulties, however, have difficulty with understanding that other people see things differently and feel differently from themselves and have different thoughts, and people with Autism invariably have this problem; namely, an inability to decouple an idea from its immediate veridical or first order representation (Frith, 1989). If the professional cannot envisage a person with special needs as having difficulties in perceiving his or her point of view, then the professional cannot sensitively communicate with that person.

It therefore seems to me that, in future, any professional who talks to people with learning difficulties, must be knowledgeable about their 'pragmatic' problems of communication, and take cognisance of the person's Theory of Mind as a cognitive explanation of autistic people's social problems, and of why other individuals with pervasive developmental disorders have social impairments. Achieving such cross-disciplinary insights where, for example, the teacher is informed by the neurophysiologist who is informed by the sociolinguist, etc, demands new forms of training and, by implication, new forms of training organisation. I shall develop ideas about 'Schools of Learning Difficulty' in the last section of this chapter.

For over 20 years, the philosophy underlying our services has been normalisation, and now in most industrially developed countries but not all, (vide Greece), ordinary lives are the standards by which the care and quality of life of those with learning difficulties are measured. Now, normalisation has been overtaken by new concepts: those of the business world, purchasers and providers, business plans, economies of scale and contracts. For most people with learning difficulties, the crucial professionals will be, as they have always been, the General Practitioner and the Teacher (therapist), to which we now add (enter Stage Right) 'The Manager'. Who now will be the guardian of the humanitarian principles of normalisation? Again I envisage a crucial role for 'Schools of Learning Difficulty' in which professionals from different disciplines can generate and acquire both a common core of knowledge and values as well as knowledge of the specialisms of one another. The graduates of such training Schools should be inspired to lifelong values – awareness of the need to regard persons with learning difficulties as valued members of society, to enable them to find meaning in their lives and to acquire new skills, as well as sensitivity to their physical and cognitive difficulties – which would guide the economic processes of budgeting. It is to the current position of the main professional groups that I now turn.

The General Practitioner

The general practitioner, with the dentist, is the service provider contacted most consistently by a high proportion of people with learning difficulties (Gollay *et al.*, 1981; Evans *et al.*, 1987, 1988). Most clients throughout the world enter the Mental Handicap Service system via a medical contact (Rowitz, 1981). Lowe and De Paiva (1990) state:

> The general practitioner plays a key role in the provision of community care and alone provides a continuous thread of medical care. The White Papers on Community Care (HMSO 1989a) and the National Health Service (HMSO 1989b) propose changes that are likely to affect general practitioner services, including larger practitioner lists which may have implications for the crucial role that general practitioners play as primary professional contact for the increasing number of mentally handicapped people living in the community.

Yet general practitioners receive little training in, or have limited experience of, people with learning difficulties (Ineichen & Russell, 1980). People with learning difficulties have difficulty communicating successfully with their doctors (Beange & Bauman, 1990) and Kinnell (1987) has suggested that the average consultation time with general practitioners was insufficient for them.

Unlike the assumed picture of the person with learning difficulties as being a child, usually with Down's Syndrome, the true presentation of mental handicap for the general practitioner will more commonly be an adult, and increasingly a severely, multiply handicapped one with little speech. At the initial interview, the medical practitioner's aims will be to discover what the problems are and to clarify them in order to ensure the appropriate management; and doing this within a circumscribed time limit. The person with learning difficulties may also be concerned about his or her health problem and want an explanation; and will expect the doctor to be interested in him or her as a person. For the person with learning difficulties the handicaps may make it difficult for him or her to hear or understand the doctor's aim, and he or she may be difficult to examine. Such experiences have led to the current practice of persons with learning difficulties being accompanied to such consultations. The doctor therefore has two sources of information and a participating role by the third person, which is often unclarified, thus changing the normal courtesies of consultation etiquette. The health care of those with learning difficulties living in the community presents problems through lack of regular screening, social impairments and their lack of ability to complain and explain to the doctor. As a group they are very vulnerable, edentulous, victims of the fast food industry, overweight, subject to poor epileptic control, particularly prone to depressive illness and stress, and particularly vulnerable to bereavement syndromes.

Those with the commonest clinical syndrome, Down's, have additional needs because of their proneness to hypothyroidism, to keratokonus in adolescence, to premature ageing and to Alzheimer-type dementia.They are also particularly vulnerable to infections and malignancies; and to atlantoaxial subluxation, which means that all those with Down's Syndrome should be screened before active sports. Despite their vulnerability, the most notable thing about people with Down's Syndrome is their increasing longevity. In 1929 their life expectancy at birth was nine years, and in 1979, 59 years. In developing countries, adults with such a condition will probably continue to be uncommon for at least a generation. It is undisputed that we are getting a better educated, more able and healthier adult with Down's Syndrome due partly to higher expectations of them by society. Their quality of life has improved but there is still evidence that particularly in medicine, expectations are lower than in education. Murdoch and Anderson (1990) have shown that parents are critical of general practitioners, not only for their reduced optimism about outcome, but also for their relative reluctance to refer for opinions on sensory deficits and failure to organise regular health surveillance. Large practices might organise other regular clinics for people with learning difficulties: epilepsy clinics, well woman clinics (although the mentally handicapped seem to have a particularly low incidence of cervical cancer, this is not true for breast cancer); regular monitoring of nutritional status, and for those general practitioners with an interest in psychological medicine, depot and lithium clinics. The general practitioner might also consider special clinics for sleep problems: not only children with Down's Syndrome have problems with sleep apnoea; some 30 per cent of families experience severe sleep difficulties with their handicapped offspring.

These additional health problems in people with learning difficulties and their families ought to present interesting challenges for the general practitioner but at present neither undergraduate nor postgraduate training equips them to meet these needs fully. The cross-disciplinary and inter-disciplinary training of 'Schools of Learning Difficulty' could provide the context for developing both more specialist and more rounded skills in general practitioners. I will expand on these ideas in the last section of this chapter.

The Teacher

I use the word teacher to mean the 'front line' professional in day-to-day contact with a person who has a learning difficulty. Other European countries have developed a training for this 'pedagogy' worker or 'conductor', part nurse, part teacher, who enables people with learning difficulties to lead ordinary lives. In the United Kingdom, there will be, as R.N.M.S. nurse training is phased out by Project 2000, no core training for people wishing to specialise in learning disability. The subject will even more be at the tailend of another trade's curriculum.

The teacher of people with special learning difficulties must be a technical innovator, replacing several of his or her former activities by computer-aided instruction programmes. Machines are cheaper than humans; there is no teacher fatigue. The teacher has to be acquainted with a range of specialised input and feedback methods. The learner can make the most basic choices through single and multiple switches, flat plates marked with coloured pictures, icons, large pads, voice keys, pointing devices such as the mouse, and the Concept Keyboard; but there is no substitute for the teacher. Computers cannot understand the cues that the teacher can, and although computers can generate speech, they are very poor at understanding it.

The teacher (with the guidance of the psychologist) must use modern technology to assess handicap. Multiple behaviour and multiple environment event recording continuously in real time by hand, has presented insurmountable problems in the past; now, however, we have laptop computers such as the Epson HX 20, the Atari and the Psion memoriser, and programmes which can record and analyse data. The 'session programme' of Repp and Felce (1990) permits the recording of up to 45 simultaneously and independently occurring events and prints them with beginning and ending times and summaries. A 'time-block programme' records a subgroup of behaviours which occur in sessions. The teacher/observer notes the people, the setting and any other information in the environment. A 'conditions programme' is like a time-block programme, except that changes in the sub-session are not based on time but based on changes in the environment, and a 'data analysis programme' provides analysis by sessions, by conditions, by environments, by events and by time. It enables, for example, analogue conditions to be examined in naturalistic studies in which the purpose is to identify antecedents or consequences in the natural environment that control behaviour; e.g. does the child become more disturbed when she gets attention, when she is ignored, or when demands are made upon her? Durand and Crimmins (1988) in analogue studies have examined the socio-communicative functions of severe injurious and stereotypic behaviours, assessing communicative intent. The commonest cause of head-banging and aggression is not for attention but in order to escape from situations which the child rejects.

What does the teacher do then? In the past, standard behaviour methods – time out, mass practice, overcorrection – were used rather unspecifically. Under this socio-communicative hypothesis of maladaptive behaviour, alternatives to aversive therapy are generated. These are often Augmented Communication approaches with which the teacher must become acquainted, but may also be forms of 'Gentle Education'. Gentle education, to quote McGee et al. (1987), "leads the caregiver to teach bonding to those who attempt to distance themselves from being involved in interactions, and is aimed at helping mentally handicapped individuals to learn the value and reward of human interaction". This, in fact, seems to me an incomplete enunciation of a fundamental Camphill pedagogue practice. Proponents of gentle teaching decry any aversive or punishment procedures in behavioural management. The arguments have become bitter. In the United States, people assume increasingly that if you are not positively enthusiastic for gentle therapy, then you are pro-aversive. Jordan *et al.* (1989) have compared the effects of visual screening and of gentle teaching in controlling self-injurious behaviour. They found no evidence of bonding and emphasised the need for further investigation of gentle teaching, and in particular, a more replicable approach. The teacher must be able to judge the evidence without emotional or doctrinal influence for and against gentle teaching. We do not know exactly what to do in gentle teaching as explicated by McGee. It is not enough to show love and tenderness when being assailed with blows and kicks. The teacher as manager must take into account other staff's ability to carry out poorly delineated but nice-sounding approaches, and ask himself or herself how long he or she can ask them to continue before burn-out.

Here Camphill practices would have much to teach us if they were articulated and incorporated into the curriculum of 'Schools of Learning Difficulty'. We require such high prestige Schools to counterbalance the magnet of the training of the traditional mainstream professionals and to provide basic, diploma and master's level of specialised experience drawing from the whole range of 'good practice' rather than simply from the orthodoxies of the day.

The Manager

The Managers, the Budget Holders (whether they be administrators, nurse managers, teachers, doctors or social workers), in the new climate are crucial. They will look at the structures we have built in the 1970s and 1980s, the Community Mental Handicap Teams (CMHTs), at the voluntary body providers like Camphill, L'Arche and Barnardos, with two overriding concerns; what are the outcomes of programmes and procedures; and what will the product cost (assuming that basic quality assurance exists)?

Concepts such as 'multidisciplinary', 'democratic' and 'social role valorisation' have little influence in a restricted budget. Already in the UK, we are seeing CMHTs being wound up, and the Audit Commission has clearly demonstrated that they wish a Care Manager, with considerable devolved authority and a budget, to minimise meetings and to get on with the job. A manager is also going to look increasingly critically at the use of professional staff time; not just into the calling of group meetings involving a large number of people to multidisciplinary groups, but also into the opportunity time lost in travel to provide community care services. He/she will be charged with identifying health gain, learning targets and client engagement as a result of specific items of therapist services. There are attractions here; many of us have been exasperated by the ponderous machinery and non-accountable bureaucracy of multi-disciplinary teams in sometimes refusing to accept as eligible certain people, e.g. those with borderline/mild difficulties, or those with severe difficulties.

The problem with the Care Manager is: how is he/she to be trained, to be sufficiently knowledgeable about all these professions to act as orchestrator and coordinator? The answers are not to be found in our current rigid, attitudinal and elitist Health, Education and Social Work Training but in the new forms of training and in 'Schools of Learning Difficulties'. At present, in each of our disciplines we have managers appointed whose knowledge of the issues of care in the community is confined to a reading of White Papers and/ or superficial recitation of the principles of normalisation as enunciated by the Civil Rights movements of the late 1960s. What is being envisaged is that no manager will be appointed unless having attended such a School for a range of exposure to the problems of learning difficulties and quality issues. The manager will have to be increasingly sensitive to consumer/customer choices in the next decade. It behoves him/her to appreciate more of the burden of the family of someone with learning difficulties.

Sustaining the Family Econiche

The 'Tom Clarke' Act (HMSO, 1986) has heralded major changes in professionals' focus towards family coping and socio-ecological factors. The importance of the everyday caretaking burden (Erickson & Upsher, 1989) in family outcomes is increasingly being appreciated. Maternal wellbeing is not depressed simply by having a child with difficulties (Harris & McHale, 1989); the diversity of child and family outcomes shows that parents' values based on social resources, experience and appraisal of handicap are important. For example, Flynt and Wood (1989) report that both black and older mothers have a lower perception of stress than white and younger mothers, possibly due to more social support. Frey et al., (1989) found that parental belief systems massively influence the perception of stress, family adjustment and psychological distress. Getting through the day – the sustainability of everyday activities – seems better to predict child and family adjustment than does the level of stimulation of the child, the 'quality of home life' (Gallimore et al., 1989). The professionals need a social context perspective. Gallimore uses the term 'ecocultural niche (econiche)' (Super & Harkness, 1986) to refer to the family's collective action to accommodate to a child with learning difficulties. Here again Camphill practices have much to teach us, and if codified, would become major principles of training in Schools of Learning Difficulty.

Families develop an 'econiche', reflected in parents' accounts of their daily routines, which is more than a home environment. Families take individual and collective action to avoid being victims of social and economic forces. Their 'econiche' reflects incomes, housing, social network but also cultural features and beliefs, and is manifest in every routine. It changes as a result of family accommodation to the many forces at work, at home, in health and in relationships that families have to react to. Gallimore *et al.* found that parents thus revealed a central dynamic of their lives; they were driven by the task of constructing and sustaining a daily routine. Such family themes may however be negative; for example, especially in middle-class families, the overvaluation of a stimulating environment may produce a frenzied set of activities.

The term 'hassle' refers to the perceived impact of the extreme behaviour problems, sleep problems, poor communication skills and physical limitations of the child which affect the family's econiche. 'Low hassle' delayed children's families look very similar to families without developmentally delayed children. 'High hassle' children's families will show heavier mother workload, more mothers deferring employment or career development, and greater engagement of siblings in childcare (Gallimore *et al.*, 1989).

Family problems were more commonly associated (Frey *et al.*, 1989) with mothers who did not have a positive belief system or non-critical family network. Frey *et al.* (1989) found that parents differed dramatically in the degree in which they view their child's disability as stressful. A comparative frame of reference – "at least she's not as handicapped as . . ." is an important way of coping. The meaning of Down's Syndrome is very different from the meaning to parents of intellectually above average children. Frey *et al.* also found that coping efforts related to beliefs held by the individual. A problem-focused coping style was related to less psychological distress, wishful thinking to higher stress. Perceived 'control' is important for maternal psychological wellbeing; parents of children with Down's Syndrome structured their interactions by assuming the role of managers and teachers (Stoneman *et al.*, 1987).

Longitudinal studies of families with a handicapped offspring and studies of older children at times of transition are still rare. As Goodyer (1990) points out: we know little of the epidemiology of life difficulties in relation to life cycle changes, e.g. school-leaving. There is a need to examine the impact of recent policy changes on young adults with learning difficulties who continue to live at home supported by their carers. Families who have been aware of the existence of institutional provision and nothing else will be anxious about new community alternatives. Sueltze and Keenan (1981) have shown that the "optimism among the parents of younger children gives way to planning for more protective employment and residential environments among the parents of young adults".

Schools of Learning Difficulties

A recurrent theme in this chapter has been the need for more education and training across the range of people who encounter those with learning difficulties, and that such training should be more often shared, and planned to be coherent and cohesive.

In the 1970s, there was a trend against centres of excellence on the grounds that they were elitist and camouflaged regions of squalor, yet most advances in our knowledge of the problems of learning difficulties have come from such centres of excellence, e.g. in this country, the Hester Adrian Research Centre. The increase in sophistication of approaches to Mental Handicap has led to an increasing demand for academic sciences combined with a gradual starvation of funds. Staff in each of the professional agencies need continuing education to keep up with necessary change. In a region it is common for there to be a university, a technical college, a training hospital and other academic institutions pursuing, without reference to each other, research and teaching in learning difficulties. The staff may not only be isolated from each other but quite hostile and even offended by each other's use of labels. The 'biomedical' staff may consider social policy and care staff to use imprecise, woolly and precious terms. Social scientists may consider the medical terminology dated and pejorative. Ignorance about the sentiments, feelings and beliefs of families and careworkers impedes genetic research; ignorance of genotype-phenotype-environtype interactions renders incomplete social policy researchers' understanding of the person with limited cognitive and emotional functioning. Different perspectives are often reflected in unnecessary tensions over the meaning of 'normalisation', care in the community, behavioural methods, the need or otherwise for medication and the requirements or otherwise of labelling.

As a first step, there is a need for meeting together: as a basic minimum, for an occasion when senior staff from institutions of Higher Education researching and teaching in mental handicap can meet; for a regular exchanged diary of events in order to enrich the various networks and to ensure that each of the research projects is greater than the sum total of individual studies.

The next step is to envisage a Board of Studies or "School of Learning Difficulties" where the entire spectrum of Mental Handicap from the high tech of molecular genetics, through psychopharmacology and psychological interventions, to research into ordinary home-making is represented; and where the entire range of activities can be acknowledged, documented and explained in terms understandable to each other and claimed for ownership by whoever works in or for such a 'School'. Throughout this chapter the need for prestigious training has been reiterated to ensure high quality leadership in service planning, management and delivery which in turn means that we require a continuing capacity for academic excellence. Training in consultation skills, training for managers in the management of change in Mental Handicap services, training in understanding the complex needs of this group of humanity, training to understand that the problems of care in the community are sophisticated, complicated and that vigilance should prevent perverse incentives to prevent real change, need constantly to be present. A substantial academic focus can provide training ranging from short courses and seminars to Master's Degrees. A research enterprise not part of such an alliance is vulnerable to being picked off in any 'cost improvement' rationalisation or retrenchment plan.

The location of such a 'School' is important. I suggest that it should be in an office setting in a town and preferably not in the environs of a hospital. Where the research happens is a separate question from where the coming together occurs. Where the teaching and resources happen it is important to be multidisciplinary. When I look as an Editor of a scientific journal at the repetitive and stereotyped, tramline character of much research at present, it is obvious that significant advance can only come through the cross-fertilisation of professions.

The goal, then, is the creation throughout Britain of a distinctive university presence similar to that in other domains of learning, offering, in addition to teaching and research, consultancy work and service inspection. In the United States, such a climate has led to the development of University Affiliated Projects, whose purpose is to teach by administration of good practice in high quality, multi-professional, medical, educational and community living projects. The John F. Kennedy Institutes throughout the United States do this; the Institute at the Johns Hopkins, for instance, has a portfolio including services for children and adults with developmental disabilities. No similar academic department developments have occurred in the UK. Here agencies which provide high quality services, e.g. Camphill, might collaborate with universities to set up such Schools. Camphill, as said earlier, has much to teach us, particularly about how to provide meaning for handicapped people's lives and how to reduce their challenging behaviour. However, Camphill also has much to learn from academia on how to learn to specify the methods that it uses to achieve its successes.

When, some years ago in the United States, I asked managers of retardation services about what were 'the best' residential services for people with learning difficulties, the response was, "Well, that's fundamentally about consumer choice – availability, accessibility and value for money, ask the Jewish people. Who do they buy services for their handicapped offspring from?" The answer was "The Camphill Communities". Why? Because Camphill Communities provide the opportunity for engagement in the world for exceptional children and adults, and in those 'small real worlds' in which these handicapped people desire to live, extra help is given thus: firstly, the knowledge of modern educational and medical techniques, with approaches built on evidence and experience rather than on doctrine; secondly, skills in managing these small real worlds, in communication with disabled people, in creating an econiche for the unusual people that live in Camphill, which understands their need for regularity, their chronobiological needs, for rhythm in their life; and thirdly, most of all, an attitude which engages and involves those with learning difficulties as valued people and understands the need for self-esteem, for purpose and meaning in their lives, the person's strivings, no matter how handicapped, to contribute, and which similarly sustains the caregivers in shared enterprises and experiences.

Had Raymond in "The Rainman" lived in Camphill, he might have said "yes" or "no" when asked did he want to go back, but there would have been with him a Camphill caregiver who would have understood what he intended, and if he had intended to leave, then he would have left that well-lit place richer from the experience.

ACKNOWLEDGMENT

Thoughts expressed in this chapter reflect discussions with Dr David Felce, Director, Applied Research Unit, University of Wales College of Medicine.

CHAPTER 4

The Task of the Handicapped: Handicap as a Force for Social Change

Stephen Sands

During the relatively short span of organised, legislated provision for the handicapped there has never been such an expressed wish for review and re-assessment as today. Equally, there has never been such a fund of educational theories, of increased attempts at inter-disciplinary co-operation and of substantial material resources. Articulated and documented methods and practices are now widely available to anyone working with the needs of those whom we recognise as special. There is an awareness today not only for the specialness of these needs (special sometimes meaning awkward) but also for the specific people with those needs. Particularly in the fields of medicine, education and social work these special needs, and these special people, address practitioners in such a way that we often feel inadequate to the task; hence there have, recently, been efforts regularly to re-evaluate responses so that they become more relevant and effective. As conscious and intellectually active people we continue developing theories about what should be done; yet the needs are so complex and diverse as to defeat simple classification. Theories can change quickly, sometimes drastically, but the essential questions of relevance and effectiveness remain. The fundamental motivation of compassion, even pity, for the handicapped has focused very much upon the needs themselves. The natural pragmatism which thus arises soon encounters the fact that the many heartfelt efforts to produce 'results' cannot adapt quickly or flexibly enough to keep pace with demands. The physically handicapped have needs different from those of the psychiatrically ill; the child needing education is different from the adult needing meaningful work; the confused and helpless elderly are different from the deprived and maladjusted teenager. In the midst of this bewildering array of challenges which face us stand the handicapped people themselves. There they confront us, more than just a compendium of needs, asking to be understood. Handicapped persons as such, whatever the disability and however severe, pose earnest moral-ethical questions to society as a whole.

This will not be an 'academic' paper, nor a research study in the usual sense; rather it will attempt to widen our view of the social questions, actually one should say the human questions, raised by the handicapped person in our midst. The experiences to which it relates arise out of the life of the Camphill Movement, its work of 50 years throughout the world and the direct involvement of the author, for nearly 20 years, with those whose needs make them special. Clearly, a tremendous amount is being done at present to meet individual special needs in different contexts, with different approaches, and the following is intended as a contribution to dialogue rather than as a definitive, exclusive statement of fact.

The growing interest with the closer relationship between the community and the individual's special needs indicates a definite change of emphasis. Behind that change one can feel the widespread hopes that, in this closer relationship, new therapeutic insights can be gained and methods developed. Broad recognition is now being given to the therapeutic value of social life itself, and what the extended community can provide for the person with special needs integrated within it has become a major area of research. I wish, however, to examine the *mutual therapeutic relationship* possible, even inherent, in the presence of the handicapped person in social life. How deeply has society as a whole recognised the extent of the challenge which this really entails?

The Question of Community

In recent years, most intensively since the 1960s, it has become quite common to speak of 'community' in a broad and undifferentiated way; an ill-defined 'some people, somehow, doing something' seems often to be enough. While frustrating for social scientists, there is something justified in this chaotic longing for community identity. One can sense that this urge for more intimate, stable human involvements emerges from a deep motivation. The element of warm, secure, co-operative contact which many had felt present in family and neighbourhood is now often felt to be missing.

As the individual personality grows in sophistication and self-reliance, and as social structures become more anonymous and abstract, the longing for open, uncomplicated relations becomes an imperative. A major theme of social research documents the statistics of loneliness and alienation; marriage ties and family cohesion dissolve; the workplace becomes harsh and depersonalised, and the urban environment uninhabitable. Words such as egotism, self-preservation, competition, or the 'profit-motive' (to use only a few of the less emotive examples) characterise the state of many modern souls. Even in children, basic human trust and openness can quickly become the exception rather than the rule. One cannot stress too strongly just how endangered fundamental social values and forms have become and how vulnerable are those who cannot 'look after themselves' mentally, emotionally or physically.

Arising out of these experiences, affecting the entire social spectrum, comes a growing urgency to find new access to others in a spirit of harmony and trust. The impulse is there not only to understand but to deepen, in concrete terms, the relation between the individual and the group. Such diverse groups as top executives, housewives, kindergarten teachers and the military are reported as seeking new social ways: methods needed to redress the balance between the reliance upon isolated individual abilities and the cultivation of the increased potentials available through, and with, others. Conscious therefore of the diverse and complex expressions of community today, let me nonetheless try to characterise it broadly for the purpose of this paper.

'Community' could simply be taken to mean a social setting expressive of the multi-faceted inter-dependence of human beings. This would allow a view as circumscribed as a family and as broad as a 'family of nations'. Each social setting will be more or less conscious of this inter-dependence, and more or less helpful in fostering it. To the extent, however, that it does consciously foster this inter-dependence, so a social organism will be able to include within it the full range of human experience. Most social organisms today have a limited, and limiting, capacity to appreciate and utilise individuals in any way beyond their ability to contribute in functional terms. How often have we all taken part in groups where the narrow definition of individual skills both factionalises the co-operative potential and allows unrealised aptitudes to remain so? In the goal-directed, task-orientated and time-determined world we live in, skills are of primary value and measurable results the criteria of success. While necessary for problem solving perhaps, the value judgements inherent in such a view of the contribution of the individual within the group have profound social consequences for the handicapped. If one equates 'usefulness' with an ascending scale of practical, increasingly intellectual, skills and with social conformity, then the person with special needs is, to put it bluntly (but so it is expressed), of little use.

Alternatively one can look to the individual in their development and see both hindrances and achievements, relative to resources. The individual possesses at birth the essentially human potential to stand upright, to speak and to think. This forms the foundation for the developing capacities necessary to establish and maintain constructive interaction with the surrounding world. On the basis of this constructive interaction moral conscience, in time, will also develop. We speak here of potentials, knowing full well that an identifiable proportion of humanity does not realise even these most basic potentials. Does this negate their individuality, their value as people?

There was a time, not so long ago, when this was the case, when the symptoms of a handicap set a person apart from others in their being, as well as in their doing. This presents a profound moral challenge to re-examine our values:

> ... the essential thing is to make a basic step forward in one's own conceptions. As long as the symptoms alone of handicap are experienced as primary – disturbed speech or movement, obsessions, convulsions, constitutional peculiarities – the perception of what is 'defective' forces itself directly upon us. Yet every handicapped child has in himself elements which are perfectly healthy, just as every healthy person can become handicapped, for instance, could have convulsions. To overcome the exclusive perception of what is defective, to gain access to that which lies to some extent 'behind' the symptoms and wishes to manifest itself as 'healthy' child or adult person; this is the task which must continually be accomplished by society and by each of us. Through the mere presence of this task a strength of humanity comes about to which we would hardly otherwise find our way. (v.Arnim, nd)

As a society we have in many ways responded with energy and creativity to the task of helping to maximise the development of skills. In this respect the physically handicapped are the most straightforward challenge, the mentally handicapped more complex and the psychiatrically ill the most difficult group to serve. Have we, however, been as creative and energetic in supporting the development of the whole human being as well as of specific skills, meeting the emotional needs, even the spiritual needs, of the handicapped person? And further, have we as a society explored the enormous potential which can reciprocally be offered by the handicapped to realise again the essential elements of our own humanity?

The Question of Special Needs

The recent use of the term 'special needs' says a great deal about how fundamentally transformed our relation with the handicapped has become. We have drawn them closer to our own realm of experience. Imbecile, idiot, lunatic, deranged, raving, deformed, were terms used in the past, the not so distant past, to ostracise and classify those 'different' from those 'normal'. Now we are much closer to the attitude which includes the handicapped person as a matter of course, and increasingly rejects the too simple division between the normal and others. The concept of normality, useful only to separate and exclude, is gradually being superseded by the reality of human reciprocity. We all have needs and some of us have special needs. What makes them special? No one would deny today the necessity for ongoing and direct assistance from a variety of specialists for generating wellbeing. The doctor, the priest, the teacher serve *basic, universal special needs*; they cultivate and stimulate the realisation of potential. Does the essential difference between needs and special needs then lie in the freedom of the person to seek and utilise such help? Personal problems and temporary incapacity are essentially different from chronic pathology, yet, despite many varied and articulate attempts to widen our perception of the essentially human in our fellow human beings, we are only just emerging from the 'cult of normality' which has done as much as anything in our century to determine our social attitudes. The bridge between the meeting of individual special needs and the reality of community life is the replacement of *standardised normality* with the concept of *developmental mutuality*.

Dr Thomas Weihs, a founder of the Camphill Movement, understood this more personally and deeply than most. He expressed it in the following way:

> From my long encounter with the handicapped I know that much of what is the least bad in me I owe to them. Everybody knows that our maturity, our potential for the good, depends on our coming into a situation in which we can do something for others. And while what we can usually do for others is pretty limited, the growth that can happen in us by being allowed to do that can be relatively great. (Weihs, 1977)

Such a view of the development of empathy, as both a tool to help others and a result of that encounter, can be felt very intensely by our modern social conscience. However, the roots of such an attitude have an historical background which it would be helpful at this point to describe.

Social Views of the Handicapped: An Historical Perspective

The development of modern social conscience can be seen against the background of slow but progressive changes in human consciousness since ancient times. As the individual developed beyond group identity to individualised self-awareness, it also became possible to express a more compassionate interest in others apart from family, tribe or blood relations.

Little concrete evidence exists of the presence of handicapped people in ancient cultures. This need not, however, be taken to mean that such handicaps did not exist. Epilepsy, for instance, was already known in Egyptian times and certain ecstatic states are described in other ancient cultures which are pictures of convulsive disorders. Physical deformity was rigorously eliminated through a 'selection process' of diet, climate, disease and warfare. It is possible that, in ancient cultures which existed before the capacity to think intellectually was fully developed, to be 'without reason' was not considered out of the ordinary; visionary consciousness was experienced as being 'close to the Gods'.

With the growth of Greek culture, more 'objective' standards of soundness, in mind and body, were applied. Physical deformity was often eliminated by infanticide and harsh social ostracism was applied in Greco-Roman times to insufficiencies in logical thinking and physical prowess. The advent of Christianity and the variety of healings described in the Gospels made *caritas* more than a question of individual compassion; it was a Christian duty. Those who suffered were considered especially close to the Son of Man, to Christ's unhesitating receptivity to those in need. The selfless will to heal flowed from love that, without judgement, recognised the suffering of the other. The first intimations that individual suffering could have meaning beyond personal biography thus came with the growth of Christianity. The Gospel healings themselves, sensitively read, are a clear description of a profoundly new relationship between the person who is ill and his or her surrounding.

During the Middle Ages the Church became the vehicle for a more organised, coherent response to human suffering. Almshouses, hospitals and hospices, the further development of Greek and Arabic medical practices, and healing centres established around the activities of saints were all expressions of the Church's commitment. The picture of the 'perfect' Greek, healthy in mind and body, was replaced by the one of St Francis kissing the leper. In the secular world, however, a great deal of cruelty, superstition and fear motivated people's relationships with those who were different. Victims of physical deformity and benign idiocy were ridiculed but generally tolerated by the general public. Distinctions were, however, beginning to be felt between 'inner' and 'outer' illness. Little pity was spared for the deranged, the convulsive or the emotionally imbalanced, and the gruesome treatment meted out to those with the 'devil within' is well documented. The prosperous, orderly and obedient conformity required of the new middle classes could not encompass the disturbed and the harsh, grim, unrelenting life of the peasant needed scapegoats upon which to vent frustration.

One fascinating exception to this picture is the figure of the fool, so well known through literature. He held a special place close to the centre of power and through his 'foolishness' transcended cold reason often to reach the truth. His value was recognised most deeply by those whom he mocked:

> In every case he was singled out from that seemingly normal circle of life to which we others belong. He was the one who was permitted, unlike others in the court, to say things without losing his head. He was, so to speak, untouchable. He could not receive additional punishment because he had come to terms with himself and his affliction. He was lifted into a special category of knowledge – of himself and of the world. (Pietzner, 1966 p.6)

The eighteenth century brought the broadest opening yet of new horizons in man's individual and social conscience. Rationalism sought the source of human development through hereditary circumstances and, while advocating a caring, paternal attitude, turned increasingly to science for the eventual 'overcoming' of mental and physical disorders. The humanists, principally Locke and Rousseau, experienced the new-born as *tabula rasa* and looked to the environment as the source of all achievement and difficulty. Through the humanists a particularly decisive step was taken in the field of social activity and social change, especially through the role of education. At the time experiments were conducted, theories argued and disputed, but not until the dawn of the nineteenth century did consistent and, importantly, legislative, action begin.

Dr Karl König's quest, to understand the origins of attitudes and approaches to the handicapped in our century, led him to examine more closely the previous century in this respect. He identified two parallel but essentially different points of reference and attempted to describe their nature (König, 1950). It is beyond the brief of this paper to describe in detail the results of this research, however it is important to sketch its outline.

König identifies one stream of development as the attempt to unite the compassionate, caring Christian attitude of the past with the clear, ordered methods of modern natural science. This he called curative education, or *Heilpädagogik*, which attempted to provide medical, educational and caring activities in an integrated context.

The work in Europe of Itard (1775–1838) and Eduard Seguin (1812–1880) had brought the needs of the handicapped out of the dark corridors of hospitals and asylums and had begun to identify individual needs. Guggenbühl (1816–1863), Troxler (1780–1866) and Pestalozzi (1746–1827) all worked not only to understand symptoms and to observe and identify specific illnesses, but had also stressed consistently the dignity, the essential humanity, of the handicapped person. They were followed in our century by people such as Dr Barnardo, and Don Bosco.

These pioneers were united by their conviction that human warmth and direct involvement were the guardians of the handicapped person's right to develop regardless of the severity of their disability. Further each individual was held to be educable so as to maximise their potentials to contribute in a constructive way to social life. This was expanded further through Rudolf Steiner's far-reaching help and advice. He used the term *Heilpädagogik* in his course of lectures (given in 1924) to a group of young teachers requesting help in their work with the handicapped and, since then, thousands have become engaged in curative educational schools and social therapeutic work with adults throughout the world.

In contrast, Dr König then points to a second, parallel, stream arising out of the scientific rationalism of the nineteenth century, deeply affected by the work of Charles Darwin, and no less dedicated to understanding the human situation and relieving suffering. At the turn of the century men such as Galton, Cattell and Binet, in conjunction with the growing science of developmental psychology, expounded theories of measurable intelligence. Man's capacity to think logically became a central criterion of normality, of educability, and soon statistical classification replaced more personal, individual diagnostic methods. Mathematically determined scales of ability identified the so-called mentally 'defective' in early childhood and isolated such a person from others. Binet himself, the main architect of these theories, complained against the 'brutal pessimism' inherent in them but it was to no avail. This too was the time when confinement in locked institutions, often for a lifetime, was a routine method of treatment.

Significant advances were made in the treatment of physical handicaps, and the social conscience more generally was aroused to correct the terrible deprivation and exploitation of children. The mentally handicapped and mentally ill were, however, generally 'dealt with' rather than treated. Slowly, very slowly, the State began to respond and significantly widened the scope of education and care. Unfortunately, such steps were also frequently accompanied by a lack of interdisciplinary co-operation, political inter-ference and were often hindered by administrative and economic considerations. Time and again sight was lost of the necessity of a flexibility of response to special needs which placed the person with those needs squarely in the centre of concern.

The changing criteria for determining the distinction between the healthy and ill since the nineteenth century have left us with astonishingly varied therapeutic methods and profound social consequences. The question of 'what to do' with the handicapped gradually has become joined by the question 'who are' the handicapped. To meet this question, the curative educational/social therapeutic approach, pioneered by Steiner and described by König, has a series of immediate responses. Are we expecting that, within contemporary social life, the person with special needs should conform to unclear and often subjective criteria such as rationality, productivity, social adaptability and intellect? What will happen to those who cannot conform? Equally, are we expecting 'objective' criteria to be found for normality and if so who will determine them? What will happen to those who cannot conform?

Experience has shown increasingly that both these expectations are simultaneously unrealistic and divisive. In both educational and social terms, to separate any individual from the wide range of human contacts, resources and experiences available through immediate interaction with others is counter-productive. Rather, the curative educational tradition has a growing conviction that *just* this contact can stimulate, even establish, the striving towards the greater realisation of potential. From this recognition we speak today of 'normalising' contact with ever widening life experiences, while at the same time accepting the need for specially adapted and guided living environments. We have only begun to realise just how profoundly beneficial this 'integration' into ever widening social settings can be for many of those with special needs. Have we, however, realised too that these profound benefits are mutual; that society as a whole can receive something from the handicapped at least as valuable as that which it can give?

The Nature of Illness and the Therapeutic Relationship

Essential to a new understanding of the social contribution of the handi-capped is a new view of the nature of illness. By achieving this we can bring enhanced meaning to the mysterious and deeply disturbing phenomena of another's suffering and helplessness. Further, we are led to examine those qualities we bear which offer the greatest help to those in need. *Therapeuia* means, in Greek, 'to accompany, to serve'. To accompany another in their suffering leads, in my experience, to the deepest re-assessment of one's own inner capacities and the therapeutic relationship as such. The empathy required to dismantle the barriers between healer and healed requires self-development; but equally it requires a starting point which significantly broadens the view of illness commonly held today:

> Disease has always been part of the human experience. Man has an inherent tendency to fall ill and to unfold a balancing, healing activity from within himself sometimes spontaneously and sometimes in response to various outside influences, whether substantial or ritual and procedural. To be ill is an experience which befalls us, but also it is a deed, an expression of our deepest being. It belongs to our biography and no account of human illness would be complete without seeing it in relation to the individual and his unique destiny and life story. This is as important as any of the other major events of life. This biographical aspect of human illness of course sets it apart from disease as it may manifest itself in the natural kingdoms . . . Man must rebel against this vision of meaninglessness, must aim at finding, releasing, creating the meaning even in disease. (Twentyman, 1989, p.11)

Until the end of the eighteenth century it was commonly accepted that the knowledge of the healer, the effective application of his or her remedies was intimately connected to a path of rigorous self-development. The expression 'Healer heal thyself' was deeply indicative of the living reality that healing forces are identical to moral forces. Medicinal substances were prescribed after the physician recognised, in the 'picture' of an illness, physical/psychic tendencies, perhaps hidden, unexpressed or benign, which were potentially present in all people, also in himself or herself. As science demanded increasingly detached objectivity, and as greater knowledge of the biological, chemical and mechanical processes of the body were acquired, this quality of the therapeutic relationship was, in the main, lost. The elimination of symptoms and the alleviation of pain has become the patient's demand and the healer's central concern. Certainly there are instances when drugs are needed to reduce acute symptoms and alter bio-chemical imbalances, when surgery is needed to correct physical damage and machines needed to replace vital bodily functions. Yet, I suggest, deep and lasting healing comes about through the intense, freely-willed, personal involvement between healer and patient. Therapy is nothing other than empathy become manifest.

While the acquisition of specific skills and the development of effective methods of physical intervention are necessities, therapy based on community begins with the inner growth of the individual. Nothing can, in honesty, be expected of handicapped people in overcoming their substantial developmental hindrances if we, as those who wish to help, do not change as well. In our essential, primary encounter with the individual with special needs, experiences of mutual recognition and relationship arise which transcend the everyday and touch the core of one's fundamental humanity. In this shared striving, the forces which can arise strengthen, potentise, the healing process to an extraordinary degree. Insights for therapeutic measures can become inspired, beyond articulated, specialised knowledge, and be moulded and adapted to the specific needs of the individual:

> Genuine help is only possible when the helper knows the needs of the other from within because he, too, has suffered them through sympathy and constantly does this. To proceed together inwardly it is necessary for the educator to experience the obstacles which the child experiences inwardly so that he himself is baffled by them and therefore seeks the ways to overcome them with even more energy. To put oneself completely into the child's soul is a spiritual process of evolving which takes place in the educator and thereby also in the person in his care. In him there grows a bond which is spiritually sustaining and which strengthens the will of the person in his care. (Vierl, 1986, p.62)

The ability to extend beyond observation and assessment and to participate deeply in the development of another is not only a task, it is a gift. More than enriching it offers concrete strength and direction in support of the resolves of self-development. This interest in the other also stimulates profound social forces. It lies at the heart of the family, it lies at the heart of friendship, it lies at the centre of communal social endeavour. Rudolf Steiner drew attention to a remarkable aspect of human 'interest' and this rings true with one's own experiences of living and working with those in special need. As von Arnim notes:

> The strange characteristic of interest is the following: that it does not so much turn to that in us which is perfect but rather to that which is imperfect. Rudolf Steiner calls this state of imperfection the 'pathological man'. We all carry something of this pathological man in us. This it is which arouses interest. Not there, where we are perfect, but there where we are imperfect and still developing, where we are in the process of becoming. This calls forth our interest. (v.Arnim, 1982, p.100)

The Question of Community Revisited

In the intentional, specific, encounter which comprises the therapeutic relationship, mutuality of an intense and intimate kind can become an instrument of healing. Suggestive of the changed attitudes which stand behind it, current policy advocates a normalisation process. The attempt is being made more easily to facilitate contact between the handicapped person and society as a whole. In time we should be able to determine more clearly which of our current methods provide the individual with the 'quality of life' which will allow personal growth simultaneous with the acquisition of skills. Tremendous challenges remain in finding social forms appropriate for sheltered, non-stressful environments which, at the same time, stimulate and maximise contact with a wide variety of other people and situations.

The question thus arises as to whether living alone is really, for everyone, an achievement or whether the appropriate challenge would rather be to live in close contact with others. How shall we balance the benefits of the hustle and bustle of ordinary life with the equally ordinary superficial and non-caring attitude of others? Where will conscious, on-going and sensitive friendships be found? It is perhaps hard to imagine that the person with special needs will easily receive a dignified and accepted place in society.

Modern civilisation is acknowledging its own struggle with a host of anti-social forces. Alienation, greed, egotism, mistrust and fear are felt to be ever more prevalent. Could we not imagine that the person with dire, complex individual special needs could become a catalyst? It may be that, through them, socially therapeutic forces could become available in response to the expressed wish that social life should change. All social change begins with the individual. Health-giving forces do become available when inter-dependence between human beings, rather than self-reliance, becomes the basis for social life. To eliminate the barriers which so easily arise between one person and another requires committed and creative effort identical to that which is required in the encounter with the person with special needs. Honest acceptance is needed that the full range of human experiences, expressed or repressed, developed or retarded, realised or hindered, belongs to us all. The needs of those whose experiences have become pathological cannot easily be ignored. No longer can we easily ignore the needs and experiences of each other and human suffering is increasingly difficult to objectify and explain away. Our neighbour cries out for our involvement in a basic and immediate way. Clearly, only enhanced contact based on mutual openness and trust will begin to heal the acute social ills of our time. The critical necessity of new community relationships only enhances our awareness of how little able we are even to begin. How can we find in ourselves those capacities required to step over the threshold of our own sense of inadequacy? Perhaps as a society we are now in a position so complex, so urgent and so crucial that the handicapped are in the position of being able to help us.

A Task for the Handicapped

A widened experience of illness and suffering can help us to understand more comprehensively the meaning of another's specific handicap. This understanding is deepened through the recognition of the affinity possible between human beings from which empathy, and thereby enhanced healing forces, can flow. Healing forces are moral forces. Through consciously acknowledged mutuality, inter-dependence, the meeting of pathological special needs can generate creative, socially healthy, interaction. The inherently noble human desire to offer, and the special needs of each of us to receive, help, demands a new responsibility.

I find it very much more helpful to speak of the task of the handicapped rather than of their mission as some have done (Weihs, 1977). Hopefully we are all growing aware of the particular contribution those in need can make to social life as a whole. However, that which now wishes to find community expression with the handicapped must, in many ways, become *joined* with our own life and work. The task of the handicapped is actually no different from our own; namely, to restore basic human dignity and meaning in each person's life in the context of a society open to receive the contribution of the individual without pre-judgement of its worth. To speak of a special mission, therefore, again distances the handicapped from us (albeit positively) and creates a new stereotype to replace the old. What needs to be renewed in social life is essential for all mankind. It would be an oversimplification to suggest that the so-called normal are more endangered. But it would be honest to say that to admit and to accept one's needs is the foundation for transforming them. We should then look for those concrete areas where mutual responsibility, community building, is possible. The influence of such mutual responsibility upon the social forms of the future will need consistent effort and creativity to maintain.

Julian Sleigh, from his own experience with those with special needs, identifies ten distinct potentials for personal growth available to the individual who allows contact with the handicapped to become a regular part of his or her life (Sleigh, 1987, p.66–67). He calls them a "schooling of the heart". They are immediately recognisable by the families of a handicapped person; they are equally familiar to educators, social workers, religious advisors, sympathetic employers, anyone who allows his or her heart to be open and his or her perceptions honest and clear. Let me summarise them (not necessarily in order of importance):

1. To learn to understand and accept another who is different.
2. To face the deep questions about the meaning of existence which arise from such acceptance.
3. To strive towards a congruent and honest perception of oneself.
4. To recognise and come to terms with one's own weakness and hurts.
5. To work towards 3) and 4) in such an open way that a bridge of trust is built towards the other.
6. As a result to work closely with others that a true community life comes about.
7. Through such communal efforts, personal and collective, love takes on a deeper meaning.
8. Allow that love for the other creates the need to understand the being of Man in depth and reverence.

9. Through understanding and love let Will arise which strives to be clear, strong and dedicated.
10. Recognise that this dedication is accompanied by powers of concentrated Will, real determination and enduring patience.

Such qualities as these are experienced time and again as gifts given by work and life with the handicapped and speak for themselves. They can pervade social life and, if allowed to grow beyond the circumscribed individual encounter, can be developed in *countless future forms*. We are only just at the beginning of our exploration of such forms. It is becoming ever more crucial that we use our heightened powers of empathy to find appropriate ways in which the immediacy of contact with the handicapped person is not diluted by too much theory. Their needs are challenging, inconvenient, even troublesome at times. Social intolerance and limited resources tempt us to find solutions which are 'realistic' but they are not always true to the actual human being served.

   In our search to 'humanise' our provisions for the handicapped, we must also face deep moral-ethical questions – questions which extend beyond the scope of this paper yet are central not only to the issue of the handicapped as contributors to social life, but to the reality of human life itself. Genetic engineering and embryonic research in themselves may not be dangerous but united with a materialistic, narrow view of human value they offer the very real possibility of 'eliminating' handicaps as such. Science left alone to overemphasise physical health and intellectual ability comes quickly to the kind of moral judgements none of us wish to make. So many have described the lovable, open, and joyous Down's Syndrome child in a way that one's compassion is moved but the present controversy about the Down's Syndrome child, now identifiable in the womb, is only the first act in the drama to come. Will one day a method be found perhaps to diagnose schizophrenia before birth? Who will protest at the parent's right to 'select'? These are emotive questions and I do not wish, here, either to criticise medical research or to take a moral high ground on exceedingly complex issues, rather, to call for alertness in safeguarding and cultivating the immense potential which the handicapped bring just *because* of their helplessness and distress.

   What of the future? Will there ever be an end of those who will need the help of others to realise their full human potential? The needs of the handicapped child widened our concepts of education and care, the physically handicapped unlocked wellsprings of ingenuity and determination in both helper and helped and the phenomenon of Autism presented questions of the accessibility of one soul to another which have revealed some hidden secrets of man's capacity to communicate. What of relatively 'new' phenomena such as schizophrenia, addiction, anorexia and syndromes (such as M.E.) which attack the individual's capacity to sustain integrated social activity; or the growing psychiatric lexicon of disturbances of old age and stress-related syndromes?

I would like to close by stating the conviction that we need not stand helpless and confused before the complex and demanding needs of our fellow men. Medicine, education and social work must continue to research, to develop, to experience and experiment on behalf of those with special needs. May the basis for new insight and the source of new inspiration and strength always be the people in need themselves. All we can do to allow ourselves the opportunity to be moved, changed and united with those who suffer will bring us closer to this source. New community forms, varied and flexible, must be sought time and again. The needs of the individual who is special are demanding and require of us faculties which are not easily available. Yet it is just in this challenge to develop, this need to overcome that which is handicapped and underdeveloped in us, that we join those we wish to help in the most intimate, important way possible.

While our approaches may be varied we should rejoice in these variations, in as much as they are united in the effort to seek the support and co-operation of the handicapped people themselves in our endeavours. As such 'community of striving' is sought, and as we listen deeply to our fellow men in need, the human encounters which arise cultivate the unlimited resource of love. This love is neither sentimental nor exclusive but can inspire deeds of commitment and sacrifice which speak more loudly than words. Community, therapy and the individual with special needs belong inextricably together. Each depends on the other two in a wonderfully balanced, dynamic way. Together they contain fertile seeds for the future which have the task of changing the quality of human relationship and social life. May our gratitude be sufficient and our resolve be clear enough warmly to accept those who suffer as our closest allies and friends.

CHAPTER 5

Community and Therapy:
What is a Healthy Community?

James A. Whyte

The word 'community' is an in-word of our time. The University Library in St Andrews has no fewer than 410 titles with the word 'community' in them. Larger libraries will have even more. A glance at these titles shows, however, that the word is used in a wide variety of senses. Many of the books relate to the European Community. There is a whole group of titles of anthropological work, studies of, for example, a village community in Mexico. There are sociological works, and books about what is now called '-Community Work'. There are even New Testament studies, concerning, for example, the community for which Luke's gospel was written. There are books about religious communities (orders of monks or nuns) and there are many books about the Church, the Christian community.

One feature which must strike almost anyone who glances through such modern literature is that the word 'community' is almost always used in a positive sense. Although it is applied to a wide diversity of human groups, its use almost always implies a positive evaluation of the group. To call a group a community is to suggest that it is a good thing. To call it a therapeutic community suggests that it is a very good thing.

For that very reason, perhaps, the apparent unanimity of the literature may be misleading. In some places the word 'community' is not a welcome word. I was once attacked by politicians of the Right for suggesting that our loyalties to the communities to which we belong had been overlooked in their political thinking. There is a strong individualism put forward today in the philosophy of the New Right. Such thinkers dislike and distrust the very concept of community, and prefer to avoid the term. Some sociologists also are embarrassed by the fact that the word 'community' has always such a strong connotation of value, and in their desire to be objective and 'scientific', would rather abandon the word.

The view put forward in this chapter is that not everything that is called 'community' in fact makes for human flourishing, and that it is necessary to seek criteria whereby we may learn to distinguish between a community which is healthy and one which is oppressive – or perhaps, to distinguish between the healthy elements and tendencies, and the oppressive elements and tendencies in all communities.

But first, it is necessary to seek some clarity in the use and meaning of this vague but fashionable word. It appears that the word was first used to indicate any relationship or association of people who had something in common. So in the Authorised Version of the New Testament the Greek word *koinonia* could be translated fellowship, communion, communication, distribution, and could equally be translated with the more modern words sharing, and community. One sixteenth-century writer could say "While God reigneth by his Spirit in us, men have a certain community with God in this world". The word also denoted the community of the town or village, such communities being centres of loyalty to those who belonged to them.

The modern interest in the word is usually traced back to Ferdinand Tönnies, and his book *Gemeinschaft und Gesellschaft* (1887). The title could be translated Community and Association, and Tönnies contrasts two ways in which human beings relate to one another, two ways of being together:

> In Gemeinschaft with one's family, one lives from birth on, bound to it in weal and woe. One goes into Gesellschaft as one goes into a strange country. (Tönnies, in Bell & Newby, 1972, p.7)

Tönnies contrasts the organic nature of Gemeinschaft with the commercial or contractual character of Gesellschaft:

> Gemeinschaft is old; Gesellschaft is new as a name as well as a phenomenon. All praise of rural life has pointed out that the Gemeinschaft among people is stronger there and more alive; it is the lasting and genuine form of living together. In contrast to Gemeinschaft, Gesellschaft is transitory and superficial. Accordingly, Gemeinschaft should be understood as a living organism, Gesellschaft as a mechanical aggregate. (Tönnies, in Bell & Newby, 1972, p.8)

It is not difficult to detect here the romanticism of one living in an urban, commercial society and idealising the old rural community of a previous age. For Tönnies there is no such thing as a bad community.

The fragmentation, loneliness and anonymity of life in the modern city can easily be contrasted with the warm sense of belonging in the country village. The desire to recover this lost age inspired much writing, religious and sociological, in the post-war years. In 1965 Harvey Cox shattered this dream in his book *The Secular City* (a book which did for the word 'secular' what Tönnies had done for the word 'community'). He sang a hymn of praise to the liberation of man by secular, urban society – liberation from 'religious tutelage' and liberation from the suffocating restrictions of the old rural life. The separation of work and home and leisure, which others deplored, was precisely what gave modern man his freedom to choose to enter into association with others (Gesellschaft) for specific and limited purposes (a Bach choir or a political party). The secular city was therefore the scene, in Bonhoeffer's phrase, of "man's coming of age".

Cox's corrective to romanticism was timely, for he saw that the religious society of the past and the village community could be places of oppression, imprisoning rather than liberating the human spirit. But he retained, essentially, Tönnies' distinction, simply turning it on its head. What for Tönnies had been good (Gemeinschaft in the village) for Cox was restrictive and stifling and what for Tonnies had been bad (urban Gesellschaft) became for Cox the instrument of liberation.

The individualism of modern political thinkers of the Right has little relation to Cox's understanding of human freedom, and stems more from the tradition, with which the name of John Locke is associated, that society arises from a contract between individuals. The individual is basic. Society is an abstraction. So, in the speech of Mrs Thatcher to the General Assembly of the Church of Scotland in 1988, the individual is contrasted with the collective. The family receives mention, but there is no mention of any community beyond the family.

On examination, however, 'the individual' proves to be as abstract and debatable a concept as 'the community'. As Raymond Plant points out in a very helpful study, "Reflection reveals that our *concept* of the individual is by no means identical with that of his physical body; rather it is every bit as abstract, as 'conceptual' as that of community and society" (Plant, 1974, p.35).

Human beings are social animals. No one is born a Robinson Crusoe, and anyone left to grow up as a Robinson Crusoe would not become a splendid individual; he or she would not develop any recognisably human characteristics. Human development requires a long period of nurture, and the skills of human living and communication have to be learned. The different ways in which these can be learned form the diversity of human culture. The primary group in which they are learned, in our society and in most societies, is normally the family, sometimes the nuclear family, sometimes the more extended family. Beyond this are wider social groupings which vary with the culture: the neighbourhood, the school, the church. All of these are or may become centres of loyalty which provide the individual with an identity, a sense of belonging, a shared history.

Any group which provides a focus of loyalty, a sense of belonging – be it family, church, neighbourhood, nation, university, company, even football club – tends to style itself, in that aspect of its life, as 'a community'. This means that any person may belong to not one, but several communities, often interlocking. Some of these groups may demand more of energy and involvement than others, though in the private hierarchy of importance these may not necessarily rank the highest.

If the word 'community' is allowed to be used in this vague way, which seems to correspond to current usage, and the emphasis is on the focus of loyalty and the sense of belonging rather than on geographical propinquity, Tönnies' sharp distinction is at least relativised. There are relations into which we enter which are almost purely functional, where the level of personal involvement is minimal. Even there, some element of personal recognition enters in, as when the man on the Tay Road Bridge says "Thank you" when I hand him my toll, and I reply in the same vein. Between that and a much higher, or deeper, level of personal involvement there will be an indefinite gradation.

A second consequence of placing the emphasis on loyalty and the sense of belonging is that the word 'community' is not confined to primary groups. The nation may be a centre of loyalty and belonging. The Roman Catholic Church is frequently described as a community, though it is an enormous organisation whose members are scattered over the whole world. So also, of course, is a great multi-national company such as ICI, but there are few people, even among those who work for it, who would regard that as a community. The emotions engendered are different. (Some firms, including some multi-nationals, seek to provide facilities for the leisure as well as the working-hours of their employees. This is welcomed by some and resented by others, who do not wish to spend their entire life within the firm.)

On the other hand, the emphasis on loyalty and belonging may enable us to read Tönnies' distinction in a different way, as a distinction between relationships of co-operation and relationships of confrontation in human affairs – Gemeinschaft being essentially co-operative, and Gesellschaft essentially confrontational. This may account for the warmth and sense of positive value that adhere to the word 'community' in modern usage. What we call 'a community' is a group where there is, it is supposed, support, nurture and co-operation, in contrast to the commercial world where the only motive is self-interest and the only maxim *Caveat emptor* ('Let the buyer beware'). But this distinction may be made too sharply, both by those who support the ideal of community and those who maintain the realism of commercial competitiveness, both of whom fail to take into account the complexities of human nature.

The individualists of today's political and economic theory act on the principle that the only motive for effective human action is the desire for profit, sheer self-interest. The attempt is therefore made to replace all relationships of trust by commercial relationships of buying and selling, and to substitute competition and confrontation for partnership and co-operation in every aspect of human life. Such an attempt cannot succeed, because, as we have seen, even in our most functional relationships a personal element keeps creeping in, and in our commercial relationships the shopkeeper has a habit of becoming our friend, and we distinguish between those enterprises that are a rip-off, and those where there is fair trading. We go to those whom we can trust, and even develop a sense of loyalty to one another.

There seems to be a pull in human nature towards trust. *Pace* Hobbes and others, our natural relations to one another are not those of war, but those of the family. The concept of community contains within it that strong belief that human relations should be based on trust, co-operation, mutual respect. This is what a civilised society should be about. This is, in a sense, a vision of the Kingdom. Self-interest (of which, to be realistic, we must take account) is destructive of the Kingdom. But the communitarian must remember that it is as impossible in this sinful world to have a society based solely on trust as it is for the individualist to have a society based solely on self-interest.

With that in mind, I should like to consider the community (as loosely defined) in both its internal and its external relationships. The individual becomes a human person through the nurture of his or her communities. If this is growth into freedom, the person thus nurtured may become critical of the ethos which upbringing has provided. The upbringing itself has provided the tools of thought and moral criticism. Such criticism may take the form of critical solidarity, attempting to persuade the community to change and improve things. It may seek to broaden the tradition, by involvement with other groups, or a concern for the whole family of mankind. It may also take the form of violent rejection of the community, or it may take the form of flight from it into other, more congenial, communities. This may happen when the community itself is particularly resistant to criticism, or hostile to freedom.

I would contend that any human community which aims at total commitment and involvement must inevitably become oppressive and tyrannical. The totalitarian community is a blight upon the human spirit. A healthy community is one which allows, indeed cherishes, the freedom of the individual. The individual depends on communities, from the family outward, to provide the nurture necessary for growth. The aim of such nurture is, or should be, the development of a mature and free person. And the mark of a mature and free person is precisely their ability to enter into free and unthreatening relationships with other persons, relationships of trust and mutual respect.

If this is the case, then the sharp opposition between the individual and the community cannot be maintained. The individual and the community are interdependent, interdependence rather than dependence or independence being itself the mark of mature relationships. The mature individual is able to enter into community; the mature community encourages the flourishing of the individual. John Stuart Mill, in his essay *On Liberty* maintained that the mark of a free society lay in its ability to tolerate, and even to produce, eccentrics. A community in which there is mutual respect will be one in which there is rejoicing in human diversity, in which people are given space to be and to become themselves.

Religious communities are particularly prone to become totalitarian communities, stifling rather than liberating the human spirit, demanding conformity and persecuting originality. The claim to an authority which derives from (or is even identical with) the authority of God, tends to give to such communities an authoritarian character, even when they do not develop an hierarchical authoritarian structure. The character of such communities may be masked by the language of love. But it is the love of the possessive mother who cannot allow her children to grow up and become free rather than that of the wise mother who is able to let go and let be. Churches are very apt to encourage the regression of their members, so that in the context of the church they are dependent children, rather than mature adults.

It is fatally easy, in a religious community (whether it is the great denomination or the small religious group) to identify the group of sinful, limited, striving human beings with the perfect community of God – to identify the church with the Kingdom of God. When the human community is thus idealised, it has no way of dealing with the badness of its members, or with the conflicts that arise among them. Denis Martin once wrote:

> Much 'Christian love' is little more than a superior brand of human kindness based upon the suppression of bad feelings . . . Too often the Church community as a whole cannot accept bad feeling in a spirit of love . . . By his cross Jesus demonstrated that real love attracts sin and bad feeling out into the open, suffers its impact to the full and only so redeems it. The conventional, respectable church community drives it underground and forces its expression in unhappiness, inhibited relationships, neurosis and disease. One of the great problems within the Church is the failure fully to acknowledge that the accepting attitude of a suffering love is more creative and contains more healing potential than control and suppression. (Martin, 1962, pp.186–187)

The idealised community deals with its badness by control or suppression. Conflict is not seen to have any constructive possibilities for change or growth. Rather it is seen always as a threat to the unity of the group, and is resolved by the schism or the exclusion of the dissident parties, or even worse, as in the past in the Soviet Union, by labelling them as mentally ill and in need of treatment.

Religious communities may be particularly prone to the problems of totalitarianism (though they also have, as Denis Martin suggests, particular resources for dealing with them), but they are not alone in this. All communities tend to idealise themselves, and so to demand that ultimate loyalty be given to a sinful and relative human group. The demands of patriotism have often been pitched at a level that is idolatrous, and even a football-club can consider its fortunes to be a matter more serious than life and death. Part of the strategy of healthy living is to recognise the relativity of the communities to which we belong, and not to give ultimate loyalty to that which has no right to it.

It may be that some of the problems facing the family today come from the idealisation of the family in the revolution of rising expectations, so that the conflicts and difficulties of marital and family relationships are treated as failures rather than as challenges, and are dealt with by schism or exclusion – by divorce or flight.

The therapeutic community may also be prone to idealisation and to totalitarianism. Years ago I came across a description of the admission of a patient to a mental hospital in the United States, run on community lines. It filled me with dismay:

> On admission, the new patient is given no special instruction regarding the rules for his group. He must rely on his contacts with the other members for his orientation. From the start he is only asked to be himself in company with other people who are being themselves. It is as though the person is entering a family again in which he may establish his own identity by learning to relate to other persons in more constructive ways.

I wondered who, behind the apparent gentleness of this account, was kidding whom. The sudden, unwelcome and anxiety-provoking event of admission to a mental hospital bears little resemblance to the gradual and natural induction into a family. Is the patient really being asked only "to be himself in company with other people who are being themselves?" Is the refusal to give him any orientation such a kindness, or is it one way of increasing his or her insecurity and therefore accelerating his or her dependence on the group?

An American hospital chaplain once described to me a group in his hospital where "We promise to be completely honest with one another, to have no secrets from one another". Again I wondered at the self-deception of this idealised community – for who can be completely honest with himself or herself, let alone with another? And if there are no secrets, the group is demanding a total surrender from its members. What group has such a right? If there are no secrets, there is no place to hide, no place where you can be alone. Erving Goffman mentions that in some mental hospitals devoted to intensive milieu therapy, "patient pairs conducting an affair may be obliged to discuss their relationship during group meetings" (Goffman, 1961, p.39). When that which is most private becomes most public, we have a violation of privacy which is a violation of the person. The right to say 'It's none of your business' is a very precious right. When any community denies its members that right it has become totalitarian, and I should consider one mark of the totalitarian community to be its disregard for privacy.

The problems of the idealisation of the therapeutic community have been dealt with by Robert F. Hobson in a paper entitled *The Messianic Community* (in Hinshelwood & Manning, 1979). The use of religious imagery seems to me significant. Hobson's honest and moving reflections on his own experience of therapeutic communities provide me with a bridge into a comment on the external relationships of communities:

> The Leader and his colleagues collude in an idealisation of himself and of the UNIT (now spelt in very large capitals), which is often personified. The good UNIT is engaged in a battle with the powers of darkness: the 'badness' outside, which is embodied in the rest of the hospital, the traditional psychiatric

establishment, or the world at large. The unit is under attack. (Hobson, in Hinshelwood & Manning, 1979, p.233)

One is reminded of Wilfred Bion's *Experiences in Groups* (Bion, 1961). The personification of the group, the belief that 'a group' exists, and that a 'group mind' exists, is evidence of 'basic assumption activity'. One of the forms of such basic assumption activity is 'the fight-flight group' – united to counter the evil outside, the threats to its very existence. Nothing unites a community so much as an external threat, real or imagined. (There are those who look back still to war-time Britain, as a time when real community existed.) If there is no real threat, it may be necessary to imagine one, for in the idealised community the badness must be outside. Some Christians believe that the Church is at its best when it is being persecuted, and would like to encourage persecution if they could. That failing, of course, it is always possible to do some persecuting ourselves.

The attempt to counter the idealisation of community must not be seen as an attack on community itself. On the contrary, we need our communities, and our existence and health as persons depends upon them, upon the support, encouragement and affirmation that they provide. But the health of our communities depends on our resistance to the tendency to idealisation.

As we have noted, the word community has always in it an element of the ideal. Commenting on the sociological literature, Bell and Newby said:

> Community simply stood for what an endless group of thinkers . . . believed to be what society *should* consist of . . . Their definitions of community have also incorporated their ideas of the Good Life. The result has been a confusion between what community is (empirical description) and what the sociologists have felt it *should be* (normative prescription). (Bell & Newby, 1972, p.xliii)

It is not possible to eliminate the evaluative element from the use of the word 'community'. It is possible, however, to prevent the ideal from becoming an idealisation, that is to avoid confusing the ideal that is aimed at and the reality that is achieved.

If we recognise, as Reinhold Niebuhr has done (Niebuhr, 1947), that while it is possible for the individual to transcend self-interest, it is extremely difficult for the community to transcend its corporate self-interest, we shall recognise that the health of our communities, and therefore the health of the individuals who compose them, depends on their capacity for self-criticism, and their response to the criticism of others. The idealised, totalitarian community cannot engage in self-criticism, and cannot tolerate criticism from its members. (Criticism from those outside is dismissed as enmity.) The free community will see in creative, constructive criticism the means to its own correction and its own growth.

The free community will therefore not be afraid to handle conflict, and will see in the diversity of human viewpoints and the uniqueness of human personality an enrichment rather than a threat. This does not mean that a community can tolerate *anything*. There will always be some things to which it has to say 'No'.

The free community will be concerned to foster the full development of individuals, and it will therefore respect their privacy. "The ideal state of a relationship is one of aloneness-togetherness" (Hobson, in Hinshelwood & Manning, 1972, p.238). The boundaries of privacy will vary from relationship to relationship, but the element of aloneness cannot be eliminated from any relationship between mature human beings, and the recognition of this must be one of the criteria of a free community.

This description of a free community itself represents an ideal. None of our communities is totally free, just as few of our communities, I trust, are fully totalitarian. In seeking the better health of our communities, we are always balancing our need for freedom and our desire for security.

The search for community may be a regressive impulse: a quest for security, a desire to recover a lost Eden, to find the primal family. The image of re-entry into a family is sometimes used of the therapeutic community. The recovery of a lost Eden is found in religious imagery. Edwin Muir's poem *The Transfiguration* is a fine example of this (Muir, 1960, pp.199–200). It ends:

> Then he will come, Christ the uncrucified,
> Christ the discrucified, his death undone,
> His agony unmade, his cross dismantled –
> Glad to be so – and the tormented wood
> Will cure its hurt and grow into a tree
> In a green springing corner of young Eden,
> And Judas damned take his long journey backward
> From darkness into light and be a child
> Beside his mother's knee, and the betrayal
> Be quite undone and never more be done.

The need to regress, to become a child again, is part of the healthy rhythm of our lives, and many of our communities, including our hospitals and our religious communities, help us to do this, and to find re-creation through it. But to be healthy, such regression can be only a temporary respite, not a permanent abode. It is not by the undoing of past wrongs, rolling back the scroll of history, that the world's redemption is to be found. Muir's is the romantic error. The true transfiguration is in the future, not the past. Not Christ the discrucified, but Christ the resurrected, his wounds still visible, is the symbol of Christian hope.

The word in the New Testament which can be translated community, or communion or fellowship or sharing is used by Paul in the phrase "the fellowship of Christ's sufferings and the power of his resurrection." The ideal of community is not the wishing away of the evil, the selfishness, the brokenness, the suffering and the strife that mar our lives and fragment our society. The ideal of community calls us to deal with these things by overcoming them, taking into ourselves the brokenness and the pain, and allowing them to be transformed by love.

It is this, as I understand it, that is the *raison d'être* of Camphill. Nowhere is the brokenness of humanity more clear than in the handicapped, especially the mentally handicapped. In many parts of our society those who most need to be included in love are those who find themselves excluded and segregated. Their difference from the rest of us cannot be disguised, and society is embarrassed by the difference – perhaps because they remind us of our own fragility and imperfection, and our dependence on one another.

The churches have tended to mirror the attitude of society. The Church of Scotland, for example, has given too little thought to the care and support of families with mentally handicapped children, and, until recently, made no provision for the Christian nurture of the mentally handicapped, or for their admission to communion.

It may be that the acceptance of the person with mental handicap has been easier in small towns and communities, where they are known and can find work within their competence. It is not so easy in the cities. Yet the concept of 'community care' has been embraced by government, and local authorities are made responsible for providing care in the community. To understand the cost of this – the cost, not in financial terms, but in love, firmness, patience and understanding – the Social Work departments and the communities they serve may need to learn from the experience of communities such as Camphill, where the costly search for a mutuality of love and respect brings its tensions as well as its rewards.

We must not pretend that our broken communities are the ideal, but we must let the ideal – the Kingdom of God – beckon us, judge us and encourage us.

CHAPTER 6

The Therapeutic Community

J. Stuart Whiteley

'*Evince a desire to show some confidence, and repose some trust, even in mad people,*' said the resident physician . . . '*not only is a thorough confidence established, by those means, between the physician and patients in respect of their hallucinations, but it is easy to understand that opportunities are afforded for seizing any moment of reason, to startle them by placing their own delusion before them in its most incongruous and ridiculous light . . .*'. It is obvious that one great feature of this system, is the inculcation and encouragement, even among such unhappy persons, of a decent self-respect.

Charles Dickens, American Notes, 1842.

The term therapeutic community came into being after the second world war following the description of experiences in two Military Psychiatric Hospitals by Main (1946) working at Northfield and Maxwell Jones (1953) working at Mill Hill. That is not to say that forms of 'living and learning' communities had not existed prior to this; indeed the roots of such can be traced through various projects with delinquent youths before and after the First World War in the United States (Father Flanagan's Boys' Town), in England (Homer Lane and the Little Commonwealth), in Russia (Makarenko and the Gorki Republics), in Austria (Aichorn) and again in England in the late thirties, (David Wills and Q Camps and Hawkspur Camp) (Bridgeland, 1971). Even these humanitarian projects, with a later input of psychoanalytic thinking and practice, perhaps owed something to the era of moral treatment in psychiatry as practised by pioneers such as Tuke at the York Asylum and Conolly at Hanwell in the mid-nineteenth century (Whiteley & Gordon, 1979). However, apart from the institution of the Planned Environment Therapy Trust by psychoanalyst Marjorie Franklin in the 1930s (Righton, 1979) there had been no real theoretical exposition of what we might now term the therapeutic community and the beginning of a qualitative validation of the subject came with the recognition of an urgent need to respond to the new problem of psychiatric casualties in the Military Hospitals of the Second World War.

63

Origins

The problem presented in the Military Psychiatric Hospitals was different, and it must be said was in part an economic problem, from that which might pertain in normal psychiatric institutions, in that the patients were all young, male, physically fit and suffering from a related form of emotional or neurotic disorder; and that engendered by a common cause, the drafting for and involvement in military service, which itself was a social rather than a medical aetiology. The situation called for an innovative approach, and perhaps most importantly, the government of the day supported an energetic response which would restore these casualties to the war effort.

At Northfield there was a legacy of a brief experiment with the then new idea of group psychotherapy (Bion, 1961) and the Northfield staff contained a high proportion of Tavistock Clinic or otherwise psychoanalytically trained psychiatrists and psychologists, thus a treatment process was developed with a bias towards psychotherapy. At Mill Hill the treatment team was largely from the more social and biologically rooted psychiatry of the Maudsley Hospital and therein a system of therapy evolved which had more leaning towards social interaction. Main and Jones were both charismatic, inspiring leaders with foresight and clarity of vision. Both saw in the war-time experiences of a therapeutic community a model for future practice in the mental health field. To some extent this has been the case and despite fluctuating fortunes, the idea of the therapeutic community has developed. Indeed it has progressed and been world-wide in its application.

As far as we know, Main and Jones did not exchange ideas nor collaborate in the war-time years, yet in many ways they wrote similarly of the philosophy. Thus, Main wrote of the therapeutic community as:

> an attempt to use a hospital not as an organisation run by doctors in the interests of their own greater technical efficiency, but as a community with the immediate aim of full participation of all its members in its daily life and the eventual aim of the re-socialisation of the neurotic individual for life in ordinary society. (Main, 1946)

Maxwell Jones (1956) wrote, "the term therapeutic community implies that the responsibility for treatment is not confined to the trained medical staff but is a concern also of the other community members." He goes on to say, however, that "there will be a single therapeutic goal, namely the adjustment of the individual to social and work conditions outside without any ambitious psychotherapeutic programme". The imprint of psychotherapy has traditionally been put upon the Main model and what we might term sociotherapy on the Maxwell Jones model but the differences have perhaps been erroneously emphasised by subsequent commentators and practitioners.

Main was primarily interested in organisational tensions and conflict between sub-groups in a community or organisation (he had advised on the resolution of the only mutiny in the British forces during the Italian campaign). He wrote of the need for analysing the inter-personal difficulties which stood between the individual and his or her participation in community life, and pointed out that the doctor no longer owned his or her captive patients and that the anarchical rights of the doctor must be given up and his or her role exchanged for that of a member of the community. His colleague Foulkes, although describing his own work at Northfield (Foulkes & Anthony, 1957) as "essentially analytical" and sitting in on the ward and workshop discussion groups as being in order to interpret behaviour, clarify problems and facilitate their resolution by the group, also wrote of the great value for the psychiatrist of being able to work in what he called the *life space* of the patient (Foulkes, 1948) moving through the ward, workshop, dining and social areas like an anthropologist learning about a strange tribe. Foulkes also commented that it was not so much the activity of a group that was the therapeutic agent but the active participation in the task that was perhaps the key feature (Foulkes & Anthony, 1957). Thus an element of sociotherapy through role exploration was present from the outset in this basically psychotherapeutic model. In a more recent account of the early days of the therapeutic community Main (1983) has described it as "a culture of enquiry".

The Maxwell Jones model incorporated *open communication, flattening of the staff hierarchy, and blurring of roles* and when it had moved on to a civilian patient group at the Belmont Hospital (later Henderson Hospital) in the post war years it was researched by a team of social scientists headed by Robert Rapoport. In the classic book *Community as Doctor* (Rapoport, 1960) they concentrated upon the social dynamics of the therapeutic community. They elicited the now well known ideological themes of the therapeutic community – *permissiveness, communalism, democracy and reality confrontation* – but also pointed out the inherent conflict between medical and nursing staff who pursued a course of treatment of the intra-personal problems of the patient and the lay workshop staff who pursued a course of rehabilitation of the handicapped individual and his or her adjustment to external conditions (without intra-personal change, as it were). Most importantly they demonstrated that it was those patients who formed close relationships with key staff figures who benefited most, which indicates an undercurrent of transference and its working through and a psychodynamic process.

Further Developments

Following Rapoport's examination of the dynamics of the therapeutic community, there have been further clarifications of the process. Thus Clark (1965) discriminated between the *therapeutic community approach*, by which he meant a more open system of treatment as adopted by many mental hospitals in the post-war years although still retaining the overall medical philosophy, and the *therapeutic community proper*, by which he meant adherence to the original visions of Main and Jones and incorporating the following features:

• less than 100 persons, small enough for everyone to be involved;
• holding regular meetings of the whole community;
• adhering to a philosophy that an individual's difficulties were largely in relation to other people and capable of resolution by discussion;
• analysing the social events of the unit;
• improving communication;
• flattening the authority pyramid;
• providing protected situations in which patients could try out new forms of coping;
• constantly examining roles and behaviour in staff and patients.

Kennard and Roberts (1983) have described the factors common to therapeutic communities operating with different patient populations as:

• the informal and communal atmosphere;
• the central place of group meetings;
• the sharing of daily work in the maintenance of the community;
• recognition of the patients as auxiliary therapists;
• the sharing of authority between staff and patients.

More recently Bloor *et al.* (1988) have identified seven aspects of practice utilised by staff in a range of different therapeutic communities in hospital, hostel, residential home or day-care based as:

• making residents (patients) responsible for keeping others in treatment;
• the after-group for promoting reflectivity;
• the attendance of residents at staff handover;
• the 'tight-house' (periodic emphasis of rules) to combat institution-alisation;
• devices to increase the resident's awareness of the possibility of change e.g. 'think' days;
• the need for junior staff to have alternative sources of satisfaction;
• selection of staff by residents.

The themes of sociotherapy and psychotherapy are central to the dynamic and design of a therapeutic community and require further exploration both of the more tangible factors as documented above and the more intangible factors such as values, belief systems, personality and attitudes of those involved.

Sociotherapy

The first impression of a visitor to a therapeutic community is that it seems highly ritualised and rigid. Rules abound, jobs are allocated to everyone, certain duties are to be performed, reports made and a busy timetable of group meetings fulfilled. But this structure is the very matrix through which communications are made, behaviour explored and interactions facilitated. No speech, action or even passing thought seems to escape scrutiny. "I even dream Henderson", commented one patient at that hospital, which illustrates a degree of involvement and identification with the unit which is to be aimed at.

Three processes of treatment then ensue: *Interaction* is promoted by the close-living, inward-looking community, somewhat cut-off from the distractions of the outside world. All decisions and all problems are referred back to the community meeting. Everyone is in some measure affected by all that occurs and there seems no escape into the diversionary behaviour which would be possible in the outside world. "It's like real life speeded up", commented one patient. "You meet in 24 hours situations you wouldn't meet in 24 days on the outside."

Then follows *exploration* of the observed behaviour, the day's activities being punctuated by reflective group meetings to comment on what has just been observed and the effect this might have had on others. The group is a rich source of varied feed-back and the formal institution of the group for this purpose allows open comment to be made. The multiplicity of rules, for instance, and their infringement offers a mechanism for behaviour to be routinely examined. A danger here is that the imposition of rigid rules and their thoughtless application in a ritualistic way as if the rules themselves were in some way curative, can obscure the very nature of the therapeutic community, as Briggs (1990) has pointed out. Yet another patient points to the therapeutic purpose of the rules in observing that "it is a crash course in living – you learn in 6 months what you should have learned between the ages of 6 to 10". This, indeed is what Piaget (1926) termed the concrete stage of personality development when social learning took place often through the imposition, testing out and playing with the rules in a rigid seeming way and where the rules of the game in playground interactions as mothers and fathers, cops and robbers etc. become rehearsals for real-life interactions. As in the playground situation, so in the therapeutic community, preoccupation with the rules of the game can become more fascinating to the players than the game itself as they seek to use the rules to better themselves in relation to others.

After having observed the behaviour in interaction and explored it in discussion, it has to be made possible through *experimentation* for the individual to try out different modes of behaviour. This may be said to him in direct advice to be more patient, for instance, but more often can be mediated best through the allotted roles of the patients' committee. These latter can vary from highly responsible posts such as chairman of the community or foreman of the workshop down to canteen assistant or the teller who counts the votes during meetings. The posts carry different expectations and call for different styles of interaction and patients will be allotted to them by their fellows not because they might do the job well but because it is seen that some aspect of behaviour pertinent to the particular job needs to be experienced by the individual. Manor (1982) researching this aspect, demonstrated how individuals came to 'live' in to the allotted role and then to feel and to act as others expected them to do. Interventions by staff can be of a socio-therapeutic nature. Matza (1969) described how deviant behaviour is a learned activity and the individual is influenced most by those with whom he or she feels most *affinity* and to whom by adopting their customs and practices he or she then becomes *affiliated*. Thereafter outside society labels him or her or awards him or her *signification* as Matza puts it, stamping him or her permanently in the deviant role and seeing all his or her behaviour as such.

The same processes can be seen in reverse during the course of therapeutic community treatment where the objective now is to learn an undeviant role. The newcomer is most influenced by his or her fellow patients with whom he or she has *affinity* and the staff need to stand back and let them deal with him. He or she knows only too well where he or she stands with staff, parent or authority figures with whom he or she has been in set manoeuvres all his or her life. Thus the co-therapist with myself in the new residents group would be a representative from the patient community.

Secondly the individual has to be *affiliated* to this new society and to feel accepted be able to join in and be one of the group. Thus the rituals, the in-group jargon and slang, the jobs and the in-jokes, together with the unchanging programme may all seem very tedious, childish and unexciting to staff who have passed this way many times before but for the new patient acquiring these 'badges' or ritualistic symbols, as it were, is being admitted to the fraternity of the community and recognised as 'one of us'.

Lastly, *signification* or the new labelling by the community of the individual as someone who is non-deviant, as someone who is worth something and has something good to say or offer is most important and often falls to the staff to remark upon, not in a patronising way but by sharing a responsibility or a decision with the patient; by seeking the patient's opinion and acting on it sincerely; by endorsing a remark a patient may make and by allowing him as well as the psychotherapist to make appropriate interpretations.

The activities in the 'life space' of the patient and separate from the formal therapeutic interchanges of the day are a valuable aspect of the therapeutic community. In an investigation of the therapeutic factors carried out at Henderson (Collis & Whiteley, 1987) we had asked patients to describe what for them had been the most important therapeutic factor of the preceding week, to describe why it was important for them and to say where it had occurred. In slightly over half the events the memorable factor was something which had occurred outside of formal group therapy sessions but still within the boundaries of the community. Sometimes it was related to a job such as "I found it real good when I was able to set-up the crisis meeting for someone who was upset and settle him down". Sometimes it was just a moment of reflection which a passing incident evoked. Thus one male patient commented, "I had become fond of a girl in the community. I noticed how upset I became when she left the room. Like a child who has been deserted by its mother". This same study also categorised the therapeutic factors into the factors listed by Bloch *et al.* (1985) as therapeutic factors in group psychotherapy[1]. The finding for the therapeutic community study was that, in the initial stages, acceptance and to a lesser extent the instillation of hope were predominant, whilst self-understanding and learning through inter-personal actions came later.

Mahony (1979) has written of his own experiences in the Henderson that:

> The groups themselves were not the places where things happened. They gave cerebral insight and stirred feelings up but it was during the unstructured times of the day, weekends, down the pub, night time when the intellectual insights percolated down to the gut. The small group, the intense group therapy meeting complete with psychiatrist evoked the highest expectation when everything was going to be explained and magically put right with a therapeutic wand, where all the high powered talking was done yet it was outside the meeting that the emotional realisation occurred, when things clicked into place.

Of the jobs he was to say,

> I had proven to myself that I could accept responsibility and discharge it as I had done in various jobs on the committee. The Henderson had been the only place out side the [Hell's Angels] family where I had been given the opportunity to show what I could do, where people listened to what I had to say, where I was treated as somebody, as a person within my own right.

Psychotherapy

The individual's progress through the unit follows a more psychodynamic but predictable course. Prospective patients will eagerly present themselves for assessment, seeking acceptance by the group and insisting that they realise the time has come for them to change their way of life. After admission, however, they are faced with the realisation that change will be traumatic, long term and involve the loss of accustomed patterns of coping, and taking on new and uncertain alternatives. Their first response is to make the situation 'viable' (Whitaker & Lieberman, 1965) i.e. to cope by using the accustomed defences that they have previously employed. They revert to old patterns whether of drinking, pairing-off, or threats of violence. The community tolerates but struggles with them as they strive to invalidate the treatment process and manipulate others to their way of interaction. After a few weeks of such confrontations the going gets tough and they realise that if they want to change they must relinquish the acting-out defences and become involved in the community ethos. Some 20–30% will opt to leave in the first three or four weeks finding the change too threatening or the course too hard – and it has to be said that for a minority the situation can also provoke a 'flight into health' .

Those who stay then experience a superficial *positive transference* to the community as a whole. They 'join' the unit by taking on all the jobs, picking up the in-group jargon and slang, learning the mythology and folklore of the unit. They enthusiastically greet visitors and assure them that 'this is the best place I have ever been'. They believe that this good place will meet all their needs but under stress they will quickly revert to the old acting-out defences and once more the community absorbs but confronts, but also supports and contains, the troubled individual. The situation is comparable to Klein's (1946) *paranoid-schizoid* position of early development where things are seen in black and white, in extremes with no compromise nor allowance for differing situations, as reward or punishment. The rules of the game are interpreted and played out strictly and crudely, but gradually the individuals form a deeper attachment to the unit and to the other residents and to staff and this may be the first real attachment and sense of belonging that they have experienced in life. They begin to trust others and allow themselves to experience feelings; they find they can survive with the support of the group, and thus the acting-out behaviour and the emotion-avoiding defences are put aside. At this stage, some three months or so into treatment, the individuals have often become depressed, anxious and feeling hopeless and may be in somewhat *negative transference* to the community, but they have progressed to the Kleinian *depressive* position where they are contemplating a state of not always being immediately gratified but sometimes left empty. 'This place has made me worse', they declaim, 'I just had a work problem but now . . .'. They are however feeling persons now and often demonstrate this as they help and support newcomers whilst struggling themselves with the new experiences of impending maturation.

Then begins the slow assimilation of the good bits and the bad bits into one perspective and preparation for perhaps the most traumatic experience of their treatment, which will be their separation from the unit and the loss of the good object to which they have become attached. Leaving can be difficult for some and unable to work towards a planned separation, they may revert to rule-breaking behaviour, so that the community has no choice but to discharge them. "It is not I who is deserting you", they seem to say, "but you who are rejecting me". When we followed-up patients who had been discharged by the community for rule-breaking, we found that those who were thus discharged in the early weeks did badly, but those who were discharged by the community after six months or so in treatment did not do much worse than those who had left in a more planned way (Whiteley, 1970).

The rule-breaking at this point seemed more a device to enable them to break off treatment which they were unable to do in a more mature and self-responsible way.

If attachment and loss seem key psychodynamic features of the therapeutic community, the psychodynamic interaction and how it is managed is of fundamental importance. Psychotherapists may fear that they lose authority or that the transference will be weakened if they interact with patients out of formal therapy sessions, but the contrary prevails. Being with and amongst the patients actually makes one more powerful and influential and may have to be guarded against, whereas the transference between an inadequate young man and his male father-figure therapist is markedly enhanced when the two are working together in the garden, re-activating either the real or the longed for situation between father and son. The therapist must be aware of this at all times. He is never out of the transference relationship and the day's activities are best seen as one ongoing group rather than as a series of different and separate activities. Often the transference is simply acted through rather than interpreted verbally, which latter process may not make much sense to a not very sophisticated client, whereas to experience a kindly or guiding, or even gently but firmly reprimanding and controlling, interaction from the therapist may be the *corrective emotional experience* which is required at that time. Despite the Rapoport finding that reality confrontation was the preferred treatment intervention, interpretations are not forbidden in the therapeutic community but must be dispensed with care. The therapist who distributes interpretations at every opportunity distances himself or herself from the patients and also finds the community members dependently waiting for the next insight rather than themselves working as a group on the task in hand. Main (1946) commented that "the psychiatrist is rarely mentioned as a therapeutic agent [in the therapeutic community] and where he or she is highly praised this is regarded as a failure of therapy". As in any group therapy, interpretations have most impact if they come from the group rather than the therapist.

Some therapeutic community practitioners will assert that the community meeting in particular is for social control (the outer world of the patient) and that interpretations are out of place therein, whereas it is the small group that deals with the inner world of the patient. This division is somewhat artificial and should not be followed absolutely but the large group is a threatening place and the pursuit of one individual by the pack of therapists and would-be therapists can become very punitive and such zeal must be contained. Main (1975) has emphasised the importance of staff involving themselves realistically in large groups (such as the community meeting) with common sense interventions and not waiting for the 'Nobel Prize' ideas to form before speaking. The so-called paradoxical injunction favoured by some family therapists has no place in the therapeutic community, which must be the bastion of openness, honesty, integrity and straight-forwardness; and the staff above all must be a model for patients in their own openness and involvement with reality and frankness of communication. There is no place for the brief or indefinite communication which allows fantasy to develop and which some psychotherapists will allege provides material for exploration of the unconscious. Questions can be answered honestly but with a query as to why the individual needs to know, which can then lead more trustworthily into the necessary exploration. Staff leadership is important and, from a psychodynamic point of view, the necessity for patients and for staff to feel an attachment to the leader and for him to accept and act upon this responsibly rather than deny it under some guise of equality is very important. Freud (1921) emphasised the need for a strong libidinal tie between leader and members of an organisation to maintain stability and function. A patient who had passed through Henderson was later to write in the following vein:

> I find that I have to consider my wife and children now which I never gave a thought to before I went to Henderson. I told you in my last letter that as I did not feel like a robot any more I was finding it difficult handling feelings. But I find it a lot better and easier now. In fact, it is quite nice. Especially towards my family. I find that I really think ahead now instead of doing things impulsively. It is very difficult to explain to you what I mean as nearly all the things I feel now are new to me. I think that when I was at Henderson I lived my life again. But whilst I was living it again I was taught right from wrong and also I was feeling things, emotions etc. also I was getting feelings from the staff to share also I was getting rid of my aggression. But you see the great thing for me at Henderson was that the staff told you truly how they thought towards you and your behaviour but still wanted to help and to understand you then help you to understand yourself at the same time. To put it in a nutshell – to me I grew up at Henderson with good foster parents – the staff.

Attachment, Loss and the Space Between

The therapeutic community offers a *truly corrective emotional experience* and the space between the vital early attachment and the subsequent management of loss, i.e. leaving, has similarities with the so-called *potential space* which Winnicott (Davis and Wallbridge, 1981) alluded to in his studies of child development. That is, the hypothetical space between infants and parents in which the infants separate from the parents and try out, often in game-playing ways, their independence yet secure in the knowledge that they can return to the protection of the parent if their experimentation becomes too stressful. For the parents the task is to stand back and let the infants explore and discover themselves, whilst the parents also learn from each infant the different and particular course taken by this particular individual.

A visitor to our therapeutic community asked a patient "What do the staff do?", and received the reply, "Ignore the staff, they are to be regarded merely as retainers". Coming from a rather middle-class and gentrified background he was using the term retainer in the sense of the old family servants. The question had come at the conclusion of a community meeting in which various patients had spoken of a fear of collapse or explosion if they spoke openly about their problems and in which staff had been actively but quietly making reference to here and now relationships in the community and linking them with real family conflicts in the outside world of the patients. The patients stayed within the community grumbling about the lack of treatment provided but fearing collapse if the community were not there. The idea of the staff as the old family servants, before whom one conducted one's business and who observed from a discrete distance, supplied what was necessary and, although poorly regarded, became indispensable to the nurturing of the family, but to whom one never spoke intimately or directly, seemed to me a very apt analogy.

The measure of success in the therapeutic community is the *growth in self-esteem* for the individual and confirmation of this at the Henderson community came from a Repertory Grid study of changes in patients during their stay (Norris, 1983). This detailed investigation compared personal change in individuals in Henderson, in a Detention Centre and in a hostel for young adults with social and personality problems. In particular, self-esteem could be measured in an indirect way by ascertaining how the individual saw himself or herself in relation to others, and to an ideal self, and the change was monitored over a period of time by serial testing. Subjects in the hostel changed little. For those in the Detention Centre self-esteem decreased whilst in the therapeutic community there was a significant increase.

Conclusions

The first *therapeutic communities proper* were residential establishments with a truly twenty-four hour treatment philosophy and the majority of the research extrapolated above is taken from such. Can the system be translated into non-residential or day-care settings? Many of the better-known therapeutic communities were founded by, or centred about, a charismatic leader. Can inspired leadership be translated into a system of action which others can follow? The early communities in the era of moral treatment, and the first essays into child care on a residential basis, could perhaps more correctly be described as *communities of therapy* – and in a humanitarian society such will continue to be needed, especially for long-term care. Can we make a distinction between such and the therapeutic community as a specific treatment approach which has a basis of scientific understanding and for which appropriate selection is required as for any other treatment?

There are tangible factors in the structure and dynamic of the therapeutic community as detailed above which can be replicated given the right amenities, living, working and recreational facilities and a facilitating sociopolitical environment. Staff can acquire the essential training in psychological and sociological skills (Royal College of Nursing, 1990) and a programme can be constructed to meet the particular needs of different patient populations (Kennard & Roberts, 1983). However, there are also intangible elements which are dependent upon personality factors, attitudes, beliefs, values and aspirations of both staff and patients which are less easily instilled. Whilst Kennard and Roberts (1986) are correct in stating that we have gone "from a movement to a method" in the therapeutic community something of that special atmosphere that Charles Dickens sensed in his visit to the Boston State Hospital in 1824 has to be present also; and this depends on the basic humanity of the individuals concerned which they in their turn have acquired from the lessons of their own upbringing and formative experiences.

NOTES

1. Therapeutic Factors in Group Psychotherapy, (Bloch *et al.* 1985): Catharsis; Acceptance; Altruism; Self-understanding; Instillation of hope; Guidance; Learning from inter-personal actions; Vicarious learning; Self-disclosure; Universality.

CHAPTER 7

Community, Therapists and Boundary Relations

Graeme Farquharson

Therapeutic communities are complex places. They are made up of assorted sub-groups: adults, young people, patients/residents and staff (different disciplines; 'therapeutic' staff; ancillary staff), men and women and different racial groups. In different combinations these people meet in specific groups for specific purposes, e.g. community meetings, small psychotherapy groups, staff meetings, work groups. In all this, there is a combination of task groups and sentient groups.[1]

Even if one said no more, the level of complexity is clear. This is a social microcosm. Numbers are relatively small (rarely more than 80–100) but the feeling is usually of something quite large or, perhaps more accurately, very intense and intensive, as the intention is to bring people into face-to-face interaction, to demonstrate how different contributions combine and to underline connectedness and relatedness within the group. The emphasis on connectedness and relatedness directly addresses the fact that usually those people who come to a therapeutic community seeking help have profound psychological and inter-personal difficulties, often with no awareness of, or interest in, the effect they have on others. Indeed many of these people have severe personality disorders (Kernberg, 1975).

Where children and young people are concerned, labels tend to be eschewed (save catch-all phrases like 'emotional disturbance') but invariably their early life experiences have gone severely awry, interfering significantly with their capacity to trust and make basic attachments. There is usually an anxiety that nothing is what it seems, no one is reliable and nothing is permanent. In short, nothing can be relied on. This usually leads to the behavioural repertoire mentioned above; little awareness of others, little concern for any impact on the other, no appreciation that the other might be taking 'me' into account.

What do we have, then? A sizeable group of deeply troubled people, plus a number of others called 'staff' who are met in a variety of small groups, all in the context of an over-arching community, a living large group: individual psychodynamics, small group dynamics, large group dynamics, all interacting within a wider professional and wider social world. Understanding the assorted phenomena which emerge from all this can be difficult, but over the years a number of very useful concepts have been called forth to describe and explain. One of the more recent, important concepts is that of 'boundary'. Over the last two decades, this idea has become increasingly central to professional thinking in this field and provides a useful means of clarifying different levels of activity and interactions between these.

Boundary

We are all of us familiar with the notion of 'boundary', of setting limits, in the ordinary, everyday sense. There will be times when this is so implicit in our interactions that it will be scarcely discernible, but it is intrinsic to all social functioning, to agreements (spoken or unspoken) of what is and what is not acceptable behaviour. At a more explicit level, we all live within a set of legal rules, the law.

The complex psychological work of the therapeutic community is underpinned by these fundamental, everyday notions (even if often as a 'battleground'), but in addition there are other, more technical, usages of the idea. Before going on to those, let us remind ourselves of yet further applications which have entered our professional language.

The Individual

One hears people talk, colloquially, of 'personal boundaries', 'professional boundaries', 'organisational boundaries' and so on. What do these mean? These are related, but different, ideas referring to different areas or levels of activity. For example, I take it that the extent to which an individual can (or cannot) maintain confidentiality, can (or cannot) keep to agreed times, can (or cannot) keep to particular relationships, are all indicative of whether or not that individual has clear 'personal boundaries'. All of these same considerations will apply at work and will be inherent in any notion of 'professional boundary', but what is pre-eminent here is that individual's capacity to subordinate his or her own needs to the needs of the task, the needs of the people seeking help. The 'personal' and the 'professional' can easily coincide, of course. For example, the therapeutic setting promotes intimacy, and erotic transference is not unknown. (Nor is erotic countertransference.) Where one or both of these occur, personal and professional boundaries will be equally tested.

What all of this already makes clear is that the pre-occupation here is with the margin: the margin between one person and another, between one group and another. Sometimes these will be in a state of juxtaposition: sometimes they will overlap each other. Again, the language of the day speaks, colloquially, of people needing 'space'. In a more formal way, one major strand of contemporary psychoanalytic thought has given specific consideration to notions of 'potential space' and of 'transitional phenomena'. This, of course, is the work of Donald Winnicott (see Davis & Wallbridge, 1981) and by extension the so-called "British School" of psychoanalysis (Kohon, 1986). This work includes detailed conceptual-isations of the process of individuation, of how it begins to be possible for the individual to differentiate between 'me' and 'not me'. So, although they will be rarely intended as such, one might say that these colloquialisms will be adult re-workings of this 'me/not me' dilemma.

The Group

In the history of understanding group phenomena and group psychotherapy, one very important strand derives from the work of Kurt Lewin (see Lewin, 1947). Lewin had been much influenced by the 'Gestalt psychologists' and wanted to think of groups as 'wholes' and the properties of those as distinct from the properties of the individuals who make up the groups. In more recent thought, these ideas have been further elaborated both within general systems theory and the small group theory which has been associated with the Tavistock Institute of Human Relations, deriving principally from the psychoanalytic group dynamic formulations of Wilfred Bion (1961) (Ganzarain, 1977).

Bion's propositions about unconscious processes in groups are sufficiently well known to require only brief recapitulation here. He identified and described major forces for regression, suggesting that groups function at, and require to be understood at, two levels. The first of these is the *work group level*: this refers to the overt task requiring to be performed. The second is what Bion calls the *basic assumption level*. At the same time as consciously meeting to perform a particular task at an unconscious level, the group may also be engaged in sabotaging its own work. Bion postulates three basic assumptions which can operate in this way. The first of these is *fight/flight* where the solution is for the group to act as if attacking or fleeing from some opponent. The second is *dependency* in which group members passively submit to an imagined omnipotent leader whose part of the bargain is that he or she will magically care for and meet all of their needs. The third of these is *pairing* where the dominant fantasy is that there will be some reproductive process giving birth to a new leader, usually some Messianic leader.

The Organisation

Bion's ideas on small group behaviours have been taken up and refined yet further by colleagues to the understanding of underlying processes within organisations. Elliott Jacques (1955), for example, has analysed the structure of social systems in terms of the functions they serve in reinforcing the defences of their members against depressive and persecutory anxiety. This was developed further, in turn, by Isabel Menzies-Lyth (1970) in her study of systemic defences in the nursing service of a large London hospital.

What can be seen from all of this work is how social structures and social systems, which are set up to perform specific tasks, and are ostensibly designed for rational purposes, also have a defensive function. The two intellectual traditions mentioned above – general systems theory and Bion's psychoanalytic group dynamics – were brought together by other workers, notably Kenneth Rice and Eric Miller. Out of this emerged the postulate that, as well as the properties of social systems which have just been described,

> the existence and survival of any human system depends on a continuous process of import, export and exchange with its environment, whether the intakes and outputs are, as in the biological system, food and waste matter, or, as in organisations, they are materials, money, people, information, ideas, values, fantasies and so on. Internally, the system engages in a conversion process, of transforming inputs into outputs (Miller 1989).

At one and the same time, all of this seems inordinately complex *and* the common or garden stuff of everyday life. And so should it be, for this is no more and no less than a descriptive account of constituent parts and processes in ordinary human intercourse.

> The boundary across which the kinds of 'commodities' just listed flow in and out both separates any given system from, and links it to, its external environment. It marks a discontinuity between the task of that particular system and the tasks of related systems with which it transacts. There has to be some degree of stability in these relations, otherwise the system cannot survive; but, as Lewin (1947) implies in his term *quasi stationary equilibrium* the stability is always incomplete. Therefore, because the behaviour and identity of the system are subject to continual renegotiation and redefinition, the system boundary is best conceived not as a line but as a region. That region is the location of those roles and activities that are concerned with mediating relations between inside and outside. In organisations and groups this is the function of leadership; in individuals it is the ego function. It is curious that the leader is often pictured, like the spider, in the centre of the web, for it is clear that effective leadership requires the boundary position. The leadership exercised in the boundary region can protect the internal subsystems from the disruption of fluctuating and inconsistent demands from outside; but it also has to promote those internal changes that will enable the system to be adaptive and indeed proactive in relationship to its environment. The health and ultimately the survival of a system – whether an organisation or an individual – therefore depends on its ability to maintain an appropriate mix of insulation and permeability in the boundary region (Miller and Rice 1967). (Miller, 1989)

So, we have moved between levels, from the individual to the group to the organisation. To develop these ideas further, let us think again of group psychotherapy in its different forms.

In a well-chosen group, there will be a real cross-section – across gender, race, class, geography and so forth. The attempt will be to provide a spectrum of experience so that no-one feels himself or herself to be totally other than fellow group members; at the same time, there will be the opportunity to recognise and tolerate difference between people. Remember here that we put people in therapeutic groups and communities for each to derive benefit as an individual, not simply to provide some experience of 'groupyness' or to provide fascinating research into how people behave when met together in small and large numbers (important by-product though that be) (Foulkes, 1964). The task of the group or community is to provide a therapeutic experience for the people who go there. The setting is designed to foster and promote emotional development within the members. To paraphrase Winnicott (1965), the intention is that the Environment will Facilitate Maturational Processes, individually and collectively. Thus it becomes possible to respect difference, to aid the development of identity and to foster relatedness based on introjective, or secondary, identification, as distinct from that based on projective mechanisms, including projective identification (see Klein, 1946; Ogden, 1982).

But all of this richness, this diversity, makes for yet more complexity. This has been well described by Kernberg (1973). One of the therapeutic community pioneers, Tom Main (1983) stated that the therapeutic community is a "hierarchy of systems". This he envisaged as a series of concentric circles. For Kernberg this will not do. He wants to emphasise the potential conflicts between "ideal value systems expressed in the psychotherapeutic culture and the constraints given by social reality", to be mindful of "economic, political, racial and other ideological conflicts". All of this leads him to conclude that traditional graphic representations of concentric circles will not do. He proposes that the various systems "-represent a 'nonconcentric' overlap of hierarchies which cannot be reduced to one" and that "the nature of the systems among which the group leader carries out boundary functions is nonconcentric".

These ideas adumbrated by Kernberg may be understood as an attempt to conceptualise all the ingredients of a given situation, especially one designed for psychotherapeutic purposes. From this, the various dimensions of the situation appear. Different levels of activity can be delineated. It also emerges that some constituents are of a different order. This rather static map provides a 'snapshot' of a complex dynamic process and identifies the many variables which must be taken into account. Somehow or another, in any given situation the worker will say something, intervene at what he/she has judged to be the appropriate level and in the most apposite area.[2] All of this is to do with leadership and the ideas are particularly germane to the leader of the community. They are every bit as relevant, however, to each individual in the areas where he/she is the leader, e.g. in a therapy group, work group, classroom setting. (For the fullest exposition of this line of thinking in current group psychotherapy, see Agazarian (1989).)

A View from Clinical Practice – Some Particular Considerations

Let me first say something of the setting in which I myself work, and of the young people whom we try to help. Peper Harow is a residential therapeutic community, set deep in the Surrey countryside, for younger and older adolescent boys and girls. They come from all over the United Kingdom and their presenting problems are almost invariably behavioural (including some substantial embryonic criminal careers). These include promiscuity, self-mutilation, violence, arson and solvent abuse, as well as a very high incidence of theft. Very few of them have experience of any length of time with two natural parents, or indeed a consistent period with substitute parents. At best, they have been badly neglected; at worst they have been very severely mistreated. Many of them have been raised in situations where violence has been commonplace. Most of them (including a number of boys) have been severely sexually abused, often over long periods, in particularly brutal ways.

Almost their whole life experience has militated against normal emotional development. Everything has gone wrong. Families have disintegrated. Parents and siblings have been lost. The backdrop has often been violent and chaotic. All of this has usually spilled over to school, where often, despite high intelligence, unacceptable behaviour has triumphed and exclusion resulted. A vicious downward spiral has then followed, perhaps including a series of unsuccessful placements, before the conclusion that "what he/she requires is a therapeutic community"!

The young person who arrives at Peper Harow is deeply mistrustful, sometimes malnourished, having invariably been mistreated. These are "the children who hate" (Redl & Wineman, 1951). What they require is consistency, predictability and regularity. They need a safe, non-abusing environment where they can begin to experience or re-experience what it is like to be cared for, where they can develop some internal sense of security which has previously been absent, and where some of the psychological and inter-personal distortions engendered by life experience can be undone. In our experience, this process takes at least three, and more likely four or five years.

It is especially pertinent to note, in a paper on this subject, that their early life experience has often been at the hands of care-givers who themselves had very poor personal boundaries. Care was spasmodic and intermittent. Limits were rarely set. They were often fed drugs or alcohol by their elders, and being drawn into/compelled into sexual activity constituted major impingement and trauma which cast them into a post-childhood, pre-adult limbo (Winnicott, 1968). This combination of un-containment and gross intrusiveness has devastating effects on the developing personality. Unsurprisingly, the consequence of such experience is frequently the development of personalities which themselves have defective boundaries. Impulses dominate and, all too often, there is no interposing thought between impulse and action.

Self evidently, there are many aspects within all this which could be illuminated by consideration of boundary phenomena. I will confine myself, however, to a brief discussion of a particularly stressful area of work – sexuality and sexual behaviour – before locating that in a more general context.

Sexuality

A visitor to Peper Harow recently said to me, "In ordinary schools, sexual attraction, infatuation between pupil and teacher, teacher and pupil is hardly unknown, how do you guard against that in the intensity of the therapeutic community?"

My answer was in the following terms. Sexual feelings exist, and are to be acknowledged. Some will be pleasurable; some will be discomforting. *Most importantly they are not to be denied.* Psychotherapy, especially the kind of modified psychotherapy which these young people require, brings near the surface in the worker many of the anxieties, excitements and fears (and dread past experience) which we all carry with us and these are often called upon for understanding, in the service of the therapeutic task. Fine judgements are often necessary to maintain the delicate balance between keeping these experiences sufficiently open so as to remain usable, while not so open as to risk being swamped by them.

Where sexual feelings do arise, these will frequently be disquieting, as *the setting is one where it is quite inappropriate that they be acted upon.* They will probably be accompanied by feelings of guilt and shame (as well as excitement and intrigue). Paradoxical though it might sound, the least damaging course almost certainly involves discussing these with colleagues in staff meetings. Here are feelings which at times may seem almost inevitable. In order to continue with the ordinary work, it is necessary to talk these through, to try to understand something of them in order to contain them. This, of course, is easier to say than to do. There are areas, and this is a prime example, where the impulse control of staff members comes under threat.

To put this in more stark form, I propose the following idea. Within families, where young girls have successfully moved to take on an adult sexuality, one of the pre-conditions for this development will have been father's recognising daughter as a sexual being, experiencing her as an object of desire, while she has felt herself to be an object of desire and will have reciprocated it, *all of this being unspoken and not enacted.* If this proposition is true, and I believe it to be, then it will be replicated in similarly successful transitions in substitute families with parental surrogates. (An identical stage will also take place between mothers and sons.) When the young person in question has had many of the early life experiences which I have described and encounters the adult/parental surrogate in a residential therapeutic setting, the pressures on both individuals are greatly intensified. Nonetheless, the developmental requirement is the same. This phenomenon ought to be fairly well understood, even expected. That is not to say that working with it is easy. These difficult, anxiety-making feelings are having to be worked with in a very public arena. The fact is, though, that this is all part of the work: it is not some extraneous split-off part, which is 'personal' and 'nothing to do with work'.

What about the situation when these arise in one of the young people?

Example

I recently interviewed a very early teenager with a history of severe and multiple sexual abuse (with a view to her admission to Peper Harow). She had been repeatedly and severally seduced by many of the men in her family and some of their friends. The seductiveness of all of this (which seems to have been without overt brutality) has left her in a highly eroticised state so that she is in a state of fairly regular sexual excitation which apparently must find expression in full intercourse. The reason for elaborating all of this is that, as one would imagine, this behaviour produces enormous anxiety within those adults who have responsibility for her care, notably her social service department. Superficially the girl herself is unconcerned. Her position is "I like to have sex – what's wrong with that?".

The interview took a fairly usual course with consideration of her present circumstances, her earlier life, hopes and aspirations, when just as we were drawing to a close, she turned to me and said, with great directness, "What do you think of me?". The manner of the question made it very clear to me that it was important to reply with equal directness. So, I gave her a summary of what I saw as some of her strengths and qualities and some of the ways in which I understood her situation to be handicapping her and, almost absent-mindedly, as an afterthought, I said to her ". . . and I've been aware that you've spent the last hour flirting with me." "What me?" she said, with a broad smile beaming from ear to ear. And, in this miniature exchange, what had become acknowledged between us was my awareness of her mode of relating and her pleasure in this being recognised. Understanding all of this, and coping with and working with the consequent behaviour are, of course, two quite separate things. It is our practice at Peper Harow, when we offer a place to new people, to ask them to write a letter accepting or declining, in the following week. A letter duly arrived, addressed to me, which said:

Dear Graeme,
I have decided to honour you with my presence and come and live with you.
Love and other indoor sports,

signed,
Flirty
xxxxxxxxxxxxxxx

(No clearer warning can man have!)

Here is an example of a young girl who can scarcely distinguish between thought and action. As soon as a sexual impulse hits, it must be acted upon. That is to say, in respect of her own sexual behaviour, she has deficient personal boundaries. This in turn places enormous pressure on the boundaries of others.

I want to reiterate that incest and sexual abuse constitute major blows to the child's attempts to maintain personal boundaries and psychological integrity. Not only have they been physically and psychologically intruded upon, but in the process parents are lost as parents. They no longer provide any kind of parental function, and the very setting, the family home, which ought to provide and epitomise sanctuary and nurture, has itself become a hostile environment (Scharff, 1982).

The shock, and the outrage, engendered by all this is such that it is usually, initially 'unspeakable' (literally) and thereafter only very, very gradually. In this slow process, the only other available means of expression is that of behaviour. As an aside here, we should remember that many of the personnel, who work with people who have been sexually abused, have themselves been sexually abused or sexually assaulted. In some ways, of course, this makes them unusually well-placed to help; in others, the psychodynamics of it all become ever more complex. I turn now to the wider context.

Regression

The mature functioning of the adult is under threat in all of this. In the literature, there are good discussions on the nature of individual and group regression, and the nature of therapeutic regression (Balint, 1969; Kernberg, 1980; Scheidlinger, 1968). The pulls towards earlier states of functioning are several.

The psychopathology, already described, of the patient/client group touches off primitive anxieties within staff. This has been particularly well described by Main (1957), who also called attention to the 'special case syndrome', the wish of the individual to be special and the corresponding need of the worker to be special. A very common trap for the novice worker is the situation where someone sidles up to him/her, confidentially uttering statements like "Don't tell anyone this but . . ." followed by some personal 'revelation', followed by the clincher, "I've never been able to tell anyone this before, you are the first person I've been able to tell". The 'hook' of flattery is almost too much to pass up. The new worker has a surge of satisfaction. "This is really what I'm supposed to be doing! Listening, allowing someone to talk . . .". Frequently, though, something else has just happened. A process of idealisation has begun, a process of pairing, and a process of splitting off the new worker from the group. It takes great self-awareness and personal resource, and not a little skill, to find the right pitch of leaving an individual feeling 'heard' while not being 'sucked into' that kind of destructive process.

Then there are the regressive group processes already identified. These are intensified by the setting of the therapeutic community. Large group processes and the residential situation both add in dimensions of a quite different order. The residential setting has two especial implications here: firstly, the therapeutic hour never ends, and secondly, the role distance between staff member and resident is a great deal less than in the outpatient setting. The operational paradox which this throws up is that, in order to achieve the necessary level of therapeutic engagement, staff members often have to function in a regressed state themselves: at the same time, however, they must keep access to higher-level, more mature functioning for the necessary, cognitive side of the work. In short, they must retain the capacity to think. Not unexpectedly, this sometimes breaks down but it is imperative that there be some self-observing capacity within the group for, left unattended, these breakdowns can be serious.

Taking all this in the round, there are clear features in this situation which can bring (within staff) aspects of sexuality and other impulses uncomfortably near the surface. Newer staff will often identify with the kids, seeing their 'normality', at first unable to see 'pathology'. Younger staff will be faced with revisitations from their own recent adolescence. Older staff will often have anxieties in respect of loss of youth, loss of potency and so on.

I have focused particularly on regressive aspects of the work with special reference to sexuality. This is because none of the staff, however mature, will be entirely free of conflicts in respect of sex or of aggression and these are psychological areas in which staff will be required to work. There is no choice in the matter. Consequently, the opportunities for things to go wrong in these areas are very many. When this happens, it is seen in the role-distance being quite skewed, i.e. individuals become hopelessly embroiled with each other or skirt far round each other avoiding any contact. There is an even more enmeshed form of engagement when it is as if two people "cannot live with" each other, but "cannot live without" each other either. It is highly problematic when this happens.

I mentioned above the need for some self-observing capacity. This is indeed the rationale for the number of staff meetings which are common in therapeutic communities. An old colleague used to say that the purpose of the staff meeting was "to scrape off all the projections" and indeed that is an important function of them. That of itself, however, is not an adequate account. Staff do reconstitute themselves by re-asserting the 'me' from the 'not me'; they also derive support from each other; and they create the opportunity to think, to learn from experience just gone and to plan for times ahead.

A reasonably mature and experienced group of staff will probably be able to do this for themselves, but increasingly the practice is to make use of external consultants. Provided these are well trained, experienced individuals (with good working knowledge of personality development, psychopathology and group processes) they will have much to contribute. The danger can then arise that staff may excessively depend on the consultants.

In those therapeutic communities which follow the precepts of Maxwell Jones (Jones 1953) there is another consideration which can cause anxiety and that is the practice of 'role-blurring'. What this means is that, instead of emphasising professional differences between disciplines, the commonalities are emphasised with specialist tasks being discharged at the margin. What this in effect means is that staff members must reconstruct their sense of professional identity. For most people that is taken up as a source of liberation, as they are encouraged to find their professional niche on the basis of aptitude, interest and ability, not on the basis of a job title. It has an integrative function for the individual, just as it does for the task, with the sense of personal self and the sense of professional self being drawn closer together. The problem which arises with this is usually expressed in the form of "what can I do next, when I leave this community?" Indeed that is a problem. To work in a therapeutic community successfully and happily requires a particular turn of mind. It is a way of working which suits some people very well and suits others not at all. Those who enjoy it enjoy the openness, the support, the shared working, the level of devolved authority and the opportunity to turn ideas creatively into practice. It also affords the opportunity for great personal development, especially in relation to that most human of dilemmas: how to be an individual and a member of the group at the same time. The problem arises subsequently, when it comes time to leave. Where to go? A not uncommon pattern is that individuals reach a point, feeling it time to leave, thinking that they have had enough of the intensity, enough of the impingement; but having actually left there comes a sense of acute loss (of all the things described above). A well-run, well-functioning therapeutic community probably offers at least as much creative opportunity as any other form of organisational setting.

There is often, too, a situational characteristic which is important in all this. In some communities, particularly those for children and adolescents, it is a requirement that staff live on site. What this means is that the balance between the public and the private is radically altered. Here one's neighbours are one's workmates. The sense of getting away from work is significantly reduced. Think of the simple matter of travelling home. In ordinary commuting, one of the functions of the journey is the separating of 'work' from 'not work' and allowing the individual sufficiently to reconstitute himself or herself before arriving home. By contrast, when one is home in two or three minutes, all the travails of the day are imported into home. The problem goes the other way too. Ill health, domestic anxieties, matrimonial disputes, all come into the public arena. At times, this is fiercely resented.

At a less obviously difficult, more everyday level, there is a sense of living in the public eye. It is not uncommon for people to compartmentalise their lives so that they reveal some facets at work and yet others at home. Whatever kind of defence this kind of separation is designed to achieve, it is no longer available in this setting. Ordinary anxieties, e.g. "Am I a good enough parent?", and other anxieties which may be projected into others, e.g. "Is my partner good enough?" are all somewhat heightened here. Going along with all this, individuals' capacity to manage envy, jealousy and the like are all fairly easily seen in every day exchange. Unsurprisingly, in all of this, issues of shame tend to be fairly near the surface. (At other times, the depth of support, which is available here and which can be fairly freely exchanged, e.g. child care, is of an order which few people have experienced.)

Nonetheless, despite all of this, I am reminded of the observation of a colleague of mine many years ago, when he said "Of course, staff always do best out of therapeutic communities." As a keen newcomer, I was bemused and somewhat depressed at this statement, but it gradually dawned on me that it could scarcely be otherwise. In a society which seems to have systematically destroyed the idea of community in so many ways over the last 20 or 30 years, the drive for communion, for belonging, for attachment, goes on as a powerful human need. Another acquaintance who works in industry recently said to me, "Of course, the work place is the only place that people get a sense of community nowadays". My reaction (in its entirety) was the same as to the previous quote.

For all its imperfections and for all the pressure that it puts on people (young and old) to face their own shortcomings, the therapeutic community ought to be able to provide all this better than anywhere.

NOTES

1. The term sentient is used here to denote groups with which individuals identify themselves and to which they ascribe their loyalty. The term is used in distinction to task groups with which individuals may or may not identify themselves (see Miller & Rice, 1967).
2. The terms 'area' and 'level' are used by and large to signify breadth and depth respectively within the social world. 'Level', for example, would differentiate between individual-small group-large group, while 'area' connotes a particular preoccupation, e.g. sexuality, which might be manifest at any of several levels.

CHAPTER 8

The Therapeutic Community in an Age of Community Care

D. W. Millard

To start on an historical note: warfare has always been a great teacher of medicine. Over the centuries, many advances in surgery, the management of shock, anaesthesia, and in tropical medicine and public health have arisen out of the care of the injured or the need to preserve the health of armies in the field. In particular, the Second World War was a great teacher of psychiatry. The military experience of psychiatrists (especially, in Britain, in the army) brought, among other things, a fresh realisation that the mental hospitals in which many of them had worked as civilians were probably doing their patients a good deal of harm. This realisation led broadly to two consequences: the first was a determination to keep as many as possible out of hospital – leading ultimately to the policy of community care – and the second, measures to improve the hospitals themselves, including, importantly, the development and propagation of therapeutic communities.

So we come to the two terms which appear in the title, and which we must first briefly consider. Fortunately, we need spend little effort on the phrase therapeutic community: the concept has been explored in detail elsewhere in this collection (by Stuart Whiteley and others). It will be sufficient here to recall the distinction cited there from the work of David Clark (1965) between the *therapeutic community approach* and the *therapeutic community proper*.

The point of Clark's work for our purposes is that it gives us some freedom to manoeuvre. The variety of forms of therapeutic community practice which occur in community care settings, broadly in hostels or day centres, place us firmly in the territory of the therapeutic community approach. The differing circumstances in which community care is practised, the range of characteristics of those using such services and the constraints imposed by the parent service-delivery agencies upon individual therapeutic communities all contribute to variety within the arrangements they make. Does this mean, then, as some critics have suggested that the whole concept runs away into the sands and that in community care we cease to be able to identify anything specific as belonging to the therapeutic community approach? I believe not.

A recent expression by Nick Manning (1989) of an essentially similar notion uses the idea of a *core* of practices. Having carefully surveyed the evolving definitions of the therapeutic community and acknowledging the existence of some confusion among both proponents and critics of the idea he writes:

> We can conclude from the review that, first, therapeutic communicates are distinct from other therapeutic practices in terms of theoretical aims, organisational structure and process, and self identity. Second, there are three broad originating streams of therapeutic work which are beginning to converge towards one general type, most clearly related to the democratic community. Third, that there is nevertheless, and not surprisingly, variation around this common core in terms of therapeutic ideology, client type and the purity with which the therapeutic community principles are put into practice. (op.cit., p.47)

Thus we are free to contemplate the application of a range of therapeutic community ideas to a range of client groups. Although most of the personal experience of therapeutic communities drawn upon in this chapter has been with 'mental illness' type psychiatry – that is, with people whose disability reflects problems in their personality, persistent severe neurosis or the late effects of psychotic disorder, the therapeutic community approach can certainly be called upon in work with other people with other disabilities: offenders, people with learning difficulties, people with age-related disorders, and perhaps others. Since its work is balanced precisely on the interface between the psychological and the social worlds it can address problems which arise equally from either world and from the interaction between them.

The second phrase of the title, however, calls for more analysis. With the *National Health Service and Community Care Act* 1990 having received the Royal Assent at the time of writing, and the dispute around the timetable for bringing it into operation still current, it is necessary that we turn next to review these concepts.

Which Community? What Care?

I shall begin by considering *care*. Perhaps the most logical starting point for this section is to notice the existence of a sequence of questions which might run somewhat as follows. We cannot ask what kinds of social arrangement allow for the best delivery of care without asking what it is that we mean by care and why any one should need it, without in turn asking what needs people actually have and why they might have them, without some further and rather fundamental enquiry into what it means to be human at all. Although we cannot possibly pursue this line of discussion here, we can perhaps briefly note a few of the assumptions embedded within it that are commonly made. Based on some moral conviction about the unique value of each person, no matter how elderly, ill, mentally disordered or otherwise socially deviant they might be, we could probably agree that individuals ought broadly to have access to life chances equal to those enjoyed by what social psychologists would call their *reference group* (Hyman, 1942), the others in society with whom they, and we, would tend to classify and compare them.

Government publications such as the important Audit Commission report *Making a Reality of Community Care* (1986) ordinarily deal separately with four main categories of those needing care: the elderly, younger physically handicapped people, the mentally ill and the mentally handicapped. In total they are numerous; the precise numbers depend, of course, on the definitions of disability, on measures of severity and the accuracy with which surveys are conducted. But the recent OPCS Survey (1988) suggests that there are some six million disabled people in Britain if all degrees of severity are taken into account, of whom 13 per cent of the disabled living at home and 56 per cent of those living in communal establishments were identified as having some form of mental disorder.

I wish to make here a major generalisation around which much of this chapter is organised. We might summarise the manifold ways in which individuals experience reduced access to life chances as representing *impaired social competence*. I used the phrase descriptively and do not wish to imply any moral condemnation; one may become less socially competent than could be wished through illness, lack of information or training or opportunity, poverty, lack of treatment or care or in many other ways. A philosophical ideal to which we might hold is that we would aim to promote, maintain and, where necessary, restore people to as high a level of social competence as possible.

Moreover if we adopt (as in practice I think we must) an interactionist view of the relationship between people and their social context, we would say that the help people need might consist partly in actions which are directed towards them individually, and which we could call treatment or care, partly in actions designed to adjust the social environment to the individuals, and usually in a combination of the two. All such action aims at improving social competence.

Although we often use the word *care* without troubling too much about its meaning, we must pause to consider this. The very first sentence of Michael Bayley's well known study of *The Mentally Handicapped in Community Care* (1973) introduced the useful distinction between care in and care by the community. By 1981 a White Paper on the elderly (*Growing Older*) was urging: "Care in the community must increasingly become care by the community" – the point being to distinguish resources fed into the community from outside, often more formal paid or professional care, from informal care provided by family friends and neighbours, usually for people in their own homes (Bulmer,1987). Increasingly over the years attention has focused on the informal carers. There are a good many of them. Hall (1990) calculates from Randall (1988) that 11 per cent of households contain a carer and suggests that one in four of all adults will be in the role of carer at some stage in their lives.

Useful, also, is a three-fold distinction drawn by Professor Roy Parker of the University of Bristol. This starts from the actual work, which he calls *tending*, involving active physical contact in activities such as feeding, washing, lifting, cleaning up the incontinent, protecting, comforting. This physical tending, often of an intimate and emotionally charged nature, is the first variant of care. The second is visiting, advice and support which may be vital in permitting a disabled person to cope with life in a non-institutional setting and which may be psychological or material, household tasks such as cooking, cleaning or washing, shopping and the like. The third variant comprises a more general expression of concern resulting in: ". . . charitable donations, in lobbying, in prayer, or in feelings of anxiety, sadness or pleasure at what happens to others." (Parker, 1981). Each of these may be thought of as in different ways contributing to the enhancement of social competence.

Against this background, we turn to consider the question of where the various forms of care might be delivered, and specifically to the notion of community care. Social scientists have worried more than most people about the notion of community. They do so because it seems that as soon as the word begins to be used seriously for the purposes of social analysis or policy formation and the planning of services, its meaning virtually disintegrates. It is not necessary here to explore in detail the sociologists' discussion of this matter – it ranges far beyond our theme (cf. Bulmer, 1987), but I will refer to it in the limited context of the use of the term community care. In this section of my chapter I shall speak of *negative* and *positive* ideas of community care, both are (as we shall see) important.[1] I intend the *negative* concept of community care to define it in terms of what it is *not*; it is any form of care delivered outside a particular form of residential institution. *Positive* concepts of community care attempt to define it in terms of particular characteristics which may be deliberately attributed to it. The negative concept of community care is of course the one I used in my reference to the influence on British psychiatry of the Second World War.

Since the negative concept of community care effectively defines it as care delivered outside a particular kind of residential institution, we have to ask specifically what kinds of institution are being rejected in its favour. It must be remembered that in the immediate post-1945 period, the places we have in mind were largely (though not, even then, entirely) closed. They were the relics of Victorian architecture and practice: geographically distant from the areas they served, with high walls or railings, locked doors, a regimented and authoritarian (though often reasonably kindly) regime, and so forth. The motives of the nineteenth century were not without benevolence, yet it was the state of patients caught in this kind of situation which eventually led to the growing concern with the oppressive features of *institutionalisation*. In Britain, the psychiatrist Russell Barton published an influential book on *Institutional Neurosis* (Barton, 1959) detailing some of the organisational and clinical practices in mental hospitals which led to this state of affairs. Probably this negative definition was developed and has been mainly used by those working within such institutions or by writers taking their perspective. In America the well-known sociologist Erving Goffman introduced in *Asylums* (Goffman, 1961) the idea of the *total institution*. The characteristics of such a place included a breakdown of the ordinary boundaries of adult life separating the activities of sleep, work and play, the carrying out of all these under the supervision of a single (and often overly controlling) authority, batch living (i.e.: a large group of individuals treated alike and required to do the same things together), and a tightly scheduled programme imposed by explicit formal rulings and a body of officials ". . . brought together into a single rational plan purportedly designed to fulfil the official aims of the institution" (op.cit.), but often, in fact, serving the needs of staff more than those of residents. Institutionalisation diminishes social competence. In the subsequent decades, other technical terms, the *open door policy*, *rehabilitation*, and later, *decanting, decarceration, case management*, and the like became familiar in the vocabulary relating to this idea.[2]

The origin of the actual phrase *community care* is obscure, but its first official use appears to be in the report of the Royal Commission on Mental Illness and Mental Deficiency which sat from 1954 to 1957 and led to the *Mental Health Act* 1959.[3] Thus, despite our continuing uncertainties about it, this particular Age of Community Care has been running for 35 years or more! In its chapter on 'The Development of Community Care', the report says:

> Community care covers all forms of care (*including residential care*) which it is appropriate for local health or welfare authorities to provide. (Emphasis added)

This is obviously an administrative definition in terms of a type of agency (local government; indeed, after the implementation of the Seebohm Report, the Social Services Departments) and says nothing of the content of such services. Historically neither in the NHS nor, as this quotation illustrates, in the personal social services has the definition of community care in fact been solely in contrast to residential care; in the hospitals, the development of psychiatric units in district general hospitals which were thought of as nearer the patients' home environment than the mental hospitals, and also hostel provision within the local authority SSD and Voluntary sectors, have been thought of as falling within that ambit.

Despite changes in the legislation, progress towards decarceration was neither rapid nor even, and pressures towards implementing this negative concept of community care were maintained by a series of scandals and hospital enquiries. The influence of these has been ably reviewed in *Hospitals in Trouble* (Martin, 1984) by Professor J. P. Martin of the University of Southampton. Starting with Ely Hospital Enquiry in 1969 and continuing through the early 1970s with Farleigh, Whittingham, Napsbury, South Ockenden and others into the 1980s, there were some 20 in all (the precise number depends on definition: they were set up under several different administrative provisions). They form a melancholy catalogue of the ills of institutionalisation, and there is no doubt that they kept the problems associated with the total institution in the public eye. Martin quotes from a Conservative spokesman in a House of Commons Debate in 1970:

> We must be very careful not to make one or two nurses or one or two hospitals scapegoats for our own failings. The basic responsibility for these troubles lies not in some remote hospital ward, which is unvisited, which is overcrowded, which is understaffed and where the conditions are completely archaic. The basic responsibility lies on the local communities and on the public as a whole who tend to ignore these services. It lies on the system itself. It lies in the lack of encouragement, the lack of inspection and the lack, of contact with the outside world. Indeed, the basic responsibility lies on ourselves as representatives of the general public. (*House of Commons Debates*, 1969–70, Vol.759, Col.1336)

With this we turn to *positive concepts* of community care, drawing again on the work of Bulmer (1987). Here there are two main emphases to distinguish: firstly, care by the whole community itself and secondly the provision of a care as close to normality as possible.

Care by the whole community is perhaps the idea of which the social scientists have been most critical:

> All attempts to give this concept (ie community) a precise empirical meaning have failed and certainly in complex societies there is *no total social system*, that is a social network within which the whole of one's life may be passed, which is also a local territorial unit . . . The concept contains a persistent romantic protest against the complexity of modern urban society – the idea of a de-centralised world in which neighbours could and should corporately satisfy each other's needs and legitimate demands for health, wealth and happiness . . . (Halsey, 1973. Italics added.)

It must be admitted that for some types of problem – mental illness, learning difficulty and the like – there is a remote and abstract justification for care by the whole community which might be found in the politically radical position. The argument is that some important aspects, if not indeed the whole essence of such problems, are actually created by a process of social definition. Then, if this be true (and it would take us too far from our theme to pursue the debate here), some fundamental reform of society might be imagined which, if not exactly abolishing such problems, would enable them to be accommodated in a quite new way. But the fact is that this particular

Age of Community Care is not one in which such radical social upheavals are on any realistic agenda, and we must proceed within a framework of more liberal assumptions.

The positive arguments advanced from the more liberal position begin with the incontestable truth that throughout human history the vast majority of acts of caring have been amateur, voluntary and informal. It follows that no proposition is sustainable which suggests that membership of an advanced society confers a right, simply by virtue of citizenship, to cradle-to-grave support delivered through state machinery. So we come to the familiar political preferences of the last decade: minimal state provision; a high evaluation of the individual, of self-help, of the family; and an emphasis on private or voluntary provision for times of need, the whole being regulated chiefly by the forces of the market place rather than by other forms of planning and control. Community care, positively conceived, seems to fit rather neatly into this political philosophy; indeed, it more or less corresponds to the *welfare pluralism* of the 1989 White Paper *Caring for People* (HMSO 1989a).

Nevertheless, we are left with a state of affairs in which the idea of a mysteriously caring local community is seen to be a myth, and it is clear that what the rhetoriticians thought they meant by this boils down to care by a number of quite specifiable individuals. These are, briefly: (a) *women*, (b) characteristically *in the 50 to 65 age band*, (c) in the large majority of cases, the *female relatives* of those needing care and (d) failing people of this sort being available in any particular case – and then only to a limited extent – *neighbours* who happen to know the person through some shared membership of an occupational, recreational, racial, religious or similar group. (It is also clear, incidentally, that current changes in the age-structure of the British population are bound during the next few decades to reduce the size of this reservoir of potential care-givers.)

There exists a large and growing literature about carers which we cannot pursue in detail here. But it is perhaps worth simply listing some of the commoner *costs* to carers. They include:

- *Employment and financial costs*: Extra expense on heating, diets, laundry, substitute care and the like; costs of providing or modifying special accommodation; loss of earnings through having to give up work or accepting part-time, low-paid employment; reduced occupational pensions; limited income from Benefits.
- *Social costs*: Isolation; loss of friendships and recreational opportunities; impaired quality of social life.
- *Emotional and psychological costs*: Stress from personality change or behavioural disorder. Tension between carers; needs for protection and support.
- *Physical costs*: Broken, sleepless nights, fatigue; ill health; general wear and tear.(Allen, 1983)

In connection with a theme to which we will return later in the paper, I wish at this point to recall the earlier reference to an *interactionist* perspective. Lists such as this, giving characteristics of either carers or people with disabilities, inevitably miss the interaction whereby we can see some scope for the disabled person to influence the extent to which their care constitutes a burden on the carer, and for the carer to influence the extent to which the disability becomes a handicap. Some well-known and rather typical examples of this kind of thing occur in chronic schizophrenia: there are studies which trace the extent to which particular aspects of such peoples' condition are burdensome to care-givers, and others which point to the influence of high levels of expressed emotion within the families may precipitate relapses in people vulnerable to this condition. There are obvious risks of a vicious cycle of mutual effects.

Finally, among the positive concepts of community care implicit in many government and other discussions of this topic is the welcome tendency to take into more general use the notion of *normalisation*. From its origin in Scandinavia in the 1960s, largely in respect of institutionalised and mentally handicapped children (Nirje, 1970), the ideal that – without denying the existence of whatever physical or mental impairment is present, or intending to promote unrealistic expectations of a person who is disabled – 'normal' behaviour cannot be encouraged in abnormal or deprived conditions remains an important guiding principle in the planning and delivery of services across the spectrum of community care. Clearly, this is close to the principles of enhancing access to life chances or of sustaining maximum levels of social competence referred to earlier.

The Therapeutic Community in the Context of Community Care

What, then, is the place of the therapeutic community in an age of community care? Plainly, we must first begin by being clear what it cannot do. Therapeutic communities are, after all, a species of social group. In the arena of community care they exist principally as residential homes or hostels, or as day care units. Thus the therapeutic community contribution to the care of individuals within their own homes (which, as we have seen, is a major thrust in the contemporary political ideology and the practice of community care) is, at best, limited. For those confined to their own homes (by, say, severe physical disability) there is no effective contribution. However, for those who are able to – or are compelled to – leave their homes, whether for short periods of respite care, or for longer stays (perhaps because no effective home is for whatever reason available for them, or because they need specific support, rehabilitation, therapy or the like), or for those who so far as can be seen will need permanent institutional care short of hospitalisation, the therapeutic community may well have something to offer.

A useful notion is that of *group care*, by which I mean to classify together residential and day care. The term has acquired this technical sense in social work (promoted, for example, by an excellent volume edited by Ainsworth and Fulcher (1981), *Group Care for Children: Concepts and Issues*). However, so far as I am aware, it is not used in any other context to make the distinction from, on the one hand, *group work* (as in stranger group psychotherapy, training or educational groups for offenders, support groups for all kinds of users, and so on) and, on the other hand, the individual focus represented by such examples as the consultation with a general practitioner or at a hospital outpatients' department, or the practice of social casework or psychotherapy. The two obvious features of particular significance in group care are *the presence of other users of the service*, and the opportunity to make *therapeutic use of the experiences of daily living*.

These are worth stressing. It is remarkable how frequently in, say, hospital work the presence of other patients is ignored. Not only does this occur in surgical and other wards in general hospitals, but also in psychiatric units where one might expect the staff to know better. Even in such places, the technical aspects of the treatment of patients sometimes goes forward on a rigorously individual basis, the staff seeming quite oblivious to the presence of other patients in the situation. Of course, the occasional need for asylum is sometimes an indication for inpatient (or other group care) admission; otherwise, where the practice is so individually orientated one wonders why such admission is ever considered,[4] since most of the technical treatments of psychiatry – drugs, ECT, giving individual advice, support, counselling or the variety of psychotherapies – may equally well be provided on an outpatient basis. The one unique feature of group care is the presence of other users. Why not, then, plan to turn this feature itself to some therapeutic advantage? The therapeutic community offers, of course, a well-considered set of techniques for doing just that. Similarly, therapeutic community principles take the daily learning/living experiences positively into the therapeutic armamentarium rather than disregarding them as no more than an inconvenient backdrop against which the real work takes place.

I wish to argue for a much wider implementation of the therapeutic community approach in group care. But we must be modest about the extent that this is occurring at present since many of the advantages of community care – broadly, those which represent a movement away from the features of Goffman's total institution – are obviously achievable without explicit reference to therapeutic community principles. The Audit Commission (1986) published figures showing the progress up to 1984 towards the run-down of hospitals and the provision of group care facilities for mentally ill and mentally handicapped people, compared to the targets set in the White Papers (1971, 1975) on policy for people with these disabilities. These (Table 5 and Table 7) are amalgamated in Appendix 1. The figures given there have of course been superseded to some extent with the passage of time.

Nevertheless, coming from an authoritative and well-known source, they act as a benchmark for reviewing policy, and a number of general points can be drawn from them. First, they give some measure of the run-down of hospital accommodation and the corresponding increase in numbers of people in community care. This is accompanied by the closure of hospital units, those which remain thus tending to serve larger geographical areas and accordingly to be further from their patients' homes. The underlying principle is that hospital services are increasingly to be reserved for those needing active, relatively short-term and, where possible, curative treatment. Hospitals, that is, are to become less places of *care* and more of *cure*. But although the distinction between these concepts works well for people with serious physical illness, when applied to the mentally ill and mentally handicapped it becomes, to say the least, blurred – or, some would argue, untenable. Much serious work therefore falls on the group care institutions in the community. Moreover, as the figures also suggest, a substantial preponderance of this work is intended to be done on a day care basis.

The point here is that the community care institutions are bound to be more numerous than Health Services units and almost always smaller in size. Moreover, they are generally nearer their users' homes and neighbourhood; indeed, where a particular facility is provided by local government its use is often confined to residents within that authority – and, as in the case of the London Boroughs, this may be a small and very strictly delimited area. Some of the major sources of institutionalisation are therefore removed.

Nevertheless, simply to organise services in this way is not enough. Recent years have brought a rising level of concern about the situation of many users of community care; it is possible for individuals to receive insufficient help, for illness to remain untreated, rehabilitation to be incomplete, apathy to triumph – in summary, for people to be left with a level of social competence markedly below that of which they are capable. There are, of course, powerful voices arguing that this state of affairs results from *underfunding*, and I would not dissent from that view. But my purpose here is not with the economics of community care, rather to suggest that whatever quantity of group care can be made available would be likely to be better in quality for adopting a therapeutic community approach to its work.

It is known that a significant number of hostels operated by local authorities in various parts of the country, as well as by voluntary organisations such as the Richmond Fellowship, Camphill Trust, 2-Care (the SOS Society) and others, and a number of day centres, employ various forms of the therapeutic community approach (Association of Therapeutic Communities, 1986). I base the final part of this chapter on work of that kind, and particularly, on personal experience as consultant to mental health day centres in an inner London borough. I shall discuss in more detail some features of the therapeutic community approach that I think could make a positive contribution to care in the community.

Therapeutic Community Theory and Practice in Community Care

First, we note that in most instances a therapeutic community is a place which persons *come to*, rather than one from which they set out. In other words, people do not constantly, or for indefinite or prolonged periods, live in therapeutic communities – they come to them from elsewhere, on a daily basis to day centres or for time-limited residence in a hostel. There are some exceptions to this generalisation. Some people choose to live more or less permanently in communities – religious houses, kibbutzim, experimental communes, and the like – and one or two of these known to me have adopted a therapeutic community basis for planning their regime. Such places, however, are private and are not our concern here.

With that exception, no-one should be a member permanently of a therapeutic community. It is of course true that there are many users of group care in the community for whom long-term provision is necessary. But even in these examples, as in many forms of mental disorder, the underlying thrust is towards rehabilitation, however slow or lengthy a process this might be. Three very important principles are related to this. Firstly, therapeutic communities are essentially places of *change*, not solely of maintenance. The expectation is that certain relevant characteristics of users of the services (which might variously be described as *functional deficits*, *symptoms*, or in some other terminology pointing to the mechanisms underlying diminished social competence) will be modified more rapidly in such a setting than would have happened spontaneously. A therapeutic community necessarily attempts to be *therapeutic*, and in this respect it must differ from some community care facilities which are no more than places for the residual support or containment (or Miller and Gwynne's (1972) deliberately pejorative *warehousing*) of those for whom no hope of change remains. Secondly, in order to accomplish this a therapeutic community must be a *special place* – unlike other places where the user might be. I have serious reservations about any residential institution which describe itself as 'homely'; if a place sets out to encourage change, and is to be effective in this objective, it will necessarily be different from home. It will not necessarily be less welcoming or comfortable (though the challenging aspects of any therapeutic regime are likely sometimes to be uncomfortable) and should certainly be no less person-centred, but the kind of features set out in Stuart Whiteley's chapter are not found in most ordinary homes! Thirdly, this implies an important emphasis upon *boundaries*. Significant parts of the life experience of the user are 'outside the boundary'. It is central to therapeutic community theory that, putting the matter quite generally, users of the community bring into the place, and replicate there, problems which are important in their life outside, while whatever changes take place as a result of their membership of the community acquire their significance in modifications in the life they live outside it. In summary, as Manning

(1989) said, ". . . therapeutic communities are distinct from other therapeutic practices in terms of theoretical aims, organisational structure and process, and self identity".

The non-existence of any genuine sense in which the local neighbourhood provides community care (as noted above) implies that the recipients of such care are expected to receive it through a *network* of social contacts.[5] Network theory requires attention both to the shape (*morphological* criteria) and the content (*interactional* criteria) of the contacts which a person has. Among the former, we can readily see that the institutionalised or 'structural' contacts which individual users of the community form with one another or with members of staff inside the community (i.e. some of the *nodes* in the individual's network) reflect and are reflected in the personal or 'informal' relationships which they may have outside (i.e. other nodes in the same network). Thus, even in cases where community care involves an element outside the institution of personal tending as well as the psychological and material support to which Parker (1981) refers, the therapeutic community may not be without influence. To understand the *content* we must also recall the earlier emphasis on an interactionist perspective. The kind of example I have in mind is of the user whose behaviour, perhaps disturbed behaviour, in the community reflects some aspect of the relationship with the carer at home, and who as a consequence of events in the therapeutic community is able so to modify her or his side of the interaction with the carer as to improve the situation. Such improvements tend to diminish the costs to the carer noted above and may also enhance the level of social competence of the user of the service.

Therapy in the therapeutic community, as elsewhere, is ultimately for the benefit of the individual. How, then – as an element in a network of community care – does it actually *work*? No doubt, a number of mechanisms might be identified operating at various social and psychological levels of analysis, but the essentials must be to do with some psychological change in the user which can, so to speak, be exported from the therapy situation. This is the emphasis of the following statement of the Association of Therapeutic Communities (quoted in Millard, 1990):

> A summary of essential principles of the theory of institutional functioning of therapeutic communities would include the following:
> (a) clients are potentially suitable if the considered judgement is that their problems (whether primarily behavioural or psychological) *include or are significantly caused by psychological events*. (This yields a wide spectrum including most varieties of mental disorder, problems in social relationships and many behavioural problems – criminal or otherwise);
> (b) such psychological events (which may be characterised according to a variety of theories, psychodynamic, system theory, cognitive) are centrally to do with the *meaningfulness of human experience and behaviour*;
> (c) therapeutic community practice aims to *operate on the meanings* which people attribute to their experience and behaviour;

(d) it does this by providing a setting in which people are allowed in a relatively non-directed environment to 'behave' and 'experience' and then by *subjecting these matters to examination, comment, experimentation with appropriate new behaviours and subsequent reinforcement* by both fellow-clients and staff;

(e) in this process, however, 'psychotherapy' alone is not enough – the model depends crucially on a *combination of interventions* into the clients' psychological world with those into their social world ('sociotherapy');

(f) the balance of psychotherapy and sociotherapy, and the detailed *arrangements for these processes* vary according to such matters as the age of the client population, the nature of the pathology, the existence of concomitant needs (for education, medical treatment, custody and the like). It is central to the theory of operation of therapeutic communities that no action-based programme is successful unless the gains (however small) made by patients are brought to some form of conscious recognition and verbal expression, and no verbal approach is complete unless the gains are tested and reinforced in action. (Blake *et al.*, 1984)

In another terminology, these psychological events may be thought of as having to do with the *rules* which link an individual to her or his social context. The central idea here is that how we act is not precisely in accordance with learned and fixed patterns of behaviour but rather in accordance with a stock of general principles which form (or generate) our action in particular social situations and which are therefore called *generative rules*. People are more socially competent because they have generative rules which adapt them well to the demands of specific situations, but people whose stock of generative rules is somehow inadequate are those whom we recognise as disabled by one or another of the mental disorders (Millard, 1981). But whether the theoretical basis is expressed in the language of rule-governed behaviour or, as in Whiteley's paper, of the learning of new and non-deviant roles, or in more psychodynamic terminology to do with reductions in resistance and acting-out, the objective remains that of encouraging the kind of internal changes which enhance the individual's competence in social behaviour.

An Example from Practice

This is, of course, a very general description and the details will vary from one situation to another. To illustrate the range of therapeutic community approaches which may be adopted we may consider work in four mental health day centres operated by a local authority Social Services Department in an area characterised by wide socio-economic variation and situated near the centre of a large British conurbation. A published account of the work of these centres (Blake *et al.*, 1984) sets out the theoretical model in operation in each as well as outlining the characteristic profile of the group users, and the corresponding regimes. In recent years these centres have not stood still. However, the progressive modifications which are a proper reflection of vitality have left them little changed in fundamentals. For the purposes of this chapter they are referred to as Units 1, 2, 3 and 4 and they may be briefly characterised as follows (typology after Wolberg, 1977):

> *Unit 1*: [Focal (Primary Attachment) Model]. Essentially a 'drop-in' centre for people with severe psychotic or borderline disorders with grave difficulty in developing successful attachments and sustaining a regular commitment to a group regime. It does, however, offer some limited groupwork (social skills, women's group etc.). There is a weekly community meeting ('forum') and members participate in staff planning meetings.
>
> *Unit 2*: [Re-Socialising (Supportive) Model]. Provides a quite structured group programme designed to support people with chronic psychotic disorders in remission who are living in the community and able to attend and participate regularly. There is a community meeting and a programme of small groups (mainly non-verbal), and members take some responsibility for preparing the mid-day meal. The longest term user has currently been a member for about 13 years. Institutionalisation is avoided by negotiating with users a general revision of the time table at intervals of ten weeks.
>
> *Unit 3*: [Re-Educative Model]. Provides a mixture of verbal and non-verbal (creative therapy) small groups and daily community meeting or large group for a group of users intermediate between *Unit 2* and *Unit 4*. Requires a substantial capacity for commitment (say, two years) but makes less demand for insightfulness and a capacity for 'internal world' change.
>
> *Unit 4*: [Re-Constructive Model]. Essentially a psycho-therapeutic community. Users stay two to three years. The daily routine (for five days weekly) provides a communal mid-day meal, business meeting and daily psychoanalytic group. Provides an uncommonly intensive psychotherapeutic opportunity for users with reasonable verbal facility and psychological-mindedness.

In Unit 1, the users are among the most obviously needy of those in community care: homeless or in very basic accommodation, not capable of paid employment and often inefficient in managing their limited welfare benefits, and typically with a greatly impaired capacity to form and sustain personal relationships. Despite the substantial modifications of the therapeutic community approach required for this user-group, many characteristic features remain recognisable in the regime. A deliberate liberty of expression (*permissiveness*) is granted (subject to the obvious restrictions concerning physical violence, explicit sexual behaviour or incapacity due to alcohol or drugs) so that users reproduce something of the impaired social competencies which constitute their disability. Yet they are responsible for shopping for and participating in the preparation of the communal lunch; there is user participation in the weekly staff planning group and the forum meeting (*democratisation*); and users know and take some responsibility for one another (*communalism*). A key worker system exists and occasional reviews are held which, along with much *peripatetic counselling*[6] offer plenty of opportunity for *reality confrontation*. The pace of change is slow, but the objectives are undoubtedly therapeutic and users frequently show significant improvements in social competence. Some can be 'rescued' from a drifting existence to achieve regular attendance, membership of groups in the centre and so forth.

In Unit 2 the users have more or less secure, if poor, homes but may be very dependent on carers for support (Parker) and, in some cases, tending. They are characteristically people with the long-term effects of severe mental illness – drug controlled or more or less in remission. Several have been attending this centre for upwards of ten years. One of the problems posed by this group is *chronicity* in community care. The regular changes in the group programme noted above, which in conformity with therapeutic community practice are themselves negotiated with members, appear to prevent this and the users remain active in relating to one another and to staff members. Considerable efforts are made by staff to understand behaviour, especially disturbed behaviour, in psychodynamic terms but such understanding is not used interpretatively. Rather it will be used by staff to guide their own social interaction with users in the centre and in advice and guidance which may be offered to members about their behaviour outside.

In Units 3 and 4 such understanding will be employed interpretatively, much more intensively in Unit 4 where users are selected specifically for their capacity to cope with such an approach and to use it therapeutically. In these centres the direct relationship between psychological, *inner world*, events and social behaviour both within the day centre and in the users' life outside is much more explicitly noted and worked with; but especially these have an overtly rehabilitative purpose: therapy is designed to enable such change as will break the readmission cycle for people with serious psychiatric histories, and encourage resettlement in paid employment and within a conventional network of social relationships.

Concluding Thoughts

Against the background of these brief illustrations two final points may be offered, one concerned with policy and the other with practice. As a matter of policy, therapeutic communities cannot exist without some protection, that is, it is necessary for the parent agency to have a sufficient degree of understanding of, and sympathy for, the approach to be willing to allow it to operate free of too much interference. The recent emphasis within community care planning on accountability does not make this always easy. For example, the parent borough in which these day centres operate has a high prevalence of mental health problems and at one time promoted the idea that the day centres should open on seven days weekly and for a longer portion of each day. It became clear in the discussion of these proposals how strongly the existing regimes depend on the existence of a time-structure including weekends and the like when the users are unavoidably thrown on their own resources. To change this even as a matter of good political policy would entail quite far-reaching modifications in the existing regime, and possibly some loss of therapeutic effectiveness. It is a difficult task in boundary management (and beyond the scope of this paper) for the staff of the units to represent such subtle arguments to their professional and political masters.

Second, there is no doubt that the community care setting does impose substantial modifications on the model of the therapeutic community proper. For example, implicit in the examples discussed in this section, and found also within residential therapeutic communities in mental health hostels and the like, is a much stronger emphasis on a one-to-one component, a direct therapeutic relationship between a staff member and individual user, than would be characteristic of the predominantly group-based traditional model. I have long held the view that this is not unreasonable. But where, as in the examples we have been considering, the distinction between care and curative treatment is uncertain (or even non-existent), and what the users need is treatment for functional deficits which lead to significant social incompetence, the contribution of the individual professional combined with and embedded in the therapeutic community regime provides the most powerful combination of aids to the individual with special needs.

NOTES

1. I use these words in somewhat the same sense that Isaiah Berlin writes of negative and positive concepts of liberty: 'negative' liberty may roughly be thought of as freedom from, and 'positive' as freedom for. (Berlin, 1969, pp.122 & 131).
2. This book is chiefly concerned with mental health and psychological disorder, but it is worth noting in passing that modern community care defined in this negative way starts with children. It was the recommendations of the Curtis Committee in the immediate post-war period (1946) which, incorporated in the *Children Act* 1948, led to a shift of emphasis in the care of children from residential institutions by specifying that wherever possible children in care should be 'boarded out'.
3. The corresponding legislation for Scotland is the *Mental Health (Scotland) Act* 1960; it includes some significant differences in procedure, although the intention that at least no undue obstacles be placed in the way of community provision was similar.
4. Apart, that is, from such non-clinical matters as economies of scale or the convenience of the professionals.
5. Social network theory has been used in social science as a rigorous analytical tool and, in this sense, it has not yet been applied to under-

standing community care as widely as it might be. But it is possible (Millard, 1984) to adapt its principles to a clinical understanding of the relationship between life inside and outside the group care institution.

6. This is a major skill of residential and daycare practice. Of course, opportunities often arise spontaneously, or are contrived, for staff to sit with users as individuals or in groups for formal therapeutic activities – exactly as they are found in individual casework or in groupwork settings. But residential and day care settings offer uniquely the possibility of peripatetic ('on the hoof') counselling. (I am not here using the word counselling to denote any specific orientation or practice – the work may be behavioural, humanistic, psychodynamic, or whatever). The particular skill is one in which work with individual users may be fragmented into quite short interventions, but where these accumulate in a coherent fashion over hours, days, months, or even years. The technique of 'holding' such a thread is demanding. The demand may be compounded by the need to hold several such threads simultaneously for different users, and to manage the complex ways in which they may be plaited together in the ever-shifting daily interactions of the unit (Millard, 1990).

APPENDIX 1

Table 1: Progress to White Paper Targets for Mentally Ill and Mentally Handicapped People[1]

	Mentally Ill[2]				Mentally Handicapped[3]			
	1974[4]	1984	Target	Progress to target	1969[5]	1984	Target (by 1991)	Progress to target
Hospitals (available beds)	104,400	78,900	47,900	45%	52,100[6]	42,500	27,300	39%
Residential places (Local authority, private and voluntary)	3,500	6,800	11,500	41%	4,300	18,500	29,800	56%
Day Hospital places	11,200	17,000	45,800	17%				
Day Centre places	5,400	9,000	28,200	16%	24,600[7]	50,500	74,500	52%

NOTES

1. From: Audit Commission (1986) *Making a Reality of Community Care*. London. HMSO. (Tables 5 and 7)
2. England only
3. England and Wales
4. DHSS (1975) *Better Services for the Mentally Ill* Cmnd 6233. London. HMSO
5. DHSS and Welsh Office (1971) *Better Services for the Mentally Handicapped*. Cmnd 4683. London. HMSO
6. Adults
7. Local Authority Training Centre Places

CHAPTER 9

The Origins and Development of the Camphill Communities

Mike Hailey

In a world which devotes an increasing proportion of its resources to providing for people with handicaps and where phrases such as 'integration' and 'equal opportunities' have become bywords, it is often difficult to realise that the position of the handicapped person in society has changed so drastically in the time span of a generation. Today, Camphill is one of many organisations working in the field of special needs and a large proportion of educational and care facilities is provided by the State. But only 40 years ago, both the level of provision and the amount of practical experience in this field were very limited. The handicapped person was excluded from, rather than included in, the affairs of the world. Camphill's attempts to establish a community where professionals lived together with handicapped children, to develop new ways of working with very difficult children, meant that the regular Superintendent's reports were sought after as sources of reference in a field where theoretical argument far exceeded practical experience. Writing in the report of 1952–1955 Dr König stated that:

> Since the beginning of Camphill, our work was arranged and conducted on lines which were unusual to many experts in this field; but, so far, the advance of time has stood on our side, and several of our principles, which may have seemed odd and absurd in 1940, are to-day generally accepted and proclaimed by those who at first belittled our efforts. Our task was to be ahead of the general convoy which moves under the flag of help for the handicapped child. (König, 1955, p.6)

In this chapter I wish to record how the Camphill Communities came about, how they have developed since the first community was established in 1940, and how they stand in the world to-day.

The inspiration behind the founding of Camphill came from one man, Dr Karl König, an Austrian who came to Scotland with a group of young friends, as refugees from Nazi Europe. Karl König had already gained considerable experience as a medical doctor who had done much of his work in clinics and institutes of curative education. By the age of 19, he was studying Goethe's scientific writings and had joined a group of doctors and students who were discussing lectures given by the philosopher Rudolf Steiner on the nature and being of man. König found in Steiner's philosophy much of what he was searching for and soon became an active member of the Society founded on this philosophy, The Anthroposophical Society. Soon after his graduation in 1927 he was invited to work at an anthroposophical clinic in Arlesheim, Switzerland, and it was here at Advent time, watching very handicapped children walking with lighted candles in a special festival, that he decided to dedicate his life to the care and education of handicapped children. He wrote later:

> It was a promise I gave to myself: to build a hill upon which a big candle was to burn so that many infirm and handicapped children would be able to find their way to this beacon of hope and to light their own candles, so that each single flame would be able to radiate and shine forth. (Cited Pietzner, 1990, p.24)

König's subsequent work in Germany in the fields of mental retardation and residential care was built on the foundations laid down by Rudolf Steiner's teachings. In addition to lectures on curative education given in 1924, Steiner had given many earlier lectures in the realm of education and the need for a new social order. Steiner's concepts include a threefold understanding of man which recognises a distinction between the spiritual life, where each person is free to develop his or her own thinking in relation to his or her work and inner development; the sphere of rights where people meet each other as equals and develop human relationships which respect the individuality of the other; and the sphere of work where each person contributes according to ability and receives according to need. This last principle was stated by Rudolf Steiner as a fundamental social law:

> In a community of people working together, the welfare of the community is the greater the less each person claims for himself the value of his labour and the more of that value he makes over to his fellow workers, such that his own needs are met, not from his own work, but from the work done by others. (Steiner, 1906)

Steiner stated that this law would only find its living expression when communities were established with a spiritual mission in which the object of obtaining a certain income and the work for one's fellow man were seen as two quite distinct activities.

When Dr König was forced to leave Germany and return to Vienna, he began to recognise the importance of bringing about social communities where these ideals might find expression. He realised that the handicapped person could play an important role in social change, acting in a way as a catalyst in ordinary human relationships, helping people to think and act for others rather than for themselves. The seed was formed which would later establish itself in Aberdeen, the first home of the Camphill Movement.

At this point, it may be helpful to look more closely at Rudolf Steiner's philosophy in so far as it affects the work with the handicapped. Anthroposophy – the knowledge of man – holds that all human beings not only have their individual existence here on earth between birth and death, but also were spiritual entities before they were born, and will continue to live on as a spiritual entities after they have passed through the gate of death. All people, whatever their mental or physical condition, are more than a body, more than a set of emotions, more than words or achievements: they each carry an infinite and eternal spiritual being. The conviction that every person has an unique individuality, and that this "I" is eternal, imperishable and of spiritual nature, is fundamental to those working out of Anthroposophy. At birth, each person brings with them a "life plan" (their karma) which is formed as a result of their previous lives on earth. Any kind of mental or physical handicap is not acquired by chance or misfortune. It has a definite meaning for the individual and is meant to change their lives and those with whom they come in contact.

Steiner explained that the teacher or therapist educating and treating a handicapped child will always interfere with the child's destiny. Such relationships help to bring about 'new karma'. Although it may not be possible directly to change the physical or mental state of a person in their present life, the fruits of curative work will appear in subsequent lives. Those who take on responsibility for the destiny of the handicapped child must therefore prepare themselves in the right way. Inner self-education, an atmosphere of human striving and the endeavour for spiritual ideals are essential for this.

Karl König recognised these points when, in 1965, he wrote about the three essentials of Camphill (König,1965a). He may also have been aware of these words of Goethe: "If we take people as they are, we make them worse. If we treat them as if they were what they ought to be, we help them to become what they are capable of becoming" (cited Frankl, 1973, p.8). These words could easily have become a motto for Camphill; they stand as a challenge to all of us, in whatever sphere we work. This challenge lies in creating the right attitude to the work; in cultivating a new kind of humility which recognises the brother in every human countenance, whatever that countenance may be. Extreme feelings of sympathy or antipathy often arise in meeting people who are not quite 'normal' whether because of a physical, mental, or social handicap. To counter this, it is necessary to cultivate feelings of humility which recognise that true help can be given only when the helper sees in his or her brother the helper and in himself or herself the one who receives help.

It was this human attitude which characterised the work which Dr König tried to bring to its full expression in the Camphill Movement. This work is given the name 'curative education' – not a common title in Britain – based on the German "Heilpädagogik". The term 'curative education' contrasts with the term 'special education' used generally in Britain; curative education is not concerned primarily with teaching or with medicine, it is concerned with developing therapeutic methods; curative education does not look at abnormalities, but rather at disturbed equilibria. In its widest aspects, it is neither an art nor a science, but a human attitude which attempts to apply 'curative' methods to restore the disturbed equilibrium in the developing child. This can be done in many ways, including music and singing, eurythmy, speech and gesture, painting and drawing, craft work and specific movement exercises. Dr König summarised curative education when he wrote:

> only the help from man to man – the encounter of ego with ego – the becoming aware of the other man's individuality . . . simply the meeting eye to eye of two persons, creates that curative education which counters in a healing way, the threat to our innermost humanity.(König 1965b)

To hold, practice, and develop such ideals in a friendly environment was itself a major task. To transfer this activity to an alien culture, and to foster its growth during a World War, was a mission which required hard work, sacrifice and grace. An account of these times can be found in the publication, *A Candle on the Hill – Images of Camphill Life* (Pietzner, 1990), especially the chapter by Bock, pp.36–55. The small group of refugees who followed Dr. König to Scotland and who helped to establish the first curative home at Camphill House in Aberdeen soon found that their work was recognised and an increasing number of children were referred to them by parents and local authorities. The community at Camphill House was the first private institution for children with special needs in Scotland. By the end of 1940, 12 children had been admitted. In 1949, there were 180 and many more on the waiting list. Fyfe Robertson writing in *Picture Post* that year, reported that "of the 180 children, about 100 are unable to use speech properly, and hardly any can move harmoniously and gracefully" (*Picture Post*, 1949). During this time more land and accommodation had been purchased in the area, so that the work was spread over four estates. The founders had been joined by more than 50 others, mostly from the Continent. A training course (The Camphill Seminar) was started to train new 'co-workers' and a school opened for co-workers' children, based on the principles of Waldorf (Steiner) Education. This period saw not only the physical struggle to expand, but the human struggle of finding new ways of working with some of the very handicapped children who came to Camphill. This challenge demanded many long hours of meetings and study, which took place only after the children had gone to bed. Dr König led this work with courage and determination, bringing new insights to the work and developing new therapies using music for deaf children, colour treatment for the blind and partially-sighted and physiotherapy for spastics.

A further major step was made in 1951. Dr König had always maintained that every child, however handicapped, should receive the benefit of education, in addition to care and therapy. At Michaelmas (September) 1951, the St John's School on the Murtle House Estate in Aberdeen was opened to all children so that children with handicaps were being educated in school, and in the same classes as normal children. It was another 19 years in England and Wales and 23 years in Scotland before government legislation followed this example, and directed that all handicapped children, regardless of their disability, should be included in the framework of special education, and 30 years before the start of integration of special needs pupils in mainstream education.

Another important element of the inclusion of all Camphill children in the St. John's School was that each child was placed in a class according to chronological age and not according to ability. The Waldorf curriculum developed by Steiner is directed at the physical, emotional and mental development of the child and it is thus important that children should experience those aspects of the curriculum appropriate to their chronological age. Many people working outside Camphill, especially as professionals in education, have found it difficult to accept that quite handicapped people can benefit from such a form of education which, prior to the introduction of the National Curriculum in state schools, contrasted dramatically with the individual pupil-based 'skills training' approach adopted in many schools. But the Waldorf curriculum adapted by Camphill teachers for their classes recognises the growing individuality of each child, regardless of handicap. The class teacher thus addresses the spiritual being living in each handicapped child.

In a memorandum written in June 1951, Dr König defined the need to educate each and every child by stating that the first part of each day should be set aside for class teaching in age groups, to be followed later by remedial work where the children would be grouped according to ability. This principle still holds good in all Camphill schools. It calls for highly creative teaching to involve a group with a wide range of ability in work on a given subject, but it also calls forth in the children and young people a very special striving and attitude of mutual help related to what can only be called their 'class spirit'.

The early years of the 1950s were important also in that they saw the first geographic expansion of Camphill work, with newly trained co-workers leaving Scotland to start new homes and schools in England: firstly at Ringwood in Hampshire, and later at Thornbury near Bristol and at the Glencraig Estate near Belfast, Northern Ireland. The money for these ventures came from friends and supporters of Camphill's work, some of whom themselves had young relatives who were benefiting from Camphill schools.

But children grow up and need to leave school. Having pioneered schooling for these young people, Camphill then did the same for the young adults. With the help of the MacMillan family, an estate was purchased at Botton on the North Yorkshire moors. This has grown to provide a home for more than 300 people, some of whom have lived all their adult life in what has become Botton Village. The foundation of Botton and subsequent centres for adults provided a strong challenge for both the people with handicaps and for those who came to live with them. Life in the schools, by its very nature, is characterised by teacher:pupil, and parent:child relationships. Such relationships are inappropriate to life in adult communities. Co-workers had to learn to accept the obsessions, deficiencies and streaks of genius in the people they now lived with. Similarly, the handicapped people had to learn that they were not necessarily going to be looked after, but needed to take on responsibility themselves. Work had to be organised more on a production basis, with each person finding the places where their contribution could be made: from each according to ability, to each according to need.

The move to Botton brought about a greater opportunity for work on the land, already pioneered in Scotland. This work is recognised for the therapeutic value which the land has for all those who work on it. But, as Rudolf Steiner had pointed to, the land also needed to be treated in a way that would foster the right forces in it. Bio-dynamic principles of agriculture and horticulture have been developed and applied in a number of Camphill centres and form an important part of the life and work of those communities. In an age when agricultural methods have been developed to exploit the land, the bio-dynamic approach brings about a healing process which stimulates the activity of the land in a way comparable to the work in curative education.

The work of Camphill continued to grow in many ways. The nature of its task expanded to embrace education, training, craft work, therapy, medicine, work on the land, production and retailing. Many new communities have been established both in Britain and abroad to meet particular needs. The Movement stretches from America to Finland, from Norway to South Africa. Over 70 communities exist in four continents in settings ranging from very rural to urban new towns. Whilst the work with some types of handicap (especially with the more physically disabled) has diminished, other work has developed to meet newly perceived needs: work with the mentally ill; further education and training for 16 to 25 year olds; alternative provision for adults unable to cope with the more production-orientated approach of the Villages; and provision for the elderly and infirm.

The recent development of Camphill has come about, not in a centrally directed way, as from a Head Office, but as a result of the initiatives of Camphill residents and co-workers, responding to the needs which they see in the world around them. That the Movement was able to grow so strongly following Dr. König's death in 1966 is a tribute both to the momentum which he had been able to engender through his leadership and to the strength which the guiding principles of Camphill gave to its co-workers.

In modern society, with greater specialisation and division of labour, the ideals set out in Steiner's 'fundamental social law' are rarely experienced. We live in an age where, for many people, work done is seen only as a means of earning an income. The product of that work and how that product serves others in the community is often not relevant to the worker. In contrast, it is a fundamental requirement in Camphill that no co-worker receives a wage or salary for the work which he or she does. Work is done because it needs to be done, by those who are able to do it. This does not mean that no one is able to spend any money! Money is not earned, rather it is made available (in limited amounts) to be administered by those who require money either for their own personal needs or for the needs of the community. Any money that remains as an excess of income over expenditure is not distributed but is used to build up the assets of the community. This money, together with donations, goes towards expansion within the community or within the Movement as a whole. Money does not become a barrier within the working environment in Camphill because it does not exist in that environment, except for dealings outside the community. Money made available to co-workers is distributed on the basis of personal need, unrelated to their work contribution. A single person, for example, may be able to work much more than a young mother, but the latter may have greater financial needs and be given more funds to meet them. It is possible to foster such brotherliness in the economic life because nearly all Camphill co-workers live within the community in which they work, sharing the daily tasks, a common cultural life and, for established co-workers, taking responsibility for the daily decisions which need to be made.

Camphill does not have an administrative head office. Each community or group of communities is administered individually. The day-to-day management of each community is carried by individual co-workers, responsible to a central body in the community. This central body usually comprises all the committed co-workers resident in the community. Within this body, there is no hierarchical structure and individuals may find themselves assuming quite different roles in different situations. The central body in each community is responsible to a Council of Management, which forms the legal framework for the community. The membership of the Council includes both Camphill co-workers and people working outside Camphill. In Britain and Ireland these Councils are constituted within non-profit making companies, registered as charities. All Camphill centres in Britain and Ireland are also affiliated to the Association of Camphill Communities, established in 1978. The Association does not attempt to be a controlling body in any sense, but rather a platform where the different communities can meet to discuss issues, such as legislative matters, which affect them all and for which agreement on a common approach or attitude is felt to be important.

It is often difficult for people, especially professional people, visiting Camphill communities to come to terms with the fact that a school does not have a head teacher or principal and adult centres have no manager or single person in charge. In the early days, Karl König was obviously 'in charge' through his physical, moral and spiritual presence. But, as Camphill grew, Dr König saw the need to decentralise both geographically, as new centres were founded in different parts of Britain and Europe, and internally, to establish an atmosphere where each co-worker was able to develop individual responsibility and an underlying commitment to the work of the community. To work effectively this approach calls forth a great deal of trust between people and also necessitates a large number of meetings where individuals can share their problems and concerns and reach common decisions. This may sometimes prove time-consuming, but it allows for the full participation of those working in the community and for something to come about in decision making which may not have been possible through an individual. This 'something' is not easily described, for it has a spiritual nature. Perhaps it is sufficient to say that a community formed by a group of individuals can bring about through its wholeness more than can be brought about by the sum of the individual actions. Recognition of this spiritual existence is an important part of the work of Camphill. Camphill is neither an anthroposophical group nor a religious sect. It is an impulse, an attempt by groups of men and women working out of Christianity to try to live and work together in common for a spiritual purpose.

During the last 50 years many people have come to Camphill as co-workers. Some have stayed to make it their way of life, many have left to pursue other tasks. For some people joining Camphill the step is an easy and natural one in their search for a satisfactory way of life. For others, however strong their ideals, the step is not so easy. Life in Camphill is very different to life in modern competitive society. The work is very demanding and demands a strong commitment. In a society where leisure time has become more and more important, the Camphill day appears long and tiring, especially to many young people. This may be so, but it is balanced by an active cultural life and the way of working with money, both of which free energy which can be put into daily work.

In the early days, the way of life in Camphill might have been described as almost monastic. This is no longer so. The standard of living in Camphill is comparable with many middle income households. In some areas this standard may appear even higher. Standards are set out of the needs of the curative and therapeutic work. The quality of life, expressed in the design and construction of its buildings, internal decor, organically grown food and concern for the environment is an essential feature of Camphill's work. But one fundamental difference remains: those living in Camphill do not own the houses, cars and other things they buy and use; they are owned by the community for the community. When someone leaves they take with them only their immediate personal possessions. Their security whilst living in

Camphill is the human community, not its material assets. But, the growing materialism in the world also affects Camphill and brings new challenges to the way of life. It is an ongoing concern to recognise that personal needs in the 1990s in terms of individual living space, free time and 'involvement with the outside world', to name but a few, are very different to those of the 1940s and 1950s when Camphill was established and that significant changes may have to come about if younger people are to be attracted to stay in Camphill. But, whatever happens, it remains especially important to continue to uphold those moral and spiritual values which are central to the being of the Camphill Movement.

Little attention has been given so far in this chapter to the training needs of both new and established co-workers. In any work with people with handicaps, the work itself is a training in the development of one's personal qualities. Much can be learned from listening to those with special needs, from close observation and by living into the situation of the other. This needs to be supplemented by study and training. Since 1949, Camphill has organised its own three-year training course in Curative Education, which is carried out at some of the larger schools. In the last ten years further courses have been developed for Youth Guidance, Social Therapy and, recently, for Mental Health. These courses are conducted by Camphill co-workers who have considerable experience in the subject, and who involve guest teachers from elsewhere – both from inside and outside the anthroposophical movement. The courses either take place at one location or move between different centres over a two- or three-year period. Study is on a part-time basis either in blocks during the week or as a series of three/four day sessions spread through the year. Additionally, many centres have their own internal introductory courses for new co-workers. In all courses, artistic work plays an important part as a balance to the more theoretical work. Meetings and conferences also provide an important forum where specialist workers – teachers, therapists, nurses, doctors, gardeners, farmers, and others – can meet their colleagues to study and to discuss themes of mutual interest.

The underlying philosophy of the Camphill approach is such that courses promoted by bodies outside the anthroposophical movement are appropriate only to a limited extent. But they are nevertheless important in providing examples of developments in the different fields of work. However, the main changes in attitude and practice which have come about in Camphill have resulted from a deeper understanding of the problems and needs of people with special needs rather than from experience or theories developed elsewhere. The needs of each new generation of people with special needs are different to the last and this in itself brings about the challenge to develop new approaches and methods.

Dr König and many of the other people who joined him in the early pioneering days were idealists with strong, individual points of view. Many of their views found expression in the development of Camphill and contributed to the professional development of the work with the handicapped. To-day, few individuals in Camphill are in such a position. Rather, it is the overall approach, the way of life, the atmosphere which each visitor experiences, the activity of community living with the handicapped, that marks Camphill's contribution in the field of special needs.

The celebration of 50 years of Camphill has brought Camphill into the 1990s. In the last few years, we have seen renewed efforts to close some of the gaps between Camphill and the 'outside world': to promote a better understanding of its philosophy, attitudes and practices; and to have Camphill's training courses validated by national agencies. But, just as importantly, we have witnessed Camphill strongly defending its position with regard to community living with the handicapped and upholding the value of curative education against pressures from the State to establish national criteria for evaluation which take no account of individual differences. Camphill has been in a period of adjustment, comparable to what has taken place in many world situations. The age of charismatic leadership passed with the death of Dr König and certain of his colleagues, such as Dr Thomas Weihs, who stood out as individuals in the professional sphere. Camphill had to adjust, to find its position in the world as a group of communities rather than through individuals. To do this it withdrew somewhat from world affairs, to consolidate its home position. This stage has now passed, although adjustments will always be necessary. Going into the 1990s Camphill is in a position to have a stronger voice in the world: the voice of a way of life. The Camphill ethos is founded on Anthroposophy and a concern to live out of a true knowledge of man. In 50 years Camphill has built up a tremendous network of supporters who have met Camphill as pupils, residents, parents, friends or professionals. This network is established on personal contacts, the meeting of 'Camphiller' and 'Visitor'. These meetings do more for Camphill than any published works or general pronouncements. Apart from its name and its buildings, Camphill exists because of the people associated with it and because it continues to reaffirm the need to treat every human being as a special person.

Rudolf Steiner's threefold social order was a prescription for the world community, not for isolated communities, even though that is where the process must start. Dr König established Camphill to attempt to bring about these ideals acknowledging that this was possible only because of the particular qualities which those with special needs bring to daily life. But, Dr König also looked forward to a time when the world would be a different, kinder place where separate communities would no longer be necessary and where, hopefully, the ideals represented in the threefold social order would have the opportunity to spread into ordinary life.

CHAPTER 10

Innovation and Regulation in the Care of those with Special Needs: The Disaggregation of Care

Stephen Baron

We may begin with two quotes from Inspections of schools of the Camphill Communities:

> It would be unreasonable and unrealistic to attempt to judge the work of the schools by criteria derived from the theories and practices current in the normal educational system. In the first place, the education of children who suffer from a severe degree of mental disorder presents problems to which no universally acceptable answers can yet be given. Secondly, the work of the Camphill schools is based on a philosophy of education which colours and informs not only the content of what is taught but also the methods and attitudes of those who teach in the schools. According to this philosophy, even the most seriously handicapped child is capable of full spiritual development; the main purpose of education is to establish conditions for this development, which proceeds along uniform lines, so that individual characteristics are of secondary importance. From these assumptions springs the characteristic concept of the main lesson, in which no concessions are made to differences in intellectual capacity or emotional maturity or to types and degrees of handicap. (HMI Report on a Camphill School, 1963)

> The underlying principles of the curriculum are derived from the philosophy of Rudolf Steiner . . . There was no evidence of the identification of pupil's strengths or of their learning difficulties. There was no evidence of planning programmes for individual pupils . . . The teachers do most of the speaking in the classes and too often the content of the lessons is pitched at a level which is too difficult for the majority of pupils to understand . . . The lessons are highly directed – even to the extent that the teacher will often guide the pupil's hand . . . For much of their school day the majority of pupils are given learning tasks which are beyond their capabilities and are faced with a use of language which is

too complex for their understanding. There is little teaching to suit the individual child. As a result many are underachieving. (HMI Report on a Camphill School, 1987)

More than 24 years separates these two HMI Reports; the former explicitly holding the assumptions of 'mainstream' special education in abeyance, the latter imposing these assumptions in a straightforwardly judgmental way. While we must allow for development during those 24 years in both mainstream and Camphill thinking (but not, I suggest, for the discovery of mythical "universally acceptable answers"), and must allow for varying qualities between different Camphill classrooms, the evaluative frame is clearly different.

In this chapter I want to explore, through a case study of the Camphill Communities, the changing nature of state regulation of provision for those with special needs, traversing the often unhelpful boundaries between 'education' and 'social care' and placing this in the context of emerging arguments about the changing nature of British society as a whole.

By taking the case of the Camphill Communities as the vehicle for this exploration particular perspectives are enabled, others prohibited. The Communities are Voluntary Organisations in current classifications, incorporated as Companies, registered as Charities, with, as Hailey points out in his chapter, a degree of formal autonomy. These legal and organisational statuses generate different determinations from those which operate on therapeutic provision located within the State itself, whether it be in the National Health Service, or Departments of Social Work (Social Services in England and Wales) or of Education. These determinations remain to be explored; my assumption is that the story would be a broadly parallel one.

Taking the case of Camphill allows us something of an *a fortiori* argument; being somewhat removed from the routine operation of State power, processes of regulation, which within the State's everyday ambit might pass quite unnoticed, have to be made more explicit and overt when applied to communities such as those of the Camphill Movement. The Communities themselves have a history of being unorthodox and innovative, and thereby generate a foil against which developments in regulatory practices may more clearly be seen. In claiming the strategic importance of studying the Camphill Communities in order to analyse changes in the processes of State regulation, no claim is being made that these Communities have any monopoly on quality, autonomy, innovation, or any other desirable qualities!

Drawing from the work of Rudolf Steiner, and later work in the anthroposophical tradition, the Camphill Communities have an explicitly metaphysical approach to special needs centred on reincarnation and karma. This holistic philosophy has led the Communities to challenge mainstream intellectual and professional boundaries in many aspects of their work and thereby to introduce new ways of living and working with those with special needs. The major innovations outlined in Hailey's chapter have, in some cases, been decades ahead of their wider adoption.

The focus of this chapter is, however, on the regulatory issues of the 1990s which represent even more comprehensive and intrusive systems of control: prescription of the curriculum, recognition by the various national Departments of Education, registration with Social Work Departments and the specification of staff qualifications. In order to analyse the development of these systems and their implications for work with those with special needs I shall look in turn at three main terms used to structure the Conference: *the Individual with Special Needs, Therapy* and *Community*.

The Individual with Special Needs

As has been repeatedly argued in other chapters, how individuals are defined as having 'special needs', how they are 'construed', 'typified', 'diagnosed' (the terms vary between different theoretical traditions) is consequential for their immediate 'therapy' and also for their wider social being. One key feature of the Camphill Communities, both innovative and unorthodox, is their anthroposophical definition of the individual with special needs as being a reincarnating spiritual entity, undamaged behind the veil of handicap, incarnating into a (damaged) physical body in a (damaged) developmental sequence. Closely allied with this is an 'historicist' conception of the appearance of handicaps: that different handicaps emerge and become dominant in different epochs and that those with special needs thus bear significant 'messages' for their Age (Weihs, 1971, 1977).

These constructions of the individual with special needs are multi-consequential. At one level they account for the derivation from Anthroposophy of the particular Camphill focus on those with special needs rather than on some other area of social life. More importantly they generate a positive, purposive insertion of those with special needs into everyday life. 'Handicap', for the individual, is treated as a challenge, an opportunity for growth with a significance beyond the 'handicap', however slow and painful this may make such growth. These difficulties are seen not only as a challenge to maximise the developmental potential but also as a stimulus to the spiritual development of the individual and to the development of those who live with the person with special needs, and to contemporary society more generally. While not denying the pain and difficulties, 'handicap' is thus ascribed a privileged place by the philosophy, an opportunity and stimulus for the individual, for the group and for social change.

This purposive construction of the individual with special needs sits alongside the more mainstream constructions which, although varied, share a 'deficit' model: 'handicap' as being a subtraction from normality. From the anguished advice to obstetricians on 'how to break the news', through the opening of Records of Needs, to the emerging Assessment of Needs for Community Care, the construction of the individual is dominated by the difficulties, the lacks, and how these may be alleviated. Strenuous efforts have been made in recent years to balance this deficit model by stressing what the person can do, by emphasising the 'rights' of those with special needs, by seeking to 'normalise' them. In many ways these efforts are an inversion of the deficit model, a liberal attempt to compensate (perhaps to overcompensate) for the attribution of deficiencies. The dimension of basic model remains: normality plus or minus.

The co-existence of these two models, the metaphysically purposive but subordinate Camphill one and the dominant, materialist, deficit model have significant effects on the work of Camphill Communities. One immediate form of this is the experience of boundary encounters with placement authorities. The focus of Camphill's assessments of the special needs of the individuals is on their whole developmental trajectory, conceived on a metaphysical plane. These assessments have to be brought into alignment with mainstream assessments heavily based around current cognitive, emotional and physical difficulties as assessed by Educational Psychologists supported by other, separate professionals brought together into a Record of Needs in an often fragmented way.

This is more than a question of words; with the criteria for making placement requests and for conducting case reviews set by outside agencies differing from the criteria for admission, care and day to day assessment set by the co-workers of the Communities, the potential for confusion is immense. At best the progress of a person understood in one set of terms can be imperfectly translated into another set of terms with all parties happy with the ambiguity; at worst progress can be assessed against outcomes which are not being sought, with consequent dissatisfaction and even withdrawal; or there can develop two, unconnected, discourses, the 'external' one for placement and review and the 'internal' one of day to day care, with consequent, potentially hostile, feelings of introspection, exclusion and secrecy.

The effects of the different constructions of the individual with special needs control the flow of 'pupils', 'trainees' across the boundaries of the Camphill Communities and thus regulate the life of the Communities in a fundamental way. For much of their history the Camphill Communities have been able to admit individuals with a broad cross section of difficulties, from across the age range; and the creation of complementary groupings has provided a basic building block in creating a therapeutic community. In recent years there was a period when the composition, and thus the functioning, of the Communities was radically altered by changes in perceptions by placement authorities of the specific therapeutic role of the Communities in the constellation of provision. These changes in referral practices led to a sudden sharp increase in the referral of older pupils with emotional disturbances (in 1980 17 per cent of admissions to the Schools at

Aberdeen were aged between 14 and 18 years, in 1990 38 per cent of admission were in this age range with the 7 to 13 years age range declining from 69 per cent to 48 per cent).

There are further effects of the different constructions of the individual with special needs at a more structural level, the discourse of 'rights' and 'choices'. The (over)compensating emphasis of the deficit model on 'normality', 'choice' and the 'rights' of the individual tends to encourage a short-time frame of reference in devising strategies of care: an emphasis on immediately articulated expressions of choice and a rejection of anything which can be seen as segregationist. Against these criteria the Camphill emphasis on an eternal time-frame, on addressing the hidden, often inarticulable, needs of the individual, on 'duties' at least as much as 'rights', and on the specific therapeutic benefits of 'special' communities, can appear as segregationist, tough-minded and patronising. I shall develop the implications of this below in the sections on Therapy and on Community.

Therapy

It follows from the arguments above that the Camphill Communities have a different 'object' of therapy (the undamaged, developing spirit taking hold of a damaged and/or delayed development in body and soul) from those working from within the deficit model (maximising developmental potential and developing compensatory skills so as to enable the individual to pass as being as close to 'normal' as possible, if not as super-normal), although the Camphill Communities do also address the issues of maximising skills. How do these two processes of therapy coexist in the field of regulation? One problem in tackling these issues is the boundaries between professions which exist, and which are stoutly defended, in Britain. While divisions of labour are practised in Camphill Communities these are less sharply specialised than in the wider society; the divisions are made along different lines and within any one Community there are complex, cross-cutting divisions. In organising the discussion below in terms of categories of medicine, education, social work, one of the most powerful regulatory mechanisms, i.e. the framework of separate professions itself, is necessarily being adopted.

Medicine

The Camphill Communities ascribe a central role to anthroposophical medicine, the holistic practice developed by and from the work of Steiner. This conception of medical practice is based on the anthroposophical Image of Man and, in its metaphysical logic, contrasts sharply with the materialist foundations of allopathic medicine. The insights of anthroposophical medicine lie at the heart of the practice of Curative Education in all its manifestations in the Camphill Communities whether in the classroom, the workshop or at home. It is no accident that two of the charismatic figures of the Communities were both physicians, and that 'Dr' is the only formal title regularly used in mundane talk in the Communities.

In Britain the right to practice as a 'Doctor' is a highly regulated one, regulation which has required Camphill doctors qualified abroad to undertake further training and experience before being granted the right to practice in Britain. With most Camphill doctors being from continental Europe, where anthroposophical medicine is both widely recognised and funded by the State, there has been a shortage of doctors thus dually qualified. This has resulted in sometimes uneasy compromises with Communities having their own 'internal' medical practice using anthroposophical methods while retaining the services of a local, non-anthroposophical General Practitioner willing to assent to, and supplement, such practices. As with referrals to specialist services in the NHS, good communication depends on the mainstream accepting the internal validity of anthroposophical medicine and its status as a complementary approach, and vice versa.

While there are overlaps and complementarities between the two different systems of medicine (e.g. in physiotherapy, in some speech therapy) the differences are substantial. At best anthroposophical practices have been permitted but are neither fully funded through the NHS nor given credence as part of the success which the Communities are seen to achieve. The therapeutic use of art, of eurhythmy, of oil dispersion baths, of coloured light therapy have to be funded 'privately' (although one non-Camphill practice in Kent has some of these funded by a sympathetic Family Practitioner Committee). These therapies, their rationale and the effectivity ascribed to them by the philosophy, are little understood outside anthroposophical circles and the reaction of the perceptive HMI Report on one school in 1963 was that they were "unorthodox (but) unobjectionable".

Such tolerance to difference in the medical realm appears to be diminishing in Britain not simply with respect to Camphill practices. The control of medicines, through the interpretation of the 1968 *Medicines Act*, is being reviewed with increased requirements for licences proposed in terms of quality, safety and efficacy. Homeopathic and anthroposophical medicines will have to gain Full Product Licences (as opposed to the existing, more permissive, Licences of Right) by meeting these criteria. While, in the abstract, such criteria seem unobjectionable (who needs poor quality, dangerous and ineffective medicines?) the procedural criteria being erected by which medicines can be shown to be good quality, safe and effective are predicated on allopathic norms. The criterion of efficacy is the most problematic one. With efficacy being interpreted in allopathic terms as the rapid suppression of the symptoms and the illness, the anthroposophical use of homeopathic and other medicines to promote self healing and long-term personal growth through the illness is being assessed, along with other systems of medicine with similar conceptions, against criteria which it does not seek to meet.

Education

The holism of anthroposophical medicine is mirrored in the conception of 'curative education'. Although many Camphill Communities conduct formal classroom work the underlying vision of education is more connected with a whole way of life rather than with the particular activities of the classroom. The adaptation of Steiner's 'Waldorf Curriculum' represents the development of an attitude, a set of social relations, as much as the use of a substantive classroom syllabus. The nature of both the classroom syllabus and the integration of the wider curriculum are confronted with regulatory issues in terms of both substance and holism.

From 1947 the Camphill Communities have provided a varied programme of in-house training with entrance qualifications more concerned with personal attitudes and social competencies than with formal educational qualifications. The training is based on living with those with special needs in the Communities, with formal input being provided largely by Camphill co-workers. In line with the nature of the division of labour within Camphill Communities, there is comparatively little differentiation in training between those who will spend much of their time in the classroom and those who will spend much of their time in craft workshops or in running households of the Communities.

While monitoring and recognising the validity of Camphill provision through placement decisions, inclusion on 'Lists' and through inspection by HMI, none of the regulatory bodies recognise the Camphill training from which this work springs even as valid for work within the Communities: the Camphill Communities are held to be staffed largely by 'unqualified' people. In Scotland, where the General Teaching Council takes a very narrow view of the qualifications appropriate to teaching, recognition of Camphill training as being teacher training appears out of the question. It is not conducted in one of the Colleges of Education, there is no school 'subject' base to the training and it crosses the Primary/ Secondary /Further Education boundaries. The Scottish Education Department Regulations for independent schools however take the most liberal view of the Education Departments; each school can employ staff qualified according to its own ethos and tradition. In England and Wales, where there is no General Teaching Council, Camphill teachers are not deemed to have Qualified Teacher Status by the Department of Education and Science and so every placement of a child at a Camphill School has to be approved by the Secretary of State. In Northern Ireland the Department of Education demands that 50 per cent of teachers have such Qualified Teacher Status if a school is to be allowed to register.

As the contrasting quotes at the beginning of this chapter suggest the relationship between the logic of the Waldorf Curriculum and that of the HMI inspecting the schools, can be problematic given the uneasy coexistence of two basic models of teaching and learning in special education. What we may term the 'mainstream' model of special education emphasises the cognitive and social skills of the individual child, the deficiencies, and the construction of individual programmes to remedy these deficiencies. Assessment is based on a relatively short time-scale, being aimed at detecting changes in the display of such skills. Classes, in this model, are little more than aggregates of individual needs, albeit aggregates which require careful and skilful planning and managing. The assumed atmosphere of the classroom is one of bright busy-ness, perhaps epitomised by the growth of computer-based teaching aids in the last decade.

This model stands in some contrast with the assumptions and ways of operating of the Camphill classroom where a distinction is drawn between 'Main Lesson' and other lessons. In 'Main Lesson', very much the core of the Waldorf Curriculum, the emphasis is on an age, and whole class, based maturation process. Within the general thesis that the path of development of each individual mirrors the development of the human species through history (ontogeny follows phylogeny), the 'Main Lesson' exposes the group of similarly aged pupils to the material appropriate to their stage of development, however impaired their overt cognitive functioning might be. The therapeutic aim of the syllabus is thus long term with assessment being of the overall development of the person rather than of the more immediate and fragmented frame of 'skills'. The development of co-operation and a strong group dynamic is sought as is a calm, peaceful atmosphere in class. In lessons other than 'Main Lesson' detailed attention is paid to individual therapies and the remedial teaching of skills in small groups more akin to the mainstream model.

The 1963 HMI Report at the head of this chapter is explicitly pluralist, recognising the different 'languages' in play and attempting a dialogue between them. In this it well represents the tone of the contact with HMI during the years from 1954 when they first visited the schools and were "agreeably surprised . . . while they saw many activities which were strange to them, they were very much impressed with the spirit of the schools" (Letter reporting on visit by HMI, 1954).

The 1987 HMI Report speaks of different times, perhaps of a lack of understanding of the principles underlying the Camphill practices, certainly of a lack of dialogue and a lack of tolerance of difference. While the small number of Reports, together with regional variations in HMI practices and variations between Camphill Communities, makes claiming a 'trend' on this basis perilous, there are cognate developments in education which also speak of radically changed conditions. The 1980s have seen a centralisation of power in education inconceivable during the 1950s, 1960s and much of the 1970s (although the administrative mechanisms of central control were developed in the latter two decades). The issues are perhaps most explicitly defined with the Standard Assessment Tasks and the National Curriculum in England, the 5–14 and the 14–18 Plans in Scotland, through which both a skills based schooling and a particular content are imposed. While the demands of the National Curriculum can be 'disapplied' for individual pupils by Education Authorities or by Headteachers, the expectation is that special education should follow the pattern of mainstream education as closely as possible. There is little doubt that this pattern is, in many ways, incompatible with curative education and the Waldorf Curriculum.

Community

In their 'community' forms the Camphill Communities provide a distinctive approach to those with special needs; each of König's three pillars of Camphill may be read as an essay on 'community' (König, 1960). The therapeutic processes of community life are an integral aspect of curative education but one which is constantly threatened by the fragmenting tendencies of the discourses of the 'professions'. The separate treatment of 'Boarding' from 'Education' in many HMI Reports does violence to this integration. So does the contrast between the detailed attention to the minutiae of physical arrangements paid by Social Work Registration Officers and their scant regard to the value of specific therapeutic practices and aspects of community life.

Where regulatory authorities do work with a definition of 'community' (implicit or explicit) there is a tendency to disqualify Camphill definitions. The contemporary discourse of 'Community Care' revolves around the polar opposition of The Community vs. Institutions. The paradigm Institution is the Victorian long-stay mental hospital which is equated with institutional living conditions, isolation, lack of patient progress (even regression), stigma, segregation, dependence: the historically aberrant provision of last resort. In contrast 'the community' is equated with home or home-like living conditions, social contact, personal development, dignity, integration, independence: the thoroughly normal site of therapy and human rights. As with all such rhetorical polar opposition the reality is more complex, but this does not negate the persuasive effectivity of the opposition. In between these poles there is something of a vacuum in contemporary thought with a dearth of positive 'not-the community' models. This places almost exclusive emphasis on 'the community' and thereby to make the presumption against any 'not-the community' form of provision. Where 'not-the community'-based care is allowed, the only real positive model available is that of more innovative homes for the elderly (with the ever present negative models of rapacious bed and breakfast landlords and Granny Farms).

It is in the field of the permissibility of provision other than in 'the community', the field of registration with Social Work Departments under the relevant Acts (*The Registered Homes Act* 1984, *The Registered*

Establishments (Scotland) Act 1987), that the logic of the Camphill Communities as communities clashes most with the assumptions of the regulatory authorities. Under these Acts the Camphill Communities are subject to a regulatory regime by which both the very existence of Communities and the details of day to day operation are determined. In the registration process the local authority have to assess the fitness of the manager and can impose any "reasonable conditions", in Scotland. Faced with the vacuum of any "reasonable conditions" Registration Officers in Scotland are impelled to generate their own set of criteria for assessing the registration status of Camphill Communities or to reach for sets of ready-made criteria. Often with a background of work with the elderly (the dominant group in residential care) the assumptions of this type of provision are carried into the assessment of the Camphill Communities.

In England this tendency is formalised with the Code of Practice generated by a Working Party convened by the Centre for Policy on Ageing being given quasi-statutory status (Centre for Policy on Ageing, 1984). This Code lays out a set of principles held to define universally valid rights of people who live in residential care settings, and some considerable detail of how these are to be achieved in practice. While entirely appropriate for provision which aims simply to provide an *individual home* for people, whether elderly or with special needs, the assumptions of "Home Life" (and similar, subsequent documents) when applied to provision which aims either to be *therapeutic* or to be a *community* (or both) are inappropriate and damaging. The biographical trajectories of the elderly and of young people with special needs could hardly be more different; the former, previously independent, socially experienced, with an increasing dependence due to physical frailty, have largely completed the major stages of personal development; the latter, previously dependent, socially less experienced, are in the midst of major stages of personal development to increasing independence. In any dispute over proper practice the onus is on the Community to appeal to tribunals or the courts against the demands of the Registration Officer.

The effects of this imposition of the assumptions of providing individual homes for elderly people or for those with special needs on the therapeutic and community forms of Camphill can be substantial. The definition of proper physical conditions applied may be termed the 'hotel model', each person having the right to a single room complete with wash basin and lock on the door. This model runs directly counter to two central, therapeutic processes of the Camphill Communities, the extended family form of *living with* those with special needs and the grouping together in accommodation of people with complementary special needs. This disqualification of the extended family form of living is reinforced by the application of Planning, Building and Fire Regulations and Codes of Practice within and outwith the registration process. In both England and Wales and in Scotland, the use of a building as a therapeutic community is classed as institutional use and such use requires planning permission. This definition is consequential not only for the hurdles of formal approval and the subsequent invocation of Building and Fire Regulations but, more significantly, in terms of establishing a firm public definition of the Community in the local area. Internally the various Regulations force institutional forms of living onto the extended family form by insisting, for example, on the isolation of different areas of one household by fire doors; on the erection of 'institutional' signs and notices in living areas; on the separation of facilities for 'staff' from those for 'residents'; or on the automatic attendance of the Fire Brigade at any false or malicious alarm.

The registration process also intrudes on the internal social relations of the Camphill Communities through its assumption of a staffing model based on the local authority or private home for the elderly. It is assumed that there is a 'manager' who is in control of the Community by means of an hierarchical staff structure. The imposition of this model on the management systems of the Camphill Communities which are both group based and, within any one Community, multiple can be damaging. In some areas this contradiction has been eased by a broad interpretation of the 'manager' as being a group of people or being the Council of the Registered Company; where a specific named individual is insisted upon the internal social relations and task related roles of the Community can be seriously disrupted. The criteria of 'fitness' for the named manager are not defined in the legislation and interpretations vary widely between different local authorities; for some 'fitness' is the absence of the negative (criminal records, a history of malpractice) while other local authorities, through an extensive list of necessary criteria combined with intensive interviews, effectively make the appointment themselves.

Assumptions about staffing as imposed by the registration process are not restricted to a single 'named' manager; in particular the relations and processes of shift work by paid employees are often assumed, and conditions which take their sense from such contexts demanded especially in terms of the production of written materials (staff procedure manual, disciplinary codes, complaints procedures, detailed record keeping on material matters). These further function to force the extended family form into an institutional mould. Staff qualifications, this time in the 'social work' area, are demanded while Camphill training is disqualified. With the publication, and widely enthusiastic reception, of the Parker Report on setting up a General Council for Social Work (Parker, 1990) such pressure seems likely to increase.

The passing of the *National Health Service and Community Care Act* 1990 also militates against the extended family, group and community forms of Camphill by its atomistic emphasis on the individual in the market place as the basic building block of a system of care. In terms of community composition this tends to disqualify considerations of the group and the community (fundamental to 'therapy') from the admission and review processes. More fundamentally it defines the relationship between co-workers and residents as being a market relationship between contractor and client for specified services, thus denying the essential "encounter of ego with ego" on which Camphill's therapeutic work is built (Karl König, quoted in Association of Camphill Communities, 1988, p.1).

The Disaggregation of Care?

The tendencies outlined, some realised, some nascent, could be read as an assorted list of unrelated problems impinging on one particular group of communities only. I shall argue that these issues are part of a wider pattern of the restructuring of British society and the State, and that the Camphill Communities have encountered them somewhat in advance of other sites due to their difference.

The issues outlined above have largely emerged as issues during the 1980s, a decade which has seen rapid structural changes in British society. These changes have been classified by Lash and Urry (1987) as 'epochal', as changes which constitute a qualitatively new type of society which they term 'disorganised capitalism' to differentiate it from the preceding epoch of 'organised' capitalism. To avoid the implication of a lack of pattern in this process I shall use the term 'disaggregation' rather than 'disorganisation'.

'Disorganised (disaggregated) capitalism' is characterised by the dismantling of the 'big blocs' of organised capitalism in favour of more *flexible* forms: production is disaggregated with plant level flexibility; the large bureaucratic mechanisms of control dwindle but the growth of the 'new' middle class accelerates with a particular emphasis on stratification through educational qualifications; the large national unions decline with a growth of non-unionised or company unionised labour; the state withdraws from providing services directly to a more regulatory role assigning the resolution of conflicts elsewhere (especially to the marketplace) (see Lash & Urry, 1987, pp.3–7 for a summary of these features).

The late 1970s and 1980s were a period of intense debate about the Welfare State, with education announced as being in crisis by Callaghan at Ruskin College in 1976. The crisis of general social work followed, with continuing high profile incidents of child abuse, until in 1984 Mishra could confidently entitle his book *The Welfare State in Crisis* (Mishra, 1984). The crisis of medicine came later in the form of renewed criticism of long waiting lists for treatment. The most prominent strategy in this attack on existing forms of the Welfare State was a deft New Right populism by which the (new, slimline) State aligned itself with 'The People' against oppressive (old) forms of the State and its personnel as being bureaucratic, inefficient, self interested and authoritarian: Less Government not More Government! In the field of education this populism took the form of 'Parent Power', an aggressive attack on the teaching profession and its responsibility for 'falling' standards with cognate, if more muted, moves in the field of medicine in terms of Patient Choice and Quality of Care. In social care, Human Rights and Deinstitutionalisation carried the critique. What is the logic of the new forms of Welfare State heralded in these critiques and brought to fruition by a spate of legislation in the late 1980s, culminating in the *National Health Service and Community Care Act* 1990?

One immediate reality is that the emerging system, while disaggregated, is more highly centralised than its predecessor, both in terms of structure and in terms of the detailed content of regulation; it is dramatically 'more' State rather than 'less'. In education the age-old complaint of the central departments about having to run a national system, administered locally, and about having no control over the 'secret garden' of the curriculum have been resolved at a stroke. The power of the education authorities has been reduced dramatically (with serious talk of complete abolition), with the central State being able to control developments, in some contexts, down to the level of single appointments. Teachers have lost discretion over the curriculum and assessment and are subject to a more intrusive, and more restrictive, system of Inspection and analysis by 'results'.

In terms of the regulation of social care the structure of the system of control is straightforward: central government controls the local authorities by approving (or not) detailed care plans in the light of its own criteria and priorities, by making funding conditional on specific programmes (while not earmarking it) and by an emerging system of Inspection. More significant perhaps is the system of control by local authorities of care provision in their area through the developing systems of Registration and Inspection by which, as we have seen, the fine grained detail of daily life can be scrutinised and regulated.

In the field of medicine equally dramatic changes are being imposed. The mechanisms for this include the 'contract' with GPs with accompanying 'norms' for achieving certain diagnostic and treatment levels on patients, as well as tightening budgets and the surveillance of prescribing patterns. In hospital medicine there is the parallel development of 'norms' and 'performance indicators', emphasising throughput, which carry significant financial consequences.

The significance of the programme of reform goes beyond a sharp increase in central State control over the daily details of welfare activities with the apparently contradictory movement of the dismantling of the blocs of the old Welfare State: schools and hospitals may 'opt out', GPs hold their own budget, while social care is to be distributed between profit making concerns, voluntary organisations, the 'informal sector' (the women of the family) and a residual State sector in a mixed economy of care. This disaggregation is driven by 'competition' both in terms of the costs of services and in terms of consumer 'choice'. While there are real, but not necessarily desirable, elements of competition and choice in the emerging system, the 'market' is heavily controlled by the State and it can be made to conform to policy preferences within broad limits. What are the implications of these movements?

Firstly, such disaggregation limits, and in the majority of cases reduces, the level of State finance available. Such reductions may be offset by 'top-ups' from either private sources or, increasingly, from supplementary insurance cover. In this way a two-tier Welfare State is emerging with a minimalist statutory provision complemented by fuller cover for those who can finance it privately. In education local management of schools brings finance calculated on a notional 'average' which, in reality, represents a cut for the majority, while the previous needs-based funding of GPs is replaced with a cash limited budget. For those wanting residential care, cash benefits at a statutorily determined level, received as of right, are replaced with services funded directly from the Social Work Department to the contractor at the minimum level consistent with an assessment of 'needs' by the same Department. The consequent transfer of money from the Social Security budget, from which those with special needs drew allowances as of right, to the general local authority fund from which Social Work Departments will receive a non 'ring-fenced' allocation can, realistically, only result in diminution of resources for those with Social Work needs. A system of care with some real consumer choice and power is thus being replaced by a system of determination by professionals who find themselves employed in a structure demanding minimalist assessments of need.

The disaggregation of the Welfare State carries cognate implications for the providers of services. At one level 'competition' for 'contract' funding removes any certainty in planning and gives pre-eminence to financial considerations on a short-term basis, factors which militate against the development of a coherent State system. There is, however, another, more fundamental function of the system: repeated restructuring of provision can simply be accomplished through the 'natural' processes of the market (the survival of the fittest), from which the State in the role of broker awarding contracts to the most efficient, and in its role as the 'neutral' regulator of markets, can effectively distance itself. Instead of slow and often bitterly contested reforms of the system as a whole there now exist the mechanisms for the State to achieve major structural reforms vicariously and relatively invisibly through the 'market'. Schools which do not 'attract' pupils will close, medical facilities which do not give 'good service' will wither, while social care provision which does not meet 'needs' will disappear. In none of these cases is the State 'responsible' nor does it have to bear the costs of restructuring. In the context of reduced funding for the Welfare State this implies not only constant, centrally controlled, restructuring but also an absolute diminution of services.

In the area of social care these tendencies have particularly profound implications. The State, as provider of services, is subject to this same process of 'competition' and this foreshadows the dismantling of substantial parts of directly provided welfare services through a process of competitive tendering. Local authorities, in their role as service providers, have relatively high fixed costs and a highly unionised workforce, and will have to compete 'in the market place' with the independent and voluntary sectors where labour organisation and the fixed costs tend to be lower (although the very costs of the regulatory process may alter this significantly). Existing experience suggests that such processes entail a casualisation of the labour force and a sharp reduction in wages unless strongly resisted by organised labour (sometimes despite such resistance), combined, in this case, with an increasing regulation of the labour market by a comprehensive system of qualifications.

While one outcome of these pressures might be an increasing role for the private and voluntary sectors, the avowed intention of the White Paper, *Caring for People* (HMSO, 1989), another outcome, more likely in my estimation, is the gradual exclusion of the private and voluntary sectors as local authorities are caught between the upper stone of being employers of a well organised workforce and the nether stone of being managers of a tight budget.

'Quality of care' (and who can be against 'high quality' care) and the registration process provide a mechanism for easing this contradiction. Under the respective Acts, Social Work Departments have almost unfettered areas of discretion to allow or disallow the existence of its market competitors in the non-statutory sectors through imposing registration conditions. Through either the imposition of its own model of care onto provision structured according to different logics, or through the imposition of expectations *above* those made of its own provision, a series of structural dilemmas of the local authorities can be resolved at a stroke, and in a manner which distances the local authority from responsibility; the removal of less costly competition on the grounds of being of poor, or insufficient, quality.

Are these developments in the State and regulation, in fact, as antithetical to innovation and high quality care of those in need of special care as I have implied? Clearly some elements of the reforms outlined above are necessary or desirable: the move of some people out of some of the 'Institutions' *is* long overdue; for some there *are* more choices; regulation *is* necessary to prevent the abuse of vulnerable people. But the overwhelming tendency of the developments runs counter to what I take to be the basic 'welfare' value of determining services by need. The populist rhetoric hides a real diminution of services and choices for the majority and a sharply increased authoritarianism. Welfare needs are being converted from being matters of public debate and responsibility into essentially 'private' matters to be defined purely on an individual basis, largely to be met by unpaid family labour. Where such needs are to be met collectively, they will be defined by the system at the lowest possible level and met by the cheapest possible method rather than being defined (except for those financially able to 'top-up') in the most developmentally advantageous way and met in the best way affordable. The labour force for welfare work is simultaneously being marginalised, polarised and more highly regulated in ways which militate against personal autonomy and satisfaction in work and which unambiguously subordinate labour to the 'demands' of the (managed) 'market'. Diversity and innovation in care, on which the possibility of real choice and progress depend, are being reduced by the universalisation of the dominant models; in short, the values of 'care' are being subordinated to the logic of profit and to monolithic State control.

ACKNOWLEDGMENT

The arguments in this paper have been developed through working, over a long period and in a variety of settings, with Nick Blitz, Tony Clark, Betty Craig, Bobbie Dickie, Douglas Haldane, Mike Hailey, Veronica Hansmann, Frank Quail and David Sutherland. While all will, doubtless, dissent vociferously from some of the arguments presented here, I owe them a great debt for their exemplary professionalism.

Part 2

Introduction to Part 2

The Conference was held in the Murtle Estate of the Camphill Rudolf Steiner Schools during a period when the pupils were on holiday.

The intention had been to have between 50 and 60 participants. Of the 56 who accepted invitations, eight were unable to attend; of the 48 members, 16 were co-workers from Camphill Communities. Each participant was already known to one or more of the Conference Organising Group; some were already known to each other in various professional contexts, but the group as a whole had never met before. An assumption in our planning had been that it would be possible to bring together a group of persons from disparate backgrounds, with widely differing experiences of the world, possibly in conflict about how best to respond to those with special needs and that they could work together in a constructive way.

The majority of the participants were resident throughout the Conference. Three of the houses were used for lunch and supper so that groups of 16 had meals together. Together with many of the co-workers who looked after us, participants shared an evening meal before the first formal session and lunch on the final day; and visitors met at breakfast and in the late evening with the houses' co-workers. They also met in five small groups on four occasions. We had planned some shared artistic endeavour for two periods each day but only one was possible: David Newbatt, artist in the Schools, helped us working together in small groups, to have "Conversations in Water Colour".

One of the participants was Jonathan Stedall, Producer and Director for BBC2 of the series of three films "Candle on the Hill", an account of the life and work of Camphill Communities in many countries. These three films – "Fifty Shades of Orange", "Botton is my Home", and "Is this Work?" – were shown and considered further in a plenary discussion, "The Media and the Representation of Special Needs". As further material for this session, participants had been sent copies of two newspaper articles on the work of Camphill, one by Alistair Warren from the *Glasgow Herald* (Education

131

Herald) of 22 March 1990, the other by Catherine Lockerbie from *The Scotsman* (Weekend) of 26 May 1990.

Throughout the Conference there was a display of photographs on the theme "Forms for Community" mounted by the Camphill Architects which also posed a problem about where best to site a building within an existing Community. Publications about the work of many Camphill Communities were available and a range of books on subjects related to the Conference theme were for sale.

All the Conference participants had had the opportunity to read the working papers, which now form Part 1 of this book. We asked three of them to undertake a particular responsibility for helping promote our work together, not as discussants, but as commentators on these papers, responding from the perspectives of their own particular interests, experience and concerns. It had become evident during the meetings of the Organising Group that a number of themes should be highlighted in our discussions and these we tried to express in the titles which we suggested to the three commentators. When thinking about the order of these presentations, we had in mind to begin from, as it were, a binocular perspective, looking at the social and community aspects of care and the handicapped; then to look at boundary issues and their management in a time of change, and finally to focus on the individual person with special needs. These three commentaries recorded at the Conference and since edited, form Part 2.

We had hoped that from the Conference and the shared preparation for it, might come more information, knowledge and understanding of the issues central to our three related themes; an extension of a supportive network; and new ways – in addition to the hoped-for publication of a book – to promote the lessons which might be learned from the work together.

CHAPTER 11

Disability, Society and Community Care: A Commentary

Chris Cullen
summarised and edited by Steve Baron

Clearly we are in a time of change where services, not just for those with learning disabilities, are in a state of transition. In such times it is useful to stand back a little and ask sceptical questions. One person asking such questions is David Rothman (cited in Scull, 1981) who describes a circle of reform whereby "the reforms of one generation became the scandals of the next; we applauded the reformers who had designed the system then applauded the reformers who exposed the system and then applauded the reformers who devised a new system and the circle moves round itself". There is a sense in which that is partly true; some of the Institutions, which we now want to get rid of, were themselves set up to save those with special needs. Nevertheless, whatever their origins, such services have to change as they are clearly not good enough. How do we change them?

The most common way to foster change is to seek an ideology to drive forward new forms of service provision. Often this is over-hasty. For example, there are reports of one London Borough placing children in foster homes which have not even been visited by social workers, such is the haste to close children's homes. If we look at services for people with learning disabilities then it is fairly clear that the fundamental ideology is, and has been for quite a number of years, that of 'normalisation'. It is, however, important to remind ourselves from whence it came and of some of the differences subsumed under that banner.

The early Danish interpretations focused very much on outcome; for example, Bank-Mikkelsen (1969) talks about achieving an existence as close to the normal as possible, a conception which had more to do with the outcome than with the process to achieve that outcome. Swedish formulations such as those of Nirje (1969) put more emphasis on the process, on patterns and conditions of everyday life which are as close as possible to the norms and patterns of the mainstream of society. In this country we have been much influenced by the formulations of the principle of normalisation of Wolf Wolfensberger (1972) who has, in a sense, put these two conceptions together.

The illusory simplicity of this notion has meant that people really do believe, once they have written the phrase into their strategy documents, that they understand it, that they know how to do it and that their services can be examples of it. Over the last ten years various organisations and people involved in normalisation have therefore felt it necessary to produce lists of what normalisation is *not* in order to counteract some of the things which were being done in its name: normalisation is *not* about making people normal; it is *not* about treating people as if they were not handicapped; it is *not* about dumping people into ordinary housing without any supporting services; it is *not* about removing special help or support; it is *not* about taking on staff with the right attitudes regardless of their (lack of) skills; it is *not* about people denying the right to be different, for example.

There are, of course, clear intellectual reasons for examining the concept of normalisation in some depth. For example Rose-Ackerman (1982) argues that the concept does not fit in with any philosophical system as a professional philosopher would understand it and that, in fact, the components of normalisation are quite contradictory. Nevertheless I think that the concept of normalisation has served a very useful purpose but that, just as it was serving this useful purpose, it was changed; Wolfensberger no longer talks about normalisation, but about social role valorisation in order to avoid some of the misunderstandings of the concept of 'normalisation'.

This has functioned to sharpen the focus of concern: it is very hard to argue with the concepts of normalisation; it is not so difficult, it seems to me, to ask real questions about the valuing of people's social role. The crucial distinction here is that it is not the people who are valued but it is the role that is valued. Unfortunately some examples of this are weak: if a person with a learning disability has an option between wearing a sweater or sports jacket and tie, he ought to be wearing a sports jacket and tie, because that is what is more socially valued. The concept does, however, make us think about what kinds of roles are valued in our society.

This is of wider significance. When I look around me and see some of the roles which are valued it makes me feel very uncomfortable. I recently read a report of a follow-up survey of Oxford graduates from 1980. One woman, now influential in the mass media, is quoted as saying in 1980 words to the effect that 'our generation believes that the future lies in self belief; if you are at all bright you screw them before they screw you'. This can be seen as prophetic of the ethic of a whole Thatcherite decade.

A friend and colleague of mine working with the Brothers of Charity in Galway put it succinctly when he said that it is not the way we deal with people with mental handicaps which is the problem but the way we deal with everyone. He elaborates on this in an article he has written about Jean

Vanier's approach in the L'Arche Communities, pointing out that there it is the person herself who is valued and not the role which she might be able to fulfil (Dunne, 1986). If that Oxford graduate is representative of the kind of society that we are in, even if only in part, then I think that we do need to be concerned about the nature of community and the part people with learning difficulties may play in it.

Margaret Flynn has recently interviewed 88 people who have moved from two big hospitals in Lancashire, Calderstones and Brockhall, into houses in Salford (Flynn, 1989). 75 per cent of them were living what their key workers described as a "successful life". However, a number of them had difficulty in keeping their homes clean, while victimisation by neighbours was a problem for 25 per cent of them. Their average weekly income was exceedingly low as you might expect and most of them needed budgeting and medical help. What is most significant for me is that nearly all of them, when asked to say who their friends were, named their social worker. Now I am sure you can be friendly with social workers, but it is a shame that the person who is paid to help you is the person that you describe as your friend. None of them, however, wanted to go back to the Institution, so they lived devalued lives in the community. Flynn's conclusion is that "in the main, people have been prepared for their independent lifestyle, and with assistance it has been sustained. However, the extent to which these people have valued social roles in the localities in which they live, is open to debate". This leads me to ask two questions: whether or not we have a clear enough understanding of the kind of communities that we think are useful for people with learning difficulties to live in; do we actually have the skills and the knowledge to enable clients to lead meaningful lives, to form social networks, to form friendships? I think that the answer to both of these is "No".

In order to address both of these questions, I would like to describe to you a fictional community from a novel published about 40 years ago. This community is very small because the people who organised the community (remember it is fictional) realised, before Schumacher, that small is beautiful; if you have a big community then your behaviour cannot be influenced by the behaviour of other people. Small communities are places where people can affect each other directly and the tenor of this community is positive rather than negative; there are no punitive practices. People are not discouraged or prevented from doing some things, rather they are encouraged or enabled to behave in ways which the community thinks are sensible ways to behave. This ties in very much with Professor Whyte's point that the idea of community is not the wishing away of evil, the selfishness, the brokenness, the suffering and the strife which mar our lives and fragment our society.

This small community is both planned and is experimental; no one knows from the outset which community and government practices are going to work so they try new ones and if they do not work, they change them. There is not a government in the traditional sense; the community is run by a set of people called planners and managers. The planners are people who cannot stay in office for more than ten years while the managers do not have any special rewards for being managers; they are simply people whose job it is to enable the community to function in a particular way. Another feature of this community is that it avoids all the competitive consumption, and the consequent pollution, which are characteristic of both socialist and capitalist societies. In an egalitarian communitarian society people are not in competition for goods and for status. Everybody engages in some physical work as a good thing in its own right, as a satisfying experience and as a focus of common striving. Unrewarding and unprofitable work is, however, avoided – you only do labour which is rewarding in some sense.

Child rearing is particularly important in the community and is done communally. The family unit is not central in this community and children are reared communally in ways which minimise negative emotions such as hate and envy. Children are taught self-control and independence. Learning is self paced and no child is compared unfavourably or favourably with other children. Another feature is that the community has rules; all communities have to have rules. If a rule becomes unnecessary it is abandoned. Outsiders who join have to agree to abide by the rules, but children who grow up in the community assimilate the rules and hardly notice that they are there. Art, music and literature are central to the running of the community but people are encouraged to engage in art, music and literature, rather than watching it.

That fictional community, one amongst many fictional communities, would be uninteresting except that there is a real community founded on these principles, Communidad Los Horcones (Horcones, 1989). In 1971 a group of people bought 35 acres of semi-desert land in Mexico. In January, 1972 they started building a school for children with behavioural deficits, in 1974 they dug a well and in 1977 they obtained a permit from the Mexican Government to form a co-operative. The members have adopted an eight-point strategy for running their community but I shall focus one only one of these strategies, experimentation.

They experiment with, for example, their system of Government: The Planner/Manager system did not work so they tried a system of direct democracy where everybody had a vote and 51 per cent of the vote was needed to carry a particular decision. They found that this direct democracy did not work either as the 49 per cent would often not work to support a decision with which they disagreed. The next attempt was to institute a different kind of Government, Personalised Government. This is a system based on equality: people do not have different statuses within the community and property is shared. The community is also based on pacificism but not pacificity; pacificism means action but non-coercive action. The community does not believe in persuading people but in modelling a new form of society; if you model a society people can come and see it, if they like it they will stay but if they see people who stay because they are afraid of leaving then they will reject it. This is a society which educates the people who want to join the community through a gradual process; its model is the fictional community, Walden II, of the American behaviourist B.F. Skinner (Skinner, 1948). Communidad Los Horcones is a behaviourist, a radical behaviourist, community.

I want to argue that five of the basic tenets of Communidad Los Horcones, and radical behaviourist tenets in general, are relevant to services for those with special needs, whether in Camphill Communities or other kinds of communities. The first tenet, probably the most important, is that of the setting of objectives. Behaviourism emphasises the setting of objectives and 'Management by Objectives' comes directly from behaviourism. In a sense all practices are run in terms of setting objectives: Millard points out that, for example, therapeutic communities are places of change and Camphill, I think, is no different. I would want therefore to know what is Camphill for? If I was a purchaser of services I would want some very clear objectives; I would want to know what Camphill is selling before I would buy it. I can see good internal reasons for Camphill not stating objectives because of its background, its own language and the possibility of alienating members of the Community through stating a formal list of objectives. The questions of 'What are we here for' and 'What are clients going to get out of it' are serious ones, and very important for communicating about communities to outsiders. If a community is described in terms which outsiders do not understand, and somebody else is talking in terms that they do understand, then people will gravitate to the latter. This necessary clarity about objectives is a hallmark of behaviourism.

A second tenet of behaviourism is that it treats individuals as part of the society in which they live. Behaviourism is not an individualist philosophy; it is not about individuals but about individuals in their social context. In order to deal with individuals with special needs their context, their environment, has to be taken into account. Clearly the Camphill environment is very different from the semi-detached house down the road and explicit statements must be made about why the particular combination of individual-and-context offered by Camphill is important and effective for its clients.

The third tenet for radical behaviourists is the value of diversity. Behaviourism is a philosophy of science which is rooted in biology. Just as species need diversity in order to evolve so individual and communities need diversity in order to evolve. I do not think it is departing from 'science' to say that we do not, and perhaps cannot, know what the one 'right thing' is for any individual or group of individuals. What is required is a patchwork of services from which people can choose.

The fourth tenet from radical behaviourism to which I want to draw your attention is its recognition of the complexity of human behaviour, a complexity which is often not recognised in attempts to change behaviour. Bronfenbrenner attacks the 'social address model' that if you move people with special needs from one location (called a big ward in a nasty hospital) and you put them in another location (called a semi-detached house in the community) then there will be a miraculous effect on their behaviour (Bronfenbrenner, 1979). We know that this simply is not true. There is no doubt whatsoever that people should not be living in big hospital wards but it is not enough to change locations because human behaviour is very complex. Often when people move from institutions into ordinary settings, but little else is changed, you see the staff struggling with problems which the hospital did not have to face because the hospital just absorbed them. For example, I have a client at the moment who is in a group home and he throws things. In hospital he did that but no one really noticed because his behaviour was not the worst on the ward by any means. In a small group home this a real problem and we are struggling to know how to deal with it.

The final tenet of radical behaviourism to which I want to draw your attention is the technical distinction between 'rule-governed behaviour' and 'contingency-shaped behaviour'. Take the skill of driving a car; when you learn to drive a car, it is almost entirely rule governed; you are given, and give yourself, a set of rules that when I do X then Y will happen. Skilful driving of a car however is contingency shaped; you are hardly aware of what you are doing most of the time, you drive along the road and your behaviour is determined entirely by the contingencies around you.

Rules are very important for forming and maintaining behaviour and have three main advantages: rules can be learnt very quickly; it very easy to profit from similarities through rules; rules can operate when the contingencies are very complex and unclear. In contrast trying to shape behaviour directly by the environment takes a long time and needs the opportunity for experimentation; imagine putting someone in a car and saying "Now, I'm not going to tell you how to do this but I want you to find out". Rule-governed behaviour is highly efficient and is the means by which our culture and our species have developed unlike other animal species. Rule-governed behaviour is however very unnatural as social behaviour. This is important for two groups with whom we are concerned, those with special needs and the staff who look after them.

Some people with learning disabilities have great difficulty following rules and therefore it is important for us to know about designing a contingency system to form and maintain their behaviour. For example, I am dealing with a client who bangs her head on the wall and kicks her family very violently and has done so for the last 10–15 years. It would be good to be able to give her a set of rules by which to conduct herself, and she certainly can follow some simple rules. More complex rules are not learnt and so we are going to have to arrange environments and direct contingencies to shape her behaviour. Whether this is possible remains to be seen as a long line of people, social workers, community nurses, psychologists, doctors, have not succeeded over the past ten years and whether such environments and contingencies can be organised in a community service is in some doubt. There is a tension here between the 'home making' emphasis in community care and the need to alter behaviour. Staff in group homes often feel that it is not their job to manage contingencies but to create a home for the residents.This may be because they may not be skilled enough; or they may not be supported enough by their managers; or they do not see their job as dealing with really difficult behaviour; or they see their job as providing a home and therefore they are not going to keep all the necessary records.

In the United States they have developed staff control into a fine art; Federal and State bureaux tie funding to the development and enforcement of sets of staff rules and so what you now have are staff who are incredibly good at following the rules. Individual care plans are highly developed and in one place in New York State which I visited recently there has to be a written programme which covers 12 hours a day of activity for each resident. If these are not produced then the State will not fund that Home. Rule-governed behaviour, as I argued earlier, is somewhat unnatural; while the staff have become good at following the rules the quality of life for the residents has not changed very much. Baron points to this as a problem of regulation for places like Camphill. If you have a local authority whose job it is to regulate a Home before they will act in their purchaser role and purchase a service, the kind of regulations that they impose may not be compatible with what that Home is trying to do.

We need a much clearer idea of the kinds of rules required and how these are likely to influence staff behaviour. I am currently doing some research where we are trying to get staff to act for contingencies rather than by following rules. We have a four phase programme aimed at getting staff to implement Care Plans; the first three phases are about training in normalisation and care planning. The fourth phase is about implementation and we have set up contingencies for the whole staff group. I had wanted to give the whole staff group lottery tickets when they had implemented a certain number of Care Plans but that is against the *Lotteries Act*. I then wanted to give each member of staff a voucher for £1 each time they met a target; these could be accumulated and spent in the local shop. This was objected to by a Nurse Educationalist as being unethical; staff should not be rewarded for work that they are already meant to be doing. Instead of these contingencies the Nurse Managers of the Health Board write personal letters to each Nursing Assistant to thank them for performing specified tasks and they receive certificates commemorating the staff training they have undergone. As Nursing Assistants have never been thanked for doing anything before, never mind have the Chairman of the Health Board come to give them a certificate for it, I am hopeful that this will be effective. Whether it is effective or not remains to be seen; it is a matter of experimentation. As with Communidad Los Horcones it is this experimental approach which is the important part of being a behaviourist.

CHAPTER 12

Community and Organisation: Managing the Boundaries at a Time of Change

Judith Brearley

The ideas which follow derive from experience in social work education and organisational consultancy. My perspective is that of an outsider to Camphill, and a learner about individuals with special needs and the communities who work with them. I shall address the concepts of change, boundaries and management in turn, using insights from the earlier chapters of this book, adding comments of my own, and shall then introduce some key theoretical ideas which I have found useful in understanding and working with change processes in organisations. Some dilemmas of practice requiring further thought will be identified briefly.

Change

An essential step is to specify the particular changes thought to be relevant. The danger is that without taking care over definition, 'change' becomes an appallingly threatening thing, an anonymous force to be reckoned with without quite knowing what its shape is. If we begin to specify, then it comes down to size. It becomes transformed into identifiable discrete elements which can be worked with. In this way a threat becomes a challenge, and this is always a step in the right direction.

The chapters are rich in this sort of healthy specification which is so useful in defining the relevant changes. For example, the introductory chapter looks not only at some of the main changes in Camphill in the last ten years, but also at parallel shifts in the wider society, and at the conceptual and practical challenges that these changes give rise to. Hailey extends the picture of internal change by giving an account of developments in Camphill over the last 50 years, while both Whiteley and Millard explore more general processes of change in therapeutic communities. Finally Baron shares some disturbing ideas about changes in state regulation in special needs provision.

Three things emerge from these accounts. First is the magnitude and the multiplicity of the changes, affecting every area and level of experience: people's needs, ways of responding to them, all the relationships involved, the nature of the opportunities and constraints offered by the environment. Secondly, a most important factor is the interconnectedness of the changes, the sheer complexity, the fact that change in one area inevitably brings about change in all the surrounding systems and sub-systems. The third striking feature is the extremely contradictory nature of the feelings aroused by the changes, with the ones seen as positive, healthy and progressive co-existing with those strongly felt to be damaging and threatening. A strong impression is that the welcome changes are more likely to be those coming from within, those we have control over, while the changes experienced as bad, regressive, or frightening are those from the outside world where people feel they have little or no say, and experience themselves as helpless victims. It is as if the environment is felt to be quite alien. These reactions are mirrored in the contradictory quality of feedback received by those working in this field; praise co-existing with criticism, pressure to expand or diversify experienced alongside threats of contraction or dispersal.

Hailey's chapter contains an interesting comment on work in the 1940s which still seems true today: "to hold, practice and develop such ideals in a friendly environment is in itself a major task, to transfer this activity to an alien culture is a mission which requires hard work, sacrifice and grace". I think we shall find it requires even more than all these good qualities.

These experiences of change are of course not unique to the field of work with individuals with special needs. They are just small examples of a global trend. Technological innovation and the possibility of instant communication force us to recognise the interdependence of events and developments world-wide. We can no longer feel immune from changes across the world, let alone changes just outside our own systems. This accelerating pace of change with its unpredictability brings disturbing feelings, confusion, questioning of basic assumptions, loss of a sense of stability and at worst experiences of chaos or even madness. Words from Yeats *The Second Coming* (1924) describe this: "The falcon cannot hear the falconer, things fall apart, the centre cannot hold." So how do we cope? Harold Bridger, an organisational consultant at the Tavistock Institute, has something to say about this. Quoting the old French saying "Le poisson ne sait qu'il vit dans l'eau que quand il est deja sur la rive", Bridger (1980, p.3) suggests we had better learn more about the turbulent, uncertain, complex and out-of-control medium in which we live.

Resistance to Change

In view of all the disturbance engendered by change, it is not surprising that, whether as individuals or in groups or as organisations, we resist change and cling to the status quo; and that we do this despite our wish and sometimes agreement to move forward and evident external pressures to do so. So what elements can we see in this reluctance and resistance to embrace change? Machiavelli addressed this issue at the beginning of the sixteenth century.

> There is nothing more difficult to take in hand, more perilous to conduct, or more uncertain in its success, than to take a lead in the introduction of a new order of things, because the innovator has for enemies all those who have done well under the old conditions and lukewarm defenders in those who may do well under the new. (Machiavelli, 1961, p.51)

Again that seems just as true now as five hundred years ago.

Continuing the theme of resistance to change, an important element is our attachment to what Parkes (1971, p.103) calls "our assumptive world". That is the familiar world peopled by all those known to us, our usual surroundings, habitual ways of working, unquestioned hopes for the future; the things that have become as comfortable as an old shoe. We strenuously cling to this assumptive world and, if forced by the circumstances to give it up, will protest vigorously and will need to mourn what is lost.

Another source of reluctance to accept and work with change is of course fear of the unknown. Better the devil you know! Who knows what is going to replace the familiar tried and trusted ways of working? Anxiety about this tends to become conviction that things are bound to get worse. Why risk losing what is precious? Of course there is always the possibility that things might get better, something new and valuable might be gained, but such an optimistic view tends to be overlooked because more primitive emotions hold sway.

Perhaps a further disincentive to embracing change is the feared loss of a reference group, a safe place among friends where it is possible for the time being to play with ideas, to share fantasies, and to behave in an 'as if' way, without being ridiculed. There has been a lot of restructuring of Social Work Departments in Scotland recently. Each time this happens, teams that were working effectively together sharing ideas and providing strong mutual support are disbanded, and lose that very precious asset of a group of familiar figures who can buttress and understand each other and take the work further. That is a very serious loss, not to be taken lightly. When those things disappear, we have to recreate them. This takes time and effort, and is not always successful.

Given that the possibility of change gives rise to such terrifying emotions, it is surprising to find little reference in the chapters to the whole idea of loss. It is only dealt with in Whiteley's chapter, yet throughout is a sense of struggling to hold on to something precious, something vitally important which is becoming increasingly vulnerable under the present circumstances. In any change there is bound to be loss, but it is as if the consequences of perhaps having to let go of some aspects cannot be faced explicitly because the prospect seems so unpalatable. The work of Marris is extremely helpful in this area. In *Loss and Change* (1986) he looks at the impact of disruption and relocation in terms of our need to search for meaning in altered circumstances. These ideas will be referred to later in relation to the management of change.

Boundary

This emerges as a central theme in the chapters, especially that of Farquharson which is entirely devoted to defining, explaining and illustrating the concept from clinical practice. The idea is dealt with fully there, so it is only necessary to highlight and develop one or two important points. I strongly agree that, when thinking about organisations, it is more helpful to think of a boundary region than a boundary line. So often we have demarcation disputes across boundary lines instead of seeing a shared area, a piece of common ground. It is like painting with primary colours where there is evidently a boundary region in which the colour is neither red nor yellow but different shades of orange. This is a very important, real aspect of living. As Farquharson points out, leadership functions are located in this boundary region, it is where one expects to find management. The term 'leadership function' is preferable to 'leader' or 'manager', which implies a single person, a fixed entity. Boundary management includes two major tasks: to protect the internal sub-systems from the disruption of fluctuating and inconsistent demands from outside; and to promote internal changes which will enable the system to be adaptive and proactive in relation to the environment. What is vital is to pay attention to *both* tasks, never losing sight of either for long. This is extremely difficult because each poses contradictory demands. One task requires great sensitivity to the feelings and pressures of those inside, a capacity to identify with the nature of their work, to know the detail of it and to understand what sort of conditions it requires to be effective. The other requirement is the ability to assess the environment very accurately, to understand and to some extent identify with its needs, to negotiate with diplomacy and to respond to demands from the outside world in a way which is neither arrogant and defensive nor subservient and compliant. I suspect we all have great difficulties achieving that sort of dual identification. It is much easier to take sides and feel more in touch and in sympathy with one than the other.

Such attributes and skills, the ability fully to understand the inside world and the outside world, and the nature of their interaction, are essential for all forms of boundary management, at whatever level, whether international relations, regional policy making, or transactions with the people next door. It is true of all types of boundary whether tangible or not. There appears to be strong agreement that however difficult those tasks are, they are absolutely vital at the present time. As Farquharson says, "Health depends on an appropriate mix of insulation and permeability in the boundary region".

This statement has close parallels with Whyte's chapter "What is a healthy community?". Two features stand out from his analysis as particularly relevant to this concern with boundaries. One is interdependence as a mark of mature relationships, and the other is the capacity for self-criticism and response to the criticism of others as a determinant of health in a community. The debate there is about maturity and health, but I think the issues at stake go even further into fundamental matters of identity and survival. Who am I? Can I continue to exist? Translated into organisational and group terms, these might be the crunch points. If that is true it will heighten our motivation to address these enormous dilemmas. Certainly the chapters give this issue a significant place. The first chapter abounds with questions like "how can groups like Camphill enter into productive dialogue with different forms of provision while maintaining necessary integrity?". Integrity clearly has something to do with wholeness and identity. "How can theories be reformulated, organisational changes negotiated, and therapeutic roles recast while maintaining essential continuity?". Hailey describes how in the last few years there have been renewed attempts to close some of the gaps between Camphill and the outside world and, just as important, to defend its position in areas such as community living.

Millard asserts that as a matter of policy therapeutic communities cannot exist without some protection. It is necessary for the parent agency to have a sufficient degree of understanding of and sympathy for the approach, and to be willing to allow it to operate free of too much interference. That is certainly a very pervasive theme. Baron, looking at State regulation, uses words like "incompatible", "inappropriate and damaging", "potentially hostile", to describe the impact of regulation on communities for people with special needs. The language in these statements conveys a sense of fighting for understanding and recognition, and the need to defend some hard-won identity against serious attack. All these are metaphors of warfare.

Part of the difficulty in really exploring these issues in depth is our ambivalence about boundaries. They are necessary, they help us to be what we are, they differentiate us, they are desired, but at the same time, by the same people, they are resented and unwanted. At one and the same time we want to merge with the other and to hold on to our separateness. This reminds me of the poem by Robert Frost, "Mending Wall" (1955, p.33). "Something there is that doesn't love a wall, . . ." The poet tells of meeting with his neighbour to build up the dry stone wall that separates their territories. The neighbour says "Good fences makes good neighbours!" but he questions that by pointing out how they are spending all their effort on repairing the wall even where they do not need it. "My apple trees will never get across and eat the cones under his pines, I tell him." This conveys very well some of the mixed feelings that we have towards boundaries.

Management

Against this background, how do we view the task of managing? We need to avoid simply reacting in a piecemeal way to whatever is the most pressing concern at a given time, and to do that we need conditions in which it is possible to look around and see what is going on, to work out what it means, to consider strategies and to identify ways forward.

Schein, a writer on organisations, said of consultancy that the task was "to help people to perceive, understand and act upon process events . . ."(1969, p.9) That is a helpful sequence. We cannot properly act until we have first of all perceived and then understood. But the pace of change is hotting up and most often there seems to be no gap in which this can happen. How do we create the space? This is where the concepts of Winnicott adapted to organisations by Bridger offer a valuable insight into the question (see Klein, 1989).

The notion of *transitional phenomena* (Winnicott, 1971, pp.1–25) is mentioned by both Whiteley and by Farquharson in their chapters. It is a highly relevant concept. What is being considered is the transition from being merged with the environment to being separate from it and yet maintaining a good relationship with it. It is a comparable process to that of a baby learning to manage the temporary absence of mother and beginning to sort out 'me' from 'not me', perhaps making use of a special ribbon, blanket, teddy bear or whatever (a transitional object) to help to do that.

So we can think in similar terms of an organisation asserting its particular identity and learning to cope with variable degrees of support and understanding from the outside world. Winnicott linked this idea of the space between, the intermediate area or field of experience between 'me' and 'not me', inextricably with play. Again something about painting comes to mind. This is not intellectual work so much as experiencing something in the particular area of our mind which has to do with creativity and imagination, rather than just getting on with the job. So not only is it all linked with play, but also with creativity and in turn with all sorts of cultural phenomena like art and religion. Something very fundamental and quite precious is being talked about.

These ideas, surprisingly perhaps, form a basis of what is called the *transitional approach to the management of change* which Bridger and his colleagues (Klein, 1989) have been developing in recent years, in conferences and consultancies with enterprises of all kinds whether multi-national industries or small voluntary organisations. This transitional approach brings together a number of features which I have already mentioned. Some of these will be familiar. One is an *open-systems perspective*, which involves balancing and optimising the interplay of forces, both within and outside the organisation, accepting the inevitable uncertainty and complexity, acknowledging the interdependence of all the parts of the system and their needs to adapt in order to change in tandem with each other, and being willing to adjust to an altered environment in a flexible way, minimising rigidities in the system.

Another feature of this approach is the notion of *potential space*. That is the space in the individual's mind within which we feel free of inhibitions of previous habits or anxieties or other restrictions, space in which ideas can be played with and imagination and perception mingle, leading to new possibilities.

Bridger is also particularly known for his concept of the *double task*. This is the idea that instead of just going through the agenda, getting on with the job, any working group could and should regularly allow space and time for monitoring, reviewing and reflecting on what is being done, whether it is the task itself, the objectives set or the way of doing the work. Are we still clear on what it is we are trying to achieve? Are we going about it in the best way? How can we learn from what has just happened? Are our basic assumptions still appropriate? I suspect that these sort of questions are neglected most of the time in most working groups, but they are the sort of questions which, if pursued, can make a significant difference to the quality of the work, to the morale of those doing it, and to the way it is communicated to other people. It is as if we give ourselves rehearsal space to articulate what the work is all about, and therefore feel identified with it and confident about it. However, certain conditions are necessary to allow that to happen. It does not occur automatically.

The concept of *transitional space* provides a way forward. This is parallel to the potential space which exists in the individual. It is like potential space held collectively. It has to be created to facilitate mobilisation of people's internal potential space. Time has to be made available, maybe just a short period in a meeting in which business in suspended, or possibly an away-day. For example, an organisation which was making a radical change in its functioning did none of its normal work and closed to users for a whole month. During that month the staff met together, visited other similar places, sat down and reviewed what they enjoyed and what they really felt proud of in the past and also what they hoped for and feared in the future. Having given themselves that moratorium on the task, they enabled themselves to go forward in a very effective way. I suspect that would not have happened without the space. Obviously sanction for this has to be given by the wider organisation, and all group members have to be willing at least to give it a try.

Loss

As mentioned earlier, even in change which is voluntary and welcomed, or even relatively minor, there is always some aspect of loss. Part of effective management of change is to understand the impact of particular losses on all those involved. It is here that Marris's ideas are worth reiterating. He is concerned not only to understand and to be sensitive to the element of loss but also to look at how such understanding influences what we do, our choice of action. The particular type of change he is concerned with is that which involves loss of things we are attached to, whether it is ways of working or working groups or people, change which cannot be reversed and where it is difficult to see meaning or purpose in it. He suggests those going through that sort of change will experience a crisis of disorientation where anxiety is predominant. I suspect that is familiar to anyone facing major change. The way this crisis is handled, he says, can quite significantly affect what then happens. His advice is to do what has just been described, to allow a moratorium, to give people space to repair what he calls the thread of continuity in their attachments and above all to recognise the element of bereavement in any major reconstruction process. He eloquently conveys how any crisis of disorientation provokes contradictory impulses. We both want to return to the past and be totally pre-occupied with what the past meant for us, and then swing towards forgetting the past and denying its significance altogether. Marris says there is no easy way through this. It has to be lived with, we have to endure the swinging between the two competing claims, struggling to reconcile and integrate them without denying either side of the equation. This of course can be done far more effectively if the right sort of support is at hand.

If disruptive change is experienced collectively, for example as a result of the closure of a unit which had developed a particular way of working in which all staff had a high investment, then the troubled feelings may well be transferred on to the institutions involved, and the conflict enacted at a wider societal level. An illustration can perhaps be seen in the scapegoating or blaming of 'the authorities' or the 'Thatcher government' or whatever. Marris says there is need for this conflict to be allowed full expression. It must not be pre-empted, especially not by rationalisation or patronising reassurance. It is not helpful to say, "There there, it's going to be all right, just you wait and see!". Each person must be allowed the right and the space to adjust. People do this in their own idiosyncratic fashion and the process needs a lot of time and patience. This is not easy work, but it is work which makes future work easier.

Metaphors of Organisational Life

Morgan, a Canadian organisational analyst, who writes about *Images of Organisation* (1986), suggests that our assumptions about managing organisational life are built on a small number of taken-for-granted images. If we examine these we can create new ways of thinking and become more adept at diagnosing and solving problems. He highlights ways of thinking based on metaphor, that is to say, an attempt to understand one element of experience in terms of another, and he offers eight or nine metaphors of organisational life. It is not claimed that any one of these offers a full picture, some are more predominant than others in different forms of organisations, and all have advantages and disadvantages. They are simply ways of seeing things, perspectives on the work which can add to our outlook and widen our range of thinking.

I shall mention four of these metaphors: organisations as mechanisms, as organisms, as cultures, and as psychic prisons. Baron's chapter about state regulation points to some of the *mechanistic* aspects of bureaucracies, of rule books, of number games, of preoccupation with money as opposed to other values, where people feel like helpless cogs in a machine, out of control of their own destiny and unsure what the whole enterprise is about. To view organisations as *organisms* reflects open-systems thinking and explores how organisations are born, grow, develop, decline, adapt to change and interact with their environment. Some of what has already been discussed implicitly reflects this way of thinking. However, it should be examined critically, not accepted unquestioningly. The notion of organisations as cultures, focuses on the ideals, values, belief systems, rituals and norms that sustain organisations as socially constructed realities. Where this is a predominant aspect, as it probably is in Camphill, then anything that threatens those ideals is very powerfully resisted. The metaphor which I find most thought-provoking is that of organisations as *psychic prisons*. The idea is that we put ourselves by various means into prisons of our own making. Morgan uses the famous allegory of Plato's Cave, in which people are chained and see only very dim and shadowy images, and yet they resist enlightenment, experiencing great pain and rejection if they try to go out into the sunlight. All sorts of behaviours result in psychic imprisonment, some of them unconscious. For example, we unwittingly split our world into 'goodies and baddies', we find ourselves caught up in organisational mechanisms of defence to cope with the anxiety, the sort of issue that Isabel Menzies-Lyth (1988) addresses. We become espoused to favoured ways of thinking. This is discussed in *On the Psychology of Military Incompetence* (Dixon, 1976), a terrifying document which details some famous campaigns in various wars since Crimea. It seems that the blinkered view of a minority of generals in those campaigns caused thousands of people to die, because they found it difficult to be flexible and take on board new understanding and new knowledge.

Just a word more about the *splitting and projection* on which polarisation of attitudes is based. These are very primitive unconscious mechanisms involving the attribution to others of our own unwanted feelings. I wonder if something of this sort is going on between the communities which care for those with special needs and the 'restrictive', 'disabling' outside agencies. Given the history of rejection in our society of those who are different, and the way in which current provision is still beset by stigmatised prejudiced societal attitudes, it would not be surprising if the workers in communities most closely identified with difference and special needs felt themselves to be scapegoated or dealt with in a hostile fashion. Some of the persecutory aspects referred to in the chapters may well be the result of unacknowledged distancing and unconscious hostility rather than the outcome of objective rational appraisal. It is all the more tragic then that this has precisely the effect of putting those on the receiving end of such attributions even further into their corner, their withdrawal apparently confirming the negative message given. The same is true in reverse; the scathing dismissal of those in bureaucracies whose task is inspection and regulation ensures paradoxically that their positive qualities such as their respect for the work and their potential for supporting it never have much chance of expression. To draw a parallel from the field of physical handicap, Dartington, Miller and Gwynne (1981) suggest that the way to deal with those expressing overt hostility to people with handicaps is not to counter this with the diametrically opposed view of "we who *really* love and care for them!", and not to assert the point and shout ever more loudly, because then no listening takes place. A more effective approach is to try to understand and identify a little with what it feels like to be the opposition. This allows a modicum of shared ground to be discovered.

Finally, I would like to identify some of the unanswered questions raised in the chapters which require more discussion across the boundaries of profession and setting and experience. The first is that of *leadership function*. Is 'leadership' an anathema to some, and if so, why, and with what results? Certainly in the chapters diametric opposites of leadership style are referred to with hierarchical state and local authority bureaucracies on the one hand, and on the other the group-based, diverse, non-hierarchical Camphill system. The question might be posed: what is in between? Work in these times of rapid change cannot be done by static hierarchies, they are too fixed, not flexible enough. It may be that organisations like Camphill have a part of a very good answer here. A number of organisational commentators, for example, Toffler in *Future Shock* (1970) advocate a move away from rigid systems towards temporary task forces, short-term groups of people with identified specialist skills who come together on a project, contribute all they have to it, and then disband once the work is completed and reform in some other way.

The second question centres on *training issues*. Hailey said in his chapter that courses promoted by bodies outside the anthroposophical movement are appropriate only to a limited extent for Camphill workers. Are we building problems into the system by that separateness in training from the very start? If at their beginning formative stages, people find themselves in separate camps, with only limited possibilities for cross-fertilisation, how can they gain a comfortable feel of what other people are about? The same argument applies to relationships between different professions in relation to the way education and training either fosters or inhibits good mutual understanding. That is worth debating.

The third question concerns the *families of those with special needs*. In the chapters there is very little reference to the experience and feelings of parents and siblings. People who live in communities have to cross and re-cross that crucial boundary between family life and community life. How do we understand and manage that boundary? How do we consult with relatives and parents, how do we understand what is going on at home as much as what is happening in the community, and enable effective transactions and movements between the two worlds?

And finally, *what is the interaction between good direct practice and attempts to influence policy?* My own conviction is that greater understanding of the boundary issues discussed above, together with developing self-awareness and on-going learning about the task, will enhance the collaborative approach which is so essential if people with special needs are to have their needs met.

CHAPTER 13

Six Ways of Dealing with Stigma: In Defence of the Ghetto

Nils Christie

One of the advantages of being a foreigner is that you are forced to reflect on language more than if you are a native speaker. I have been given the task of reflecting on the "Individual with Special Needs", but I must say that the term is not precisely precise; people are all individuals with special needs. Such a lack of clarity usually has a reason; in this case the reasons are obvious. We do not dare to put words to, to put precise concepts on, what we are to describe. The whole area of labelling surveyed in this book is a minefield of terminological bias.

This is the same danger which you meet in conversations on Israel or Ireland. Saying 'Northern Ireland' and the 'West Bank', you align yourself with the states of Great Britain and Israel; saying 'the Six Counties in the North' and 'The Occupied Territories', you align yourself with Irish Nationalists and the Arabs. It impossible to talk without taking a stand, and without saying much more than the words superficially seem to convey. We have to live with this. If one is forced out of the native tongue and into another these problems become more obvious; but this disadvantage can be turned into an advantage. As a foreigner one is permitted to make errors, and one is also permitted to take a more detached view when it comes to the final choices of what we shall express.

What, then, should we call those at the centre of our attention? I assume that we all would like to make choices whereby we at least try to minimise the stigmatising effect of what we are saying. Reflecting on this issue I have come upon six basic terminological solutions implicit in the earlier chapters and in our discussions.

Euphemism

The first solution is in heavy use these days. Eagerly listening to discussions in the Conference, and reading the earlier chapters, I have been brought to

151

the understanding that there are several words which I am supposed not to use here: of course not 'idiot', even if it means peculiar. We probably all think we are peculiar, so it is very strange that we cannot call other people idiots! More subtly, I am not supposed to talk about 'handicapped people' but 'people with handicaps'.

This first terminological solution we can call the solution of euphemism, probably the most commonly applied solution to the problems we have in this area. It is widely used elsewhere; it is a very familiar solution to me working in the field of crime and crime control. I meet the solution all the time; for example in my country we do not have any prisons, they do not exist! We do, however, have 'Institutions'. We don't have 'prisoners', we have 'inmates'; we don't have 'cells', we have 'rooms'; we don't have 'punishment cells', we have 'single rooms'; we don't have a Ministry for Prison Affairs, we have a sub-ministry 'for the Care of Those in the Hands of the Crime Control System'; we do not 'punish' people if we can avoid the term, we apply some form of 'measures', or we can, of course, 'treat' people and we can call what we do 'compulsory treatment'. The systematic attempt is to avoid the harshest words. This is an old tradition, the use of euphemism.

Non-Conceptualisation

Another solution is the solution of non-conceptualisation. What do I have in mind? I could also call it the mother-in-law technique. That term came to my mind when I was thinking back on a meeting in this country many, many years ago. There was a meeting in the British Anthropological Association and they had asked as their invited guest George Homans, a marvellous man and also both a very good sociologist and social anthropologist. He described a personal dilemma he had: at any particular time there are certain words which have suddenly become taboo due to social change. At this time, Homans maintained, it had suddenly become impossible to say what he could have said quite simply before the Second World War, but not after, namely 'mother-in-law'. At that time the 'mother-in-law' was, in a way, only a comic figure; it was derogatory to call a person 'mother-in-law'; previously it had been acceptable to call someone my 'mother-in-law' – she had a natural position and you called her that. But, after the Second World War, there had been so many jokes about it, and the 'mother-in-law' was generally held to be such a terrible person, that he felt he could not use the term. On the other hand he could not use her first name because that would have been lacking in respect. What do you do in that case – if there was a telephone call for his mother-in-law he felt he could not call out "You – it is the telephone for You". His solution instead was to go and fetch her so that she could go to the telephone without having to be addressed directly by name or status.

This is the solution of non-conceptualisation, of avoiding classification. Of course in most cases you can call people by their first names and thus avoid classification. This is the technique used in Camphill, everybody is on first name terms and the problem is solved. It is the same in many organisations; people jump into calling each other by their first name because then you escape the general concept which might classify people as 'subordinate' or 'superior'. Names are without all of this so they can hide the outer structure of status and stigma.

Skill Enhancement

A third possibility, much in evidence these days, is to attempt to change those we talk about so that stigmatising labels will not be quite that easy to apply. Bill Fraser in his chapter talks of the possibility of training into normal ways of life. It is quite clear that Bill Fraser does not overestimate the limits of this possibility – you can train people to operate a bit more as if they were not extraordinary and thereby minimise the temptation to use stigmatising terms but they remain extraordinary.

Educating the Labellers

A fourth possibility for dealing with stigma is to educate those who do the labelling. Ivana Markova and Andrew Jahoda give some relevant examples of the use of advertisements to challenge dominant terminology. Bill Fraser in his chapter however reflects on how Medical Practitioners seem to get detrained in medical schools and further detrained with age so as to be less and less capable of handling interactions with an extraordinary person and, by extension, less and less able to see the ordinary in that person and the limited need to have special terms.

Changing the Preconditions for Labelling

A fifth way to deal with this whole dilemma has to do with changing the basic conditions of the person whom you are labelling. Ivana Markova and Andrew Jahoda give some examples of this but maintain that if the basic conditions are not changed then nothing will change in the terminology. We may coin new words, make new sounds about those of whom we are speaking, but the effect will last only a little while until these new terms take on the same stigma as the old terms. There are endless possibilities in rushing ever newer and newer labels fresh from the printer but, after a very short time, they are worn out. Why are they worn out? As Markova and Jahoda say so clearly, changes in terminology will be fruitless if they are not accompanied by implicit and explicit changes in values, representations and conditions; the change in labels and names would only be temporary because the new terms would quickly acquire the meaning of the discarded terms and the renaming could start all over again. I think this is the crux of the matter. There is no hope whatsoever of removing a population from this unhealthy cycle of labelling if nothing else is changed.

In Camphill we have an example which is fascinating and so important for the rest of us, we have an example where the basic conditions for using terms on other people have been substantially changed. But even there, even in Camphill, there are terminological differences. I do not know of any social system which has gone so far in reducing the difference between Us and Them, but still in Camphill the cleavage is maintained. Camphill has two basic terms in, for example, its village settings: 'co-workers' and 'villagers'. Co-workers one would expect would mean everybody who was working in the community; but no, co-workers means those who are supposed not to be dumb or idiots. The other group is called villagers; again it is completely illogical because the whole community lives in the village, but only half of the population is called villagers.

So, in the most advanced system I know, social realities seem to force differences in terminology but there is an important additional point here. Although Camphill has these two words it is not at all obvious if these represent a status difference; it is not quite clear who is at the top! Because of their conception of the human being as containing a reincarnating spirit, the comparative stratification of these two conditions is not straightforward - "OK now you are a villager but next time round you might reappear as a co-worker" (or the other way around). This is not simply a dialectical point but it is a lived reality: many co-workers in the Camphill villages I know best would say that the ideal is to become a villager in basic attitudes and social form.

Accepting the Condition

It will not surprise you that I want to put forward another solution which is not discussed very much in Great Britain; the attempt to turn stigma into honour. In history there are many examples of this and I would like to highlight an example from Scandinavia, the Movement of the Mad.

This is a movement in Scandinavia, particularly well developed in Denmark which is often advanced in such matters, for and among people who have been declared by doctors to be insane; they are roaring mad. In Danish and Norwegian the word for mad is *gale*. But that is also the word for the crowing of the cock; the Movement of the Mad therefore is also the Movement of those who Crow. *Gale* also means to cry out and so we also have the Movement of those who Cry Out (at what people do with you when you are mad). This Movement is trying to organise the Mad, and on 1 May last year they had a special section in the procession with a special banner proclaiming the Movement of the Mad. So instead of saying "Don't call us mad, remove our stigma" they are saying "I am mad! Isn't it OK to be mad?".

Is not this only further self deception? There have been several discussions on this in the Mad Movement and the general conclusion is that it is very painful to be mad. Most people who are mad have gone through severe trauma and have reasons for being mad; it is a painful condition. But there is much to be learnt from mad people; their experience is often expensive and, if we listen, we can learn a lot. Gaining such insights necessitates paying very close attention to what mad people are saying both about their background and about their experiences of professional systems. Too often, in pursuit of a fast diagnosis, they are not listened to or understood. The life experience of the mad is not taken into our cultural fabric; the mad can say "Listen to this in another way; we have values to which you ought to listen. Since we have these values we are valuable; and since we are valuable it is OK to be mad". This way of reasoning has, in many ways, great attractions.

So we can now return once more to our specific theme and ask "Is it OK to be less able in certain activities than most people are?". Is it not painful or, perhaps, obviously more painful than not, to have Downs Syndrome or whatever? It is very complicated to have any view on this and it is probably a mistake to pose the question in that way; who can say if one life condition is more or less painful than another.

It is terribly difficult to answer the question of 'what is pain?'. Writing *The Limits of Pain* (Christie, 1982) I came to the conclusion that I did not know what pain was. In the autobiography of a blind man from the French Resistance Movement (Lusseyran, 1963) who was placed in a concentration camp you find his testimony that never in his life had he been more happy than in the impossible situation of the concentration camp.

The same thought struck me just two Sundays ago when a woman visited me to tell me about her rather desperate situation. She is mad; she said she was mad, but had played at being not mad for the doctors in order to be let out. She said that she was so happy, and is so happy, in her madness; it was the best experience of her life, a fantastic period. The only inconvenience was that they placed her behind bars in the mental hospital.

Living with the Dumb

I recount these stories only to complicate the usual simplifications on pain. With regard to supposedly dumb people I must say that their life does not look painful; unless we say they ought to suffer, or unless we actually make them suffer, then it often looks as if they are not in great pain. I cannot evaluate this from the point of view of those living these lives; my only solution is to try to evaluate it from the point of view of myself. If, for me, they seem to be OK then for me they *are* OK, and I can tell them that I think that they are OK.

I cannot say if it is OK to be in other people's shoes. I can say that, for me, it is good that these people exist. Taking this very egocentric view I can say it is OK for me that they exist as they exist, and it might be OK for them. Maybe life might be even better for them to know that I think they are OK for me as they are. But I cannot say if they are OK for themselves. Without descending into banalities an example in terms of purely physical conditions might help: when city plans and house plans are drawn up so that they are good for people who have one sort of handicap or another, then usually those cities or those houses are better for me also. If we take a set of stairs where the bannister is poorly placed it is dangerous for all of us. But if it is in a house where a lot of people with disabilities of various sorts live then we would be spurred to alter the bannister more quickly to prevent accidents. It would be good for them and, thereby, it would be good for us.

This is also the case in intellectual relationships. Having partners in discussion who have great difficulties in understanding, forces me in new directions which are good for all the listeners. If I know I have some half deaf people in the audience, of course I talk as loud as possible. If I know that I have people there whose training in reasoning is not the same as most people's training in following logical arguments, of course I try to illustrate my arguments with body language, with examples, with different ways at looking and understanding. It is perfectly possible to express most arguments in relatively uncomplicated concepts. If I know that there are people in the audience who are not well trained in this, and who might be expected not to keep their interest alive for a very long time, I shall cut out a lot of the usual academic embroidery. We are trained very much to symbolise that we really are well trained; but this is not essential for the core of what we want to say. I am personally absolutely convinced that since I accidentally came into some of the Camphill Villages many many years back, they have helped me enormously in my ordinary lecturing for ordinary students. I have been able to cut out a lot of the nonsense and have been forced to behave in a more decent way when I have a mixed audience of people with varying possibilities for understanding what I am saying. It has been a blessing for me and I am sure it has been a blessing for my ordinary students; so it is OK for me!

A further illustration of this point which I regard as crucial is that to lecture in the Camphill Village at Vidaråsen is so pleasant. Musicians coming to Vidaråsen say the same thing; they are willing to travel a very long way, for very little money to play there because they have an audience which is so interested, and one which will not simply listen but also react. It is an audience where emotions are easily activated, are easily displayed, and where there is an atmosphere in the room which is on a much higher level than among the ordinary audiences one meets. I spent some terms lecturing in Berkeley shortly after the student revolution; Vidaråsen reminds me of Berkeley. I have never met an audience so close to the Berkeley experience as there has been at Vidaråsen. People cry, shout and show that they are following; they also interrupt. If I really get the lecture going there is a lot of turmoil. I have had to admit defeat several times when I have not been well enough prepared and I have slipped into the usual academic role; that is a very easy and comfortable role to slip into where you can talk and talk because most of us can talk for hours but without coming to the real core of the matter. People at Vidaråsen will listen politely but it is clear that it is a total failure.

What I take out of these examples is the possibility of putting aside the endless regress of changing the labels and instead going more on the offensive, saying, "Some people are seen as different. They are seen as dumb but is being dumb not OK? Probably they are OK.".

Is this not a sort of romanticism while in reality these people are suffering? I hope I have put that argument away. I am arguing that maybe we should be more frank in our terminology; in the same way as we have a Movement of the Mad, could we not have a Movement of the Dumb, claiming "I am as I am why don't you accept it?". I can imagine several people in Vidaråsen who would stand up and say this; some actually do when using the telephone for example. In my study of the Camphill Village at Vidaråsen, *Beyond Loneliness and Institutions* (Christie, 1989), I give the example of the man who asked for the times of a bus in Vidaråsen. When he was given poor information he said, "You see I am mentally retarded you will have to tell me this in a bit more of a clear way". I think it is great that it was possible to convey that message over the telephone lines.

If the dumb are OK then they should feel able to preserve that 'OKness' themselves. I think that the Camphill Communities are very good at this; this is one of their strengths. But could we not also help those who are not inside Camphill? One way to approach this is to try to educate the public generally and the 'professionals' specifically to be more accepting of the dumb as they are, to preserve their identities as dumb people. This means dropping notions of the dumb being 'clients' with all the implications of relations of domination and subordination. This means dropping notions of 'integration' where the identity and communality of the dumb are lost. It means dropping the unrealistic pretence of the dumb being normal participants in social interaction.

Personally I do not want to spend most of my time alone with one other person who I think is rather dumb. It is difficult, if not impossible, to respect the 'OKness' of the dumb in a social situation where I am alone, or nearly alone, with him or her; there is no social system generating challenges, I do not have enough to talk with him or her about, I have my other work to do and the social life would not be organised to take care of my needs. If I am placed in such a context I shall of course be polite, but I shall not initiate a lasting contact based on friendship. I am sure that most ordinary people would react that way.

The reason that the Camphill Communities are so fantastic is precisely because you have so many encounters; you have the company of co-workers, you have the dense cultural life and you have all the challenges of community living. It is this turmoil in Camphill which makes it bearable, not only bearable but an extremely good life. I would have liked to have such a life in Oslo, I would have moved in immediately, but not with the person called mentally retarded as my natural choice of sole interactional partner. I just would not do that.

Who should do it? We know from many of the chapters, and from our experience both in Camphill and outside Camphill, that people who are dumb are not the first choice among ordinary people for friendship, or for routine interaction. We may try to be idealistic, but we must accept that other people are not idealistic in this way, and so it becomes a lonely life for the dumb.

In Defence of the Ghetto

We currently have a taboo against certain views on this matter and we thereby tend to underplay the only sensible solution to this problem. The only sensible solution is that dumb people should be with other people who are the same, in the same condition, whether it be in a Camphill Community or in another life setting. The reality is that these people choose each other as the only available, long term, interactional partners. It is the last choice but it is better than nothing. Of course we hesitate to say "Yes" to that solution and we spread the dumb out; in my country it is a wide spreading out so as not create a ghetto.

I wanted to call my study of Vidaråsen *In Defence of the Ghetto* but they talked me out of it for understandable reasons; in many ways the Camphill Movement is not a ghetto, and the term does not fit. I am sure of that. But I do want to put forward what seem to me to be powerful arguments in favour of the ghetto, even if the Camphill Communities do not fit the term. As the process of de-institutionalisation progresses and we push dumb people out into the ordinary community then we should ensure that they live close together, that they can reach each other all the time and meet each other as if they were living in a ghetto. Misplaced thoughts of equality are creating a handicapping situation for a lot of dumb people.

If you look at the United States you will find a general returning to ethnic roots; people now want to be identified as 'Mexican' in New York for example. Inside the European Community a similar process is in train; as the nation states begin to lose their pre-eminence so minorities are beginning to assert their identities more; in Norway when immigrants or refugees arrive they want to be close to others from their background but we insist, out of our goodness and concern for them, on spreading them out all over the country so they do not create a ghetto. Of course they want to create a ghetto, and of course they are better off in a ghetto. We, the rest of us, we allow ourselves the luxury of choosing our friends and where we live. The only good argument against the ghetto which I can see is when the powerful create a ghetto and force the subordinate into it. But to deny the possibility of forming the ghetto, with all the benefits of solidarity and community, to those without power, people who are denied so many other things, is particularly bad social policy.

External Control

By way of conclusion I want to make two points, one specific and the other general. The earlier chapters leave me with a certain uneasiness about the functions of control exercised by the Social Services on places such as the Camphill Communities. This is a double-sided problem. From the point of view of Camphill such control is threatening because it might paralyse the dynamic of the system, its independence, and thereby abolish everything which makes the Camphill Communities similar to families, to ordinary family life. If a lot of external controls are established then family life is not family life any more; the Communities would have to adapt to so many demands that they would become institutions. This is a realistic possibility, and a problem.

On the other hand it is quite clear that many dumb people are in rather vulnerable positions, so it is also quite legitimate that people feel responsible and that those with administrative responsibilities see to it that the dumb are treated in the best possible way. It is easy to accept this when it is a matter of the Fire Regulations and perhaps, from the perspective of the Social Services, if it is a question of whether the room is big enough. But if the issue is whether the social milieu is good or not, who should decide on that?

One possibility raised earlier in our discussions is that a panel of lay people would be the best mechanism to evaluate such questions. This could take the form of some sort of enquiry proceedings or some sort of organisation charged with resolving conflicts. The attraction of this is that it moves away from leaning too much on the authority of one profession which is supposed to know better.

A parallel issue to be resolved is that of where should the control agencies devote their attention? I have no ready answer to this question but am concerned that all the attention to the fine detail of life in, say, nursing homes not only may force institutionalisation on them and restrict innovation but it also may generate a sense that "We have the situation under control" and thus blunt our critical faculties.

Lives Worth Living

A much more important point has to do with our dominant pattern of thinking. These days this seems to be narrowly utilitarian – things should be useful and people should be useful, and that useful solutions are most readily available through 'science'. When it comes to people who are not as most people are, is this not a dangerous thing?

Maybe I am only reawakening old ghosts but I have an older identity where my major task was to work with horrors of the concentration camps. One of my first scientific studies was to investigate concentration camps to find out why so many Norwegians had killed people in those camps (Snare & Christie, 1975). I think I found the solution. People were so reduced in the concentration camps that they no longer appeared human and this made it more easy to kill them.

Now, at the other end of my life travel, I am in the second phase of this research and, in this new phase, I have been obliged to reframe the question. It is no longer to me a question of "Why did some people kill?"; it is more a question of "Why did some people *not* kill?". I think the layer between us and normal existence, and between us and the most terrible things is a very, very thin skin. In the first wave of studies on concentration camps it was thought that the horror was due to bad people, ultimately the politicians. As I found in my study the Norwegians who had killed blamed, of course, the S.S., who were just above them. The S.S. blamed the central command in Oslo and central command in Oslo blamed people in Berlin. Those people in Berlin blamed their bosses and some of the politicians; those people were hanged and we were supposedly rid of the problem. In this second wave of studies therefore it is more usual to observe that the willingness to kill is common; it is more of a surprise that somebody will not kill.

There is now a cognate literature on the scientific aspects of this killing; this literature in English is dominated by Robert Jay Lifton who has written a book with the sub-title *Medical Killing and the Psychology of Genocide* (Lifton, 1986). Lifton's argument, supported by other work in both English and German, is that the whole movement towards concentration camps and the 'Final Solution' had started by 1933 with enforced sterilisation of some people under the banner of 'life not worth living' (a concept with which the contemporary British High Court is familiar). In Nazi Germany there was a gradual increase in the scope of this category until it included physically handicapped children, the mentally retarded, the mad, the maladjusted, alcoholics and finally those with the wrong genetic content (the Jews, the Gypsies and people from Eastern Europe).

What was so important in this story is, first of all, that the groundwork was laid, and much of the killing done, *before the war*. This was a very unpopular project in Germany and Hitler tried, partially successfully, to conceal his involvement. The strength of the protests, particularly the protests of Catholics, nearly brought a halt to the process, but the machinery was set up and when the war came the whole machinery was sent to the East.

The second point of this history is that the whole operation was kept very clearly within the framework of medical thinking. It was seen as a medical operation on two levels; firstly in terms of individual 'cases', it was the doctors who decided if the person had no chance to live a life worth living;

secondly the medical model was extended from the biological body to the social body. The concept of 'Folk' or 'community' was taken from the German sociological tradition and assimilated to the medical model: if the body has a sick part you cut it out; if the social body has a sick part you cut it out, all in the name of preserving the health of the whole social body. This was utilitarian thinking in the extreme and the 'problems' were handed to the medical profession for resolution. It is important to note that the medical profession made virtually no protest at this.

In Saxenhausen, when the train came, the selection procedure on the platform for life or death was under medical control at the insistence of the medical profession. Such was the power of the medical model that, if there were no medical doctor available, dentists and also a pharmacist were put in charge of the selection. Now, as then, it is the image of the medical operation, dispassionate, highly competent technically, beneficial, in short, scientific, which allows us to contemplate horrors with equanimity.

This example shows how quickly scientists like myself are without defences when we are grabbed by one Big Idea, namely the primary distinction between what is useful and what is not useful. Once that framework is adopted there are no limits to what can be done.

I have raised very unpleasant issues in order to argue against the dominant ethos of utility and to argue for self control in assessing, for others, their 'utility' or 'quality of life'. Maybe I am calling up the ghosts of half a century ago, the ghosts which stimulated the foundation of Camphill, but I ask myself what would happen if there were a new crisis, perhaps a war on home territory with food shortages, with shortages of medical equipment, who would be the first to the wall in such a situation?

I see no solution to this except a cultural one: we have to raise these questions again and again; we have to try to create a sort of anxiety so that people can see how very close we are constantly to catastrophe; we have to resist such utilitarian patterns of thinking, and their consequent measures, even if they seem to be essential to the preservation of 'life worth living'. One part of this cultural process, whether in Camphill or outside, must be to underline the dignified character of people independent of their supposed abilities. Only this provides a bulwark against the repetition of the most horrible sights of human society.

Part 3

Introduction to Part 3

In Part 3 we bring the project to a completion. In accounting for the conference we do not seek to summarise it; less do we seek to present its deliberations as encapsulating *the* solution to each of the dilemmas outlined in previous chapters. In this final Part we seek to take from the conference those themes which seem to us to carry the potential for high quality innovation and to develop them further.

The conference was, by all accounts, an unusual experience: the work rate was fierce but there was little evidence of stress; the participants were diverse, and often placed in oppositional roles elsewhere, but the discussions were friendly and supportive without ever being bland. The occasional set speech, striking pose, laboured theme or empty rhetoric was thus more than usually incongruous. A space was created in which differences were explored in a spirit of active tolerance, mutual elucidation and critical debate. Brearley's warning about the dangers of the metaphors of warfare and mechanism captured a reality of this experience. The changing realities of power by which the aims and pace of change are being determined hierarchically, and in an accountancy framework, were discussed, but the conference did not address alternative ways of determining priorities. In so far as the conference reached a 'conclusion' it was that there is a need for developing 'networks' for interchange in which the processes of power could be held in abeyance and held up for scrutiny. One expression of this conclusion is that a series of workshops in different parts of the UK is being planned. Here, in both Chapters 14 and 15 we reflect on this process and the creation of such spaces under other conditions.

We had not intended, or hoped, that the work of the conference would focus on Camphill, or that it would become a dialogue between Camphill co-workers on the one hand and others; but we were the guests of the Camphill Schools. The films in particular, but also the exhibition, displays and living environment, powerfully brought to the forefront Camphill policies and practices. It became clear that, for a number of participants, their intention in

163

attending had been to find out more about the Camphill system. In Chapter 14 we develop arguments about some of the positive contributions which the Camphill model may make to the care of those with special needs. The conference was by no means uncritical of Camphill ways, especially the image conveyed by some co-workers and sympathisers of community living as being relatively free of conflict; but these criticisms were not elaborated to the stage of abstracting general principles. We have not tried to undertake this task in this context but have published a preliminary sketch elsewhere (Baron & Haldane, 1991).

One feature of the conference, replicating wider tendencies, was the use of a myriad of polar oppositions to reference the field (for example, Institutions-The Community, Normality-Difference, Professional-Lay). Such polarities are powerful cultural tools needing careful use, but currently they tend to be used more for caricature/disqualification, and consecration/celebration, than for exploring the diversity and subtlety of different forms of provision. Opting *for* one *against* the other has the appeal of simplicity and commitment, but fails to capture the complexity and uncertainty of the empirical world. In both Chapters 14 and 15 we try to move beyond such an *either-or* framework to bring key polar oppositions into a more fruitful relationship. In so doing we do not seek any 'middle ground' in terms of ad hoc aggregations of features from either pole, but seek more active combinations creating new forms of social relations and care. In Chapter 14 we address the polarity of Normality-Difference as applied to persons, while in Chapter 15 we address this polarity as applied to communities.

Negotiating Polarities

Douglas Haldane and Stephen Baron

Normality and Difference

In the plenary sessions and the small group workshops of the conference, Julian Sleigh, one of the group of Camphill co-workers responsible for the Camphill Villages in South Africa and for their emphasis on racial integration, argued that the Camphill Movement had lost sight of the *tragedy* of handicap; in particular it had lost sight of the loneliness of the adult with special needs who had not forged an intimate personal relationship in young adulthood. Nils Christie, in his commentary on the working papers for the conference, argued the case for establishing 'The Movement of the Dumb' to proclaim the 'OK-ness' of being dumb.

These perspectives provoked lively debate about whether it was legitimate to speak of handicap as tragedy, or of those with special needs as 'dumb'. Underpinning these arguments are two polar ideal-typical positions: that handicaps are part of the range of normal human variation, no different in essence from other forms of human variation; that handicaps are a class of variation which, in their essence and in their consequences, make different those who bear them. In this the conference reflected tensions in the wider discourse of special needs.

The argument that those with special needs are essentially different finds its strongest expression, and historical roots, in what we may term the 'medical model'. Based in biological sciences this model (dominant in medicine, psychiatry and psychology) centres on a strong, if not always clear, conception of normal functioning against which the person with special needs is measured, and found wanting. With a conceptual division between conditions which are chronic and those which are susceptible to remediation, the emphasis is on the containment of the chronic, and the minimisation of effects, and on treatment of the not-chronic. The strengths of this model lie in the development of specialist services which counter the handicap, with the increasing life expectancy of those with Down's Syndrome as an example of major achievement.

The argument that those with special needs are, in essence, no different from 'normal' people (all of whom have special needs also) is rooted in what we may term a 'social work model'. Based on a set of core values – dignity, respect, privacy, confidentiality, choice, protection against abuse and a commitment to the strengths and skills of local communities – this model emphasises the communality of those labelled as having special needs and those not so labelled (CCETSW, 1989). The strengths of this model lie in the celebration of the value of the individual irrespective of difficulties and in the celebration of a tolerant social solidarity.

From the perspective of the 'social work model', the 'medical model' has stigmatising and segregationist tendencies; from the perspective of the 'medical model', the 'social work model' is unrealistically optimistic about individual and societal potentials, and thus fails to acknowledge and meet real needs. Actual practice, of course, contains elements of both models but with policy moving decisively, if somewhat uncritically, towards this 'social work model' there is a danger of the field polarising into two hostile camps, one assumingly dominant, the other resentfully subordinate.

Currently the two models co-exist in rather ad hoc ways. To our knowledge there does not exist a seamless and reasoned continuum of provision ranging from that dominated by the 'social work model' to that dominated by the 'medical model'; indeed there appears to be little work which seeks to integrate the strengths of both models into a new whole. The consequent dangers of arbitrary differences in the treatment of similar people in different areas or in the treatment of the same person through time and space are all too evident in the case of people we know: small changes in individuals (or in the availability of resources) may lead to dramatic and disorienting change from a 'social work' regime to a 'medical' regime (or vice versa); in some parts of their lives people may be subjected to one regime while, without any coordination, subjected to another regime in another part of their lives.

These problems of practice are, at heart, problems of philosophy, of how we constitute the person and their needs. Here the conception of the individual with special needs which generates Camphill practices, offers *one* creative synthesis of the two positions, minimising the problems we have outlined. The difference, the deficits and pain of handicap are there accepted and dealt with as real and consequential, but the rights of those with special needs to dignity and fulfilment are also powerfully realised. Diagnosis and treatment through a medical model lie at the heart of a practice which is thoroughly social and integrationist. The key to this synthesis is the conception of handicap as a karmic challenge, as a difficult incarnation on the spirit's journey. As Sands, Hailey and Baron argue in their chapters this attributes to those with handicaps both a positive personal life-task and positive social roles in the primary group and in society as a whole. Our purpose in using Camphill as an example of the synthesis of the 'medical' and the 'social work' models is not to suggest that it is the only such model, nor that it should be simply adopted by other agencies, nor that it is unproblematic; but that it contains ways of thinking about, and relating with, those with special needs, which could act as analogies for cognate developments.

The Camphill model is based on a specific metaphysic from the German Idealist philosophical tradition which is discordant with the more Empiricist Anglo-Saxon philosophic tradition, a contrast well illustrated in the chapters by Sands and Cullen respectively. As part of a pluralist system of welfare, let alone as part of a pluralist society, this difference seems to us to be healthy, even if threatened by encroaching State regulation; but we neither realistically expect, nor would we want, the Camphill model to be propagated as a new orthodoxy. Other metaphysics, and the range of materialist philosophies, generate different models of good practice essential to pluralism and choice. In the Camphill model however there are ways of negotiating the Normality-Difference polarity which can be separated from the metaphysics and which hold the potential for stimulating new practices in wider arenas. None of these elements is unique to Camphill although it is arguable that this is true of their combination. The Camphill construction of the individual with special needs as growing personally through the significant personal challenges of handicap, stands as a bulwark (as Christie argues) against utilitarianism. This philosophy is inherent in the 'medical model', is increasingly dominant in contemporary discourse and constantly poses the question of 'which lives are worth living?'. By standing for the worth of the individual not simply as an abstract value but as an ongoing process, the Camphill conception counters this tendency. In this there is clearly much shared ground with other religiously-based approaches to special needs; the links with the intrinsic value ascribed to the process of 'reality confrontation' by psychoanalytical and existentialist inspired approaches remain to be explored. We turn to the questions of welfare pluralism and of political alliances in the final chapter.

More acute, given current political trends, is the relationship between these conceptions and those values of the 'social work model' which are increasingly being held to be universal both in principle and in detail. Here the Camphill emphasis on personal growth, and community role and status as depending significantly on the performance of 'duties', offers an important complement to the emphasis on 'rights'. Historically these two concepts have been closely linked, often two sides of the same coin, but they have become separated in the discourse of special needs, with damaging consequences. The emphasis on the 'rights' of those with special needs without a corresponding analysis of their 'duties' re-ascribes an essentially passive role to them as the consumers of social goods largely offered by professionals. We find it difficult to imagine 'social role valorisation' working in this essentially passive and deficit based manner. In the Camphill context, 'duties' may range from specific tasks performed for the larger good, to the more diffuse value which a person's being brings to the community. We turn in the final chapter to the problem of how practices with different core values may relate to each other.

It is in the 'integrated therapeutic community' form of the Camphill Communities that there are many elements of practice which offer ways forward for other forms of provision. The positive conception of the individual with special needs entails a shift in the 'geometry' of the social relations of special needs. This manifests itself in a variety of ways united by the practice of reciprocity. The sharing of daily life between co-workers and those with special needs in Camphill Communities presents a model of 'integration' in practice more thoroughgoing than the 'Pub and Post Office' model of normalisation. The separation of financial matters from the labour process throws the emphasis of 'work' onto its intrinsic values, particularly the human encounter and human consequences of shared efforts. As the emphasis of national policy shifts towards a 'social work' model there is a sharply paradoxical move towards the increasing professionalisation of those who work with special needs; a shift strengthening both notions of detached expertise derived from the 'medical model' and the instrumental relations of the contractor-client relationship. The mutuality of the Camphill model stands as an alternative to this increasing instrumentalism and suggests ways of meeting needs such as those found by Flynn (cited in Cullen's chapter). In offering a conscious and organised realisation of the two-way process of care, the teacher is also taught, the therapist is also healed, the carer is also cared for. This transforms the dynamic of care beyond professionalism and beyond altruism; those with special needs are cared for not because of expertise (certainly present), not because of compassion (certainly present) but through the self development and self fulfilment of the co-workers.

These elements have, to date, found their combination in therapeutic community type settings, relatively enclosed and separate special societies. Whether the elements described can be translated individually into different settings, or whether the combination is indivisible, remains to be explored. Similarly it is unclear whether the positive elements of the Camphill Communities can be translated from their special community setting into settings with a less structured internal social system and more fluid boundaries: those Camphill Communities attempting this are having mixed experiences. While Millard's chapter reports positive experiences with day-care therapeutic communities, Christie argues for the necessity of 'ghettos'.

We do not hold, nor did the conference experience, the Camphill model as unproblematic. At the conference what we have called the 'positive conception' of the individual with special needs was challenged as being a mass idealisation, a re-stereotyping of handicap. This is a criticism with which it is easy to agree. Stereotyping, however positive, negates the individual; but a world without classification would be a 'blooming, buzzing confusion', the actors blind, deaf and dumb. How then can we classify without negating the individual? Such concerns pinpoint one of the tensions of the Camphill philosophy, and its German Idealist origins, between the encounter with the concrete individual 'as-is' and the 'reading back' from that specificity to the 'essence'. In terms of Camphill practice this manifests itself in multiple ways and we shall focus on one aspect of this, diagnostic classification.

The diagnostic classifications used by the Camphill Communities share many of the labels of the orthodox 'medical model' but have a different logic, rooted in the anthroposophical Image of Man, and carry much fuller attributions of spiritual and social traits. While this accounts for much creativity in approaching those with special needs it, simultaneously, carries the danger of ossification: Down's Syndrome are . . ., Autistics are . . ., Hysterics are . . . The delicate dialectic between the specificity of the individual and the essence of his/her handicap contains, because of the elaborated thinking about the nature of handicap, a pull to reification: the working hypothesis may become the total truth, the theoretical model may become the empirical reality. In terms of Schutz's phenomenology the 'course-of-action' type, necessary for making sense of the world when first encountering some new or difficult aspect of it, may dominate the 'personal' type, our complex and conditional typification of the specific individual (Schutz, 1962).

The obvious counter to this tendency is to maximise the contexts in which the individual is met both as bearing a syndrome *and* as a complex, concrete person. The sharing of daily life in Camphill Communities offers such a maximisation but this is endangered by the nature of the differentiation between long-term co-workers and the constantly changing population of short-term co-workers. The bulk of the daily 'encounter of ego with ego' tends to be between the short-term co-worker and those with special needs, with the long-term co-worker taking a more distant, 'management' role. This not only increases the tendency of long-term co-workers to rely on 'course-of-action' typifications; it emphasises the power of a small group of initiates who, somewhat remotely, 'read' the essence of those with special needs and set out the developmental challenges for them. We have laid out our general objections to this authoritarianism elsewhere (Baron & Haldane, 1991) but note that, in these dynamics, the Camphill Communities are analogous to the institutional practice of other therapeutic communities. Here it is sufficient to suggest that the successful propagation of positive conceptions of the individual depends, in our analysis, on those in power having dense and detailed personal knowledge of those with special needs. This analysis runs quite counter to the current sharp polarisation of the social care labour force into an elite of case managers and a mass of carers. It is to the polarity of Professional-Lay that we now turn in search of a new professionalism.

Professional and Lay

In contemporary discourse there are two major versions of the Professional – Lay polarity, the 'Expert' version and the 'Power' version. The former revolves around the polarity between knowledge and ignorance and carries themes of science and disinterest. The latter revolves around a restrictive practice – free-market polarity and carries themes of vested interests acting against the common people. The past decade has seen a dual movement by which sturdy commonsense has been celebrated, while reforms have been introduced which centralise power in the hands of a decreasing number of professionals, often of new 'disciplines'. Opting for one or other of the four poles does not seem to us to be an adequate strategy for the future and we dissent from the authoritarian logic of the current subtle combination of populism and centralisation.

Creating a new mode of 'professionalism' and forming new relations with lay people are key issues for the realisation of *community* care. The conference reflected, and did not resolve, many of the tensions of this process. Firstly, only professionals were invited, an omission for which Christie took us to task not so much in terms of 'representation' as in terms of the clarity of thought that the presence of 'the dumb' would have demanded to debate issues in simple but rigorous terms. Given its composition the conference could largely assume current forms of professional-lay relations without challenge: there was competition between different professional groups for the *voice*.

One possible exception to the assumption of current professional-lay relations were those people who conceived their professional role as that of 'enabler' in 'self advocacy' – professionals one of whose main tasks is to counter other professionals. Starting from the populist poles of the Professional-Lay polarity such work emphasises the self determination and self development of those with special needs: abstract values with which we have no quarrel. The pull from this position is, however, to assume that the path of self determination lies immanent in each individual, needing only the stripping away of constraints for full realisation to be possible. This ignores, and is limited by, what we see as two major realities; as well as being limited by the problem of the re-production of those with special needs as passive, consumers of rights *given by others* to which Baron has referred.

Firstly the capacity of individuals for self determination varies. Clearly for some people, for example those who can manage in sheltered accommodation, a normal degree of self determination is a reality and entirely appropriate; equally clearly there are those whose faculties are so damaged that gauging whether they are more or less happy in a context depends on the intimate personal knowledge and interpretations of an observer. Fraser's example of 'The Rainman' is instructive; the two doctors' lack of engagement with Raymond, and their denial of his capacity to decide, are held up for criticism by the structure of the film. Fraser's conclusion, however, is not that Raymond could achieve self determination unaided but that it would depend on the detailed knowledge of a caregiver who understood the unspoken. What is still not clear to us (and we do not pursue here) are the principles by which different degrees of self determination can be held to be appropriate, who makes such decisions and what is the manner in which people are to be involved in the process of making life decisions for another person.

The second reality which limits a simple self-advocacy model is its liberal, almost free market, assumptions that stripping away the power of professional intermediaries enables freedom of choice. The denial of this particular power relationship does not negate other power relations and, in many cases, it enhances the power of other, more exploitative and damaging, systems. Fraser, for example, writes of those with special needs as being victims of the fast food industry, while self determination for Farquharson's 'Flirty' would seem to be the continuation of abusive and exploitative sexual relations. Those with special needs are not unique in being victims to burgers or sexual exploitation but they are more vulnerable. Underpinning our arguments there are unexplicated notions of 'reasonableness': the capacity to make reasonable life decisions, the nature of a proper diet, appropriate expressions of sexuality. Elaborating the principles and processes for determining 'reasonableness' in all its manifestations seems to us to be a key task for developing community care. Locating such decisions simply in the hands *either* of professionals *or* of those with special needs are not tenable strategies. We return to such issues below and in the final chapter.

Having suggested that the arguments from the populist poles for self determination are grounded in values to which we subscribe but that these are not currently complex enough, we now turn to discuss the continuing value of elements from the professional-as-expert pole. The willingness to deal with acutely difficult human and social problems, problems which are often otherwise denied, ignored or hidden, is one underlying feature of professionalism, as is performing this in a thorough, well-informed and reflective manner. Properly carried through, professionalism displays a difficult combination of interest and disinterest in the individual and has a more strategic and collective view of the issues of special needs. It is difficult to think of 'enablers' who would dissent from these qualities of professionalism. Current dissatisfaction with professionalism focuses on the unilateral power that it can generate in which the person (whether patient, client, trainee, resident) is reduced to the status of a passive object of the actions of others.

The implication of our arguments against the unilateral versions of both 'professionalism' and 'self advocacy', and against the current combination of populism and centralisation, are to seek a different combination of professionalism and self determination. 'Dialogue' seems to us to offer the possibility of a different combination of 'professional' and 'lay'; it recognises the reality of different perspectives without simply exalting one; it depends on clear speech and, more importantly, clear listening; it revolves around the negotiation of differences either to a consensus or to an explicit disagreement. In this we draw from the work of Habermas on 'systematically distorted communication' in which he argues that only when communication is freed from the relations of power and coercion can a rational consensus based on truth, freedom and justice emerge (Habermas, 1970a, b). These are qualities which are sorely needed for 'community care'. In medicine there has been a recent trend towards a greater emphasis on 'informed consent' which, at best, displays some of these features and this could provide a starting point in the field of special needs.

'Dialogue' on its own is not a sufficient model; as Fraser and Christie point out in different ways, those with special needs are not easy interactional partners and a greater degree of interpretation than normal may be necessary. More importantly the model of 'dialogue' is a version of 'methodological individualism' in taking the interaction of Ego and Alter as the basic building block of social analysis. From such a starting point it is difficult to build powerful analyses of *collectivities*; it is the analysis of the collective issues of special needs which we see as crucial and which is currently being disqualified by the atomistic tendencies of 'community care' and by the sociological naivety of 'social role valorisation'.

In trying to move beyond the model of dialogue to a more structural conception of how 'professional' and 'lay' might relate while maintaining the advantages of the dialogue model we find suggestive the work of Gramsci on "The Philosophy of Praxis" (Gramsci, 1971). Gramsci starts from the contention that all people are 'philosophers' in that they develop and use conceptions of the world and that these 'spontaneous philosophies' are shared by social groups expressing their past, present and possible future social existence, a conception in which 'philosophy' is expressed in 'action' rather than in formal written or verbal statements. Indeed Gramsci sees immediate and explicit verbalisations of philosophy as being relatively uncritical, being rooted in received knowledge, in comparison with the philosophy implicit in action, being rooted in existential struggles. The commonsense of any particular person for Gramsci is thus a complex mixture of such philosophies rooted in a wide variety of different social groups:

> The personality is strangely composite: it contains Stone Age elements and principles of a more advanced science, prejudices from all past phases of history at the local level and intuitions of a future philosophy which will be that of a human race united the world over. (Gramsci, 1971, p.324)

For Gramsci social development depends on social groups criticising their own make up, seeking to deconstruct the 'strange composite' and to reconstruct it as coherent, united and active – a 'critical elaboration' "to order in a systematic, coherent and critical fashion one's own intuitions of life and the world" (Gramsci, 1971, p.327). The starting point for this is "'knowing thyself' as a product of the historical process to date which has deposited in you an infinity of traces, without leaving an inventory" (loc. cit.). This entire process is not one of abstract thought but one where thought and social action in a determinate context are held together in the dynamic of a self-modifying spiral. Such critical elaboration is not achieved in a vacuum but in the context of, and in conflict with, the philosophies and action of other social groups.

As a starting point for developing a new identity and existence with those with special needs this seems to us to offer many advantages over current conceptions: it attributes a collectivity to those with special needs; it roots development in the current experiences and actions of concrete people without suggesting that their future lies immaculate awaiting revelation; it recognises that development demands difficult struggles with self, with reference group and with opposing groups. In this process Gramsci attributes a special role to the 'intellectuals', those who, whatever formal position they hold, abstract and make coherent the principles which the social group is partially living and struggling to articulate. Such "organic intellectuals" are characterised by their necessary difference from the social group in question *and* by their intimate connection with the social group from which their insights derive. It is on such a dialectical basis that new forms of 'professional' and 'lay' relationships might be built to foster the self determination of those with special needs as a group as well as, indeed through, taking advantage of the benefits of rigorous intellectual work. It is how this might be fostered in an era when authoritarian centralisation is rampant that we turn in the last chapter.

CHAPTER 15

About your House, St Augustine

Stephen Baron and Douglas Haldane

Scene: An Oaken Portal

Social Worker: Under the *Registered Homes Act* the Local Authority is empowered to make any reasonable requirements of any establishment which offers personal care and, in this, I represent the Social Work Committee which makes the decisions.[1]

St Augustine: D. V.

Social Worker: I understand you care for elderly brethren here. Under the same Act I am empowered to enter and inspect such premises at all times.

St Augustine: So Be It.

Social Worker: Could we start with meals? *Home Life* stipulates that "flexibility in the timing of meals is a significant factor in normalising life" . . .

St Augustine: Let them not take any nourishment except at the customary hour of repast!

Social Worker: *(concerned)* I see . . . "consideration of residents' dietary needs and wishes should be seen as integral to the philosophy of the home" . . .

St Augustine: Keep the flesh under by fasting and abstinence from meat and drink as far as health allows!

Social Worker: *(brightly)* How about clothing? *Home Life* clearly says that "the practice of supplying clothes from a communal pool is never acceptable" . . .

St Augustine: Keep your clothes in one place; let your clothes be provided from one wardrobe; regard it as a matter of no importance whether each of you receives the very same article of clothing which was formerly worn!

Social Worker: *(anxiously)* *Home Life* also says that "residents should be

St Augustine: encouraged to bring with them as many personal possessions as can be accommodated in their rooms".

St Augustine: Let those who had worldly goods when they entered the monastery cheerfully desire that these become common property!

Social Worker: *(worriedly)* I see – some more personal issues now. *Home Life* insists that residents "should have normal opportunities for emotional expression, in particular the freedom to have intimate and personal relations within, and outside, the home. General rules which totally ban sexual relations within the home are undesirable."

St Augustine: Those things which are practised by the immodest in shameful frolic and sporting with one another ought not even to be done by those of your sex who are married, and much more ought not to be done by chaste virgins dedicated to Christ by a holy vow!

Social Worker: *(assertively)* *Home Life* says that "privacy of space is important, as is the right to hold and express opinions or keep them private" . . .

St Augustine: Guard your chastity by watching over one another!

Social Worker: Um, *(incredulously)* St Augustine, *Home Life* does say that rules should be kept to a minimum and residents should be involved as much as possible in making decisions concerning the way in which a home is run . . .

St Augustine: Obey the Superior as a Father! The Lord grant that you may yield loving submission to all these rules! Let this little book be read to you once a week!

Social Worker: But St Augustine, *Home Life* does say that residents have the right to live in a manner and in circumstances which correspond as far as is possible with what is normal for those who remain in their own homes. Are you *(nervously)* . . . challenging *Home Life*?

St Augustine: You must meet Brother Armand de Rance down the road – he's just opened a Trappist House and may need to register . . .

Social Worker: Poverty . . . Chastity . . . Obedience . . . SILENCE *(fleeing)* It's the Committee which makes these decisions.

St Augustine: Would you like to borrow a copy of my Epistles . . . Number 211 sets out a clear statement of the aims and objectives . . . Hello . . . page 18 of *Home Life* refers . . . hellooo . . . D. V. . . . So Be It.

The conceit is not entirely fanciful: current moves to the tighter regulation of provision for vulnerable groups are bringing different sets of basic assumptions face to face (and presumably such a dialogue will have to take place in Houses across the country). The tension which has yet to be resolved is between an espousal in policy of diversity (together with the practical need for it) and the need for regulation to prevent abuse of vulnerable groups.

Currently this tension is not creatively managed; ready-made manuals such as *Home Life* or *Homes Are For Living In* are either given direct statutory force or are an immediate point of reference for exercising the open-ended discretion of any 'reasonable condition' (Centre for Policy on Ageing, 1984; Department of Health, 1989). Baron argues that these offer a coherent model for one type of care for one type of person but that their current use presents these specifics as universals (one of the hallmarks of a limited and limiting 'ideology'): the philosophy of *Home Life* is claimed as 'universal', its articulation of rights as 'basic' (Centre for Policy on Ageing, 1984, p.10, p.15); the basic values of *Homes Are For Living In* are claimed as 'natural' (Department of Health, 1989, p.7).

Home Life tries to avoid this problem ("what might constitute appropriate levels of care in one home would be unnecessary or unworkable in another" p.10) and tries to strike "a fine balance . . . between an over-rigid application which treats the Code as a handbook, and adherence to those recommendations which stem directly from particular principles" (loc. cit.). The example given of a principle which directly generates a practice, that all residents should be offered single rooms, is instructive. While appropriate and desirable for the care of the elderly whose previous social existence was one of independence in private space, such a principle cuts directly across a fundamental process in the group therapeutic care of young people with special needs, part of whose problem is often associated with too much private space.

One of the most systematic attempts to establish the quality of care in provision for the elderly by the Social Services Inspectorate found that "it is difficult to identify simple indicators of either good management or good quality of care and quality of life: all are complex and diverse areas of activity" and it concludes "the picture is, however, very complex and it is not possible to point to any one factor which has a clear relationship with 'good care' or 'quality of life'" (Social Services Inspectorate, 1989, p.3, p.7).

The implication of these findings, and many others from similar fields, is that it is not possible to develop a set of checklists by which alone quality can be assessed. The ever-present danger is that of forcing complex, qualitative and holistic phenomena into a set of fragmented and narrowing categories which, at best, misunderstand the nature of the beast and, at worst, damage it. The Social Services Inspectorate conclusion does not seem to have inhibited the State from developing and imposing just such checklists on its competitors; one such example contained nine pages of largely Yes/No questions about physical structure, administrative procedures, etc, with an open-ended question for the Registration Officer: "What was general impression of quality of care?", with 10mm for writing the answer! In the context of such administrative procedures provision which is different from this model of care as applied to some elderly people finds itself in an *objective* confrontation over core values and practices. For organisations seeking to maintain difference and the possibility of innovation strategies may be seen at three, overlapping levels.

The basic strategy is to maintain contact with the various regulatory authorities in order to participate in formal consultations and to present the case for 'difference'. As noted in the first chapter there is an important, but never easy, distinction to be drawn between individuals in their multiple professional and personal roles, and the structures in which they work; a distinction which allows us to explain the simultaneous lauding and criticism of, for example, the Camphill Communities by individuals of high personal integrity and standing. This is not a simple distinction between the Individual (Good) and the System (Bad) but a complex web of determinations which allows greater or lesser discretion to officers of the regulatory authorities in different contexts. From this complexity we may isolate two crucial dimensions: case officer-policy officer, and central-local government. Our experience suggests that the value of a diversity of provision is appreciated more in the case officer-local government combination than in the policy officer-central government combination; and that if the experience of the former can be incorporated into the frame of reference of the latter then policy can be significantly more sensitive than it might otherwise be. This implies a strategy for the non-statutory sector of not only vigorously presenting their own case at requisite opportunities but also of seeking to ensure that the day-to-day professional judgments of case officers inform the policy frame of reference. While highly significant individual successes of this strategy can be enumerated, it would be unrealistic to expect this to produce structural change.

A second, complementary, group of strategies is for the non-statutory sectors to organise themselves more 'politically' on both an individual and collective basis in order to act as 'pressure groups'. While there are variations in constituencies for pressure groups based around single sites, most organisations will have geographic concentrations of residents, the families of residents and supporters together with local political structures (Councils and MPs) on which to put pressure. While the effectiveness of this strategy for single, relatively specific issues can be significant it is doubtful whether this can affect more global policies. Individual organisations may group themselves together into associations in terms of their shared approach to special care in order to make representations at a national level, or to seek some form of 'representation' by a sympathetic national figure. The success of both of these in matters of national policy seems limited, while the symbolic costs of seeking political patronage may be heavy. In the new age of a 'mixed economy of care' potentially more fruitful strategies, at both local and national levels, might be to organise both 'sectorally' (i.e. the Voluntary Sector, the Independent Sector) and cross-sectorally (i.e. the non-statutory sectors) in alliances which seek to ensure that promised diversity is, in fact, realised. While some elements of this exist already (especially national, sectoral organisations) coverage is patchy and co-ordination seems limited. It is significant that the almost universal, but somewhat fragmented, opposition to the non ring-fencing of former Social Security funds was not successful.

The key stake for such alliances is the structure and operation of the Registration and Inspection systems. For present purposes we shall ignore the structural issues around 'arms-length' inspection and focus on the criteria for assessing 'quality' in care. Having rejected currently articulated criteria as falsely universalising, how can we seek to establish a set of criteria which are both sensitive to difference and prohibitive of abuse? The current checklist approach seems to us to conflate three different sets of criteria: substantive criteria to be sought in all forms of provision (Level 1); the criteria by which any specific provision builds and monitors its approach (Level 2); meta-criteria by which the adequacy of criteria at Levels 1 and 2 may be assessed (Level 3). The fault of *Home Life* lies largely in attributing the status of both Levels 1 and 3 to criteria which are properly Level 2. These arguments are more fully developed in a paper in response to the Scottish Office Consultative Papers on Registration and Inspection (Association of Camphill Communities, 1990)

Level 3 criteria are over-arching; how can different approaches be evaluated within one framework? Clearly such criteria cannot in themselves be value-free but equally clearly they should be able to encompass wider human experience than the historically and culturally specific one of living alone in a single room. The first such Level 3 criterion which we propose is that any form of provision should have a publicly articulated philosophy of care which is consistent and comprehensive, thus enabling public debate about the value of that provision. A second Level 3 criterion should be that the philosophy of any form of provision centres on a construction of the individual to be cared for which is positive both in the sense of focusing on abilities rather than disabilities, and in the sense of seeking the positive aspects of such disabilities. A third Level 3 criterion which we propose is that the philosophy should contain no elements which can be shown to be damaging to the individuals concerned. In this we follow Barrington Moore (1970) who argues persuasively that human happiness is infinitely diverse and, as such, impossible to codify, whereas the factors generating human misery are, historically, overwhelmingly constant: war, poverty, hunger, disease, injustice, oppression and persecution for dissident beliefs. Relying on the absence of these thus provides a secure base line for the diversity of happiness and a tolerance of different ways of seeking it.

In the light of such Level 3 criteria Levels 1 and 2 can be specified more briefly. At Level 1, i.e. criteria to be met by all forms of provision, a distinction can be drawn between operational criteria and procedural criteria. The former can be derived from Barrington Moore's 'unity of misery' – that provision is made to keep people safe, properly fed and healthy and that the regime meets general standards of fairness and tolerance. Here Christie's suggestion of panels of lay people as the arbiters of which conditions are 'normal' carries great weight; not only would this counter increasing the power of state professionals and help form a wider constituency for special needs but it could also foster the role of those with special needs as a force for social change (as Sands argues). Central to this are the procedural criteria that each form of provision should make available information in suitable forms for each person to make an informed consent and that there should be established procedures for reviewing the nature and operation of the provision. *Prima facie* St Augustine's House could thus seem to be a place of misery (Poverty, Chastity and Obedience) but through consent to the explicitly stated Rule these 'negatives' are turned to a positive for a higher good.

Level 2 criteria are self defined, self evaluative criteria – the articulation by any particular unit of its philosophy and the various operational standards it needs to meet in order to fulfil its conception of 'good care'. We would expect such criteria to cover areas such as how the individual with special needs is defined, how these needs are to be met, how the 'group' is to operate, how the community is to be involved in this, the physical structures necessary for this work, staffing, admission and discharge, relationships with family and professional supporters together with the administrative procedures necessary to maintain these; or, alternatively, we would expect arguments why this list of areas was inapplicable and why another list was more appropriate. We turn now to the third group of strategies for organisations trying to maintain space for innovation and diversity.

The final group of strategies, if attempts to negotiate any non-consonant regulations away fail, revolves around issues of compliance, non-compliance, avoidance, appeal. Here core issues of the integrity of a project are entailed. Compliance to regulation which adversely affects desirable but non-essential features of an approach, may be thought appropriate and action taken to minimise the real impact (and the resources wasted). If regulation threatens definitive features of an approach then rights of appeal or legal challenge may be operated, an onus which currently rests by default on the *regulated* and which thus constantly places those who are different as *appellants*. The costs of this in financial terms and in terms of adverse publicity and damaged relations with regulatory bodies make this option one very much of the last resort. A middle ground of the creative, still legal, avoidance of regulation by exploiting definitions, gaps and loopholes seems a major way forward, especially if the (tacit) agreement of individuals in the enforcement authorities can be gained.

A Space Between?

In commenting on an earlier version of these arguments, Brearley in her commentary points, quite correctly, to our use of the metaphors of warfare and of state organisations as mechanisms. These she contrasts with two more favoured metaphors: the open systems perspective which "involves balancing and optimising the interplay of forces, both within and outside the organisation, accepting the inevitable uncertainty and complexity . . . being willing to adjust to an altered environment in a flexible way, minimising rigidities in the system"; and the metaphor of organisations as potential psychic prisons by which we chain ourselves into prisons of our own making. From these perspectives resistance to change is intimately linked to the possibility of anxiety and loss; to the scapegoating of those in authority; to the use of the primitive unconscious mechanisms of splitting and projection which attributes our unwanted feelings onto others.

These are helpful metaphors and important warnings which we want to bring into alliance with the metaphors of warfare and mechanism rather to replace the latter as is the *tendency* of Brearley's commentary. The 'open systems perspective' and the depth analysis of 'psychic prisons' can both be insightful but both tend, perhaps necessarily, to be blind to processes outside the group or organisations, processes of the social structure. The open systems perspective, based in an ecological analogy of the organism, can be limited by functionalist concepts. Concepts such as 'adaptation to an altered environment', tend to take external change as the given in any analysis, as the reality to which all should adjust itself. There is little conceptual space in such perspectives for the analysis of the nature of that change, the acceptability of its logic and how that logic itself might be altered. An analysis of psychic prisons needs to be tempered by the analysis of 'ideology', the *super-individual* chaining of perception by relations of power.

The strategies we outline above are very much boundary-defining and boundary-maintaining strategies, essential we think to combat increasing authoritarian centralisation but also, we acknowledge, carrying boundary-ossifying tendencies. Brearley's analysis suggests three modifications to these strategies: that the metaphors of warfare and mechanism need to be used consciously, selectively and reflectively when major issues of principle are at stake rather than as a metaphor of first resort; that these strategies define the issues in terms of power, those who resist as victims, and thus have a tendency to generate hostility and an increasing spiral of conflict which *may* be counter-productive; that complementary strategies need to be developed using other metaphors of first resort.

It is to the last of these to which we finally turn. Here the ideas of the 'transitional approach to the management of change ' outlined by Brearley are very fertile. The processes we have outlined for each form of provision developing their own set of evaluative criteria would encourage the exploration of 'potential space' and tackling 'the double task' systematically. On a more structural level the idea of 'transitional space' is important – as the collective space to play with ideas, to cross boundaries, to imagine ourselves in quite other states of existence. Developing and exploring such a space has the possibility of limiting some of the damaging potential of the other metaphors outlined above and of linking with more structural strategies we have outlined; it should provide one context for the 'critical elaboration' of the lived intuitions of those with special needs and thus provide one moment in the formation of 'organic intellectuals' in Gramsci's terms; it should provide a stimulus for defining different versions of Level 2 criteria not in oppositional terms but in the context of a sharing and cross-fertilisation of perspectives.

For a 'transitional space' to function in these ways a variety of conditions are implied. If different versions of good care are to be explored and developed in tandem, then people of different persuasions need to be present; the metaphors of warfare and mechanism, and their necessity, need to be disqualified. This suggests that such a 'space' should consciously have no 'organisational' status; no remit, no set agenda, no powers beyond itself, no claim to authority other than that of rational and perceptive dialogue. Those participating need consciously to step outside the organisational roles which they carry in part of their lives and thus minimise the contradictions and conflicts often generated by speaking as agents of structures so that different kinds of reality can be explored. The participants in such a space would, if the professional-lay opposition is to be transcended, need to be drawn from a wide range of life situations and include those usually inserted in the discourse of special needs as the passive objects.

Our project has thus come full circle: we set out to celebrate the fiftieth anniversary of the Camphill Communities by fostering the "full exchange of cognate but different experiences". The chapters in this book stimulated and reflected on this process and, in this final chapter, we have come to a clearer understanding of this process itself, how it was and how it might be; and we have come to a clearer understanding of some of the processes necessary for advancing the cause of those with special needs. The next steps are practical.

NOTES

1. The dialogue is either direct quotation from or a gentle paraphrasing of (in order):
Social Worker: *Registered Homes Act* 1984 9 a)–c), *Registered Homes Act* 1984 17.2, *Home Life* pp. 35, 34, 19, 19, 17, 15, 21, 15.
St Augustine: Epistle 211 (in Augustine, 1875) pp. 396, 396, 400, 395, 403, 399, 403, 404.
The last three utterances are simply mischievous.

List of Conference Participants

Baron, Mr Stephen, Lecturer in Sociology and Social Policy and Warden, Murray Hall, Stirling

Blitz, Dr Nick, Medical Officer, Camphill Rudolf Steiner Schools, Aberdeen

Brearley, Ms Judith, Senior Lecturer in Social Work and Organisational Consultant, Edinburgh

Calderwood, Mrs Agneta, Co-Worker, Tigh A' Chomainn Camphill, Aberdeen

Christie, Prof. Nils, Professor of Criminology, Oslo

Cullen, Prof. Chris, Professor of Learning Difficulties, St Andrews

D'Agostino, Mr Vincent, Co-Worker, Camphill Rudolf Steiner Schools, Aberdeen

Dell, Mr Geoffrey, Retired HMI, Coupar Angus

Dickie, Ms Bobbie, Central Regional Council Social Work Department, Stirling

Dumbleton, Mr Paul, Lecturer in Further Education, Jordanhill College, Stirling

Durno, Dr Denis, General Medical Practitioner and Parent and Member of the Council of the Camphill Rudolf Steiner Schools, Aberdeen

Farquharson, Mr Graeme, Group Analyst and Director, Peper Harow, Godalming

Findlay, Dr Anne, Medical Officer, Scottish Home and Health Department, Edinburgh

Fraser, Prof Bill, Professor of Mental Handicap, Cardiff

Hailey, Mr Mike, Co-Worker, The Mount Camphill Community, Wadhurst

Haldane, Dr Douglas, Psychotherapist and Consultant, St Andrews

Hansmann, Miss Veronica, Co-Worker, Camphill Blair Drummond

Hansmann, Mr Henning, Co-Worker, Camphill Rudolf Steiner Schools, Aberdeen

Harris, Miss Ann, Co-Worker Delrow College and Rehabilitation Centre and Director, Camphill Village Trust, Watford

Hartnoll, Miss Mary, Director of Social Work, Grampian Regional Council, Aberdeen

Hills, Mr Charles, President, Six Circles Group, Edinburgh

Jahoda, Dr Andrew, Psychologist, Solihull Health Authority, Solihull

Luxford, Mr Michael, Co-Worker, The Pennine Community, Wakefield

McClintock, Prof. F.H., Professor of Criminology and the Social and Philosophical Studies of Law, Edinburgh

Millard, Dr David, Lecturer in Applied Social Studies and Fellow of Green College, Oxford

Newbatt, Mr David, Artist and Co-Worker Camphill Rudolf Steiner Schools, Aberdeen

Nicol, Mr Bill, BBC Television and Parent, Camphill Rudolf Steiner Schools, Bridge of Earn

Noble, Mr Tony, Economic Development Officer, Middlesborough Borough Council, Middlesborough

Parsloe, Prof. Phyllida, Pro-Vice Chancellor and Professor of Social Work, Bristol

Peter, Mrs Margaret, Editor, British Journal of Special Education, London

Poole, Mr Nicholas, Co-Worker, Botton Village, Whitby

Radysh, Mr Wolodymyr, Camphill Architect and Co-Worker, Newton Dee Village, Aberdeen

Reed, Mr Jack, Garvald Centre, Edinburgh

Reinardy, Mrs Rasheeda, Co-Worker, Camphill Rudolf Steiner Schools, Aberdeen

Schad, Mr Georg, Co-Worker, Camphill Blair Drummond

Seed, Mr Philip, Senior Research Fellow, Dundee

Sheldon, Miss Betty, Retired Social Work Lecturer, Aberdeen

Singh, Mr Neville, Senior Nurse Psychotherapist and Staff Support, Edinburgh

Sleigh, Rev. Julian, Minister of the Christian Community, Camphill Village, Kalbaskraal, South Africa

Stedall, Mr Jonathan, Documentary Film-Maker, Painswick

Taylor, Miss Margaret, Chartered Psychologist and Consultant to the Camphill Rudolf Steiner Schools, Aberdeen

Warren, Mr Alastair, Retired Editor, Glasgow Herald, Castle Douglas

Werthmann, Mrs Valerie, Co-Worker, Newton Dee Village, Aberdeen

Whiteley, Dr J. Stuart, Consultant Psychotherapist and Organisational Analyst, Brockham

Whyte, The Very Rev. Dr James, Professor Emeritus of Practical Theology and Christian Ethics, St Andrews

Williams, Dr Tom, Senior Educational Psychologist, Saltcoats

Bibliography

Agazarian, Y.M., 1989, Group-as-a-Whole Systems Theory and Practice, *Group*, 13, 3&4, pp.131–154.

Ainsworth, F., & Fulcher, L. C., 1981, *Group Care for Children: Concepts and Issues*, Tavistock, London.

Allen, I., 1983, The elderly and their informal carers, in DHSS, *Elderly People in the Community; Their Service Needs. Research Contributions to the Development of Policy and Practice*, HMSO, London.

v. Arnim, G., nd, *What is Curative Education*, unpublished Working Paper, Association of Camphill Communities, Aberdeen.

v. Arnim, G., 1982, Soul Forces in Human Encounters, *Journal for Curative Education and Social Therapy*, Vol. 1, No. 4, 1982.

Association of Camphill Communities, 1988, *Camphill Communities: Social Renewal through Community Living*, Association of Camphill Communities, Aberdeen.

Association of Camphill Communities, 1990, *Standards, Identity and Choice: Criteria and Roles in the Registration, Inspection and Quality Assurance of Residential Units*, Association of Camphill Communities, Aberdeen.

Association of Therapeutic Communities, 1986, *Directory of Therapeutic Communities in Great Britain*, ATC, London.

Audit Commission, 1986, *Making a Reality of Community Care*, HMSO, London.

Augustine, St A, 1875, *The Works of Aurelius Augustine, Bishop of Hippo*, Dods, M. (ed.), Vol. 13, T & T Clark, Edinburgh.

Balint, M., 1969, *The Basic Fault – Therapeutic Aspects of Regression*, Tavistock Publications, London.

Bank-Mikkelsen, N.E., 1969, A Metropolitan Area in Denmark: Copenhagen, in Kugel, R., & Wolfensberger, W., (eds.), *Changing Patterns in Residential Services for the Mentally Retarded*, President's Committee on Mental Retardation, Washington D.C.

Bank-Mikkelsen, N.E., 1976, Denmark, in Flynn, I. & Nitsch, R.J. (eds.), *Normalisation, Social Integration and Community Services*, University Park Press, Baltimore.

Baron, S., 1988, Community and the Limits of Social Democracy, in Green, A. G. & Ball S. J. (eds), *Progress and Inequality in Comprehensive Education*, Routledge, London.

Baron, S., 1989, Community Education: From the Cam to the Rea, in S. Walker & L. Barton (eds), *Politics and the Processes of Schooling*, Open University Press, Milton Keynes.

Baron, S., & Haldane, D., 1991, Approaching Camphill: Some Notes from the Boundary, *British Journal of Special Education*, 18, 2, pp. 75–78.

Barr, M.W., 1904, *Mental Defectives: Their History, Treatment and Training*, Blakinston, Philadelphia.

Barton, R., 1959, *Institutional Neurosis*, Wright, Bristol.

Bayley, M., 1973, *The Mentally Handicapped and Community Care*, Routledge and Kegan Paul, London.

Beange, H. & Bauman, A., 1990, Health Care for the Developmentally Disabled. Is it necessary?, in Fraser W. (ed.), *Key Issues in Mental Retardation*, Routledge, London.

Begab, M.J., 1975, The mentally retarded and society: Trends and issues, in Begab M.J. & Richardson S.A. (eds.), *The Mentally Retarded and Society: A Social Science Perspective*, University Park Press, Baltimore.

Bell, C. & Newby, H. (eds.), 1972, *Community Studies*, Allen & Unwin, London.

Berlin, I., 1969, *Four Essays on Liberty*, OUP, Oxford.

Binet, A.S.T., 1905, Enquête sur le mode d'existence des sujets sortis d'une école d'arrièrees, *L'Annee Psychologie*, XI, pp.137–145.

Bion, W. R., 1961, *Experiences in Groups*, Tavistock, London.

Bishop, D. & Adams, C., 1989, Conversational Characteristics of Children with Semantic Pragmatic Disorders, *British Journal of Disorders of Communication*, 24, pp.241–263.

Blake, R., Millard, D. W., Roberts, J. R., l984, Therapeutic Community Principles in an Integrated Local Authority Community Mental Health Service, *International Journal of Therapeutic Communities*, 5, pp.243–274.

Bloch, S. and Crouch, E., 1985, *The Therapeutic Factors in Group Psychotherapy*, Oxford University Press, Oxford.

Bloor, M., McKeganey, N., and Fonkert, D., 1988, *One Foot in Eden: A Sociological Study of a Range of Therapeutic Community Practice*, Routledge, London.

Bridgeland, M., 1971, *Pioneer Work with Maladjusted Children*, Willmer Bros, Birkenhead.

Bridger, H., 1980, *Consultative Work with Communities and Organisations: Malcolm Millar Lecture*, Aberdeen University Press, Aberdeen.

Briggs, D., 1990, *Therapeutic Community: Comments on Order and Structure*, Unpublished Paper.

Bronfenbrenner, U., 1979, *The Ecology of Human Development*, Harvard University Press, Cambridge.

Bulmer, M., 1987, *The Social Basis of Community Care*, Allen and Unwin, London.

Burford, B., 1988, Action Cycles; Rhythmic Actions for Engagement with Children and Young Adults, *European Journal of Special Needs Education*, 3, pp.189–206.

Card, H. & Horton, J., 1982, *Reassurance or Action? The Accommodation Needs of Mentally Handicapped Adults in Eastbourne Health Authority as seen by their Parents or Caring Relative*, Community Mental Handicap Team, Eastbourne Health Authority, Eastbourne.

Cattermole, M., Jahoda, A. & Markova, I., 1988, Life in a Mental Handicap Hospital: the View from Inside, *Mental Handicap*, 18, pp.136–139.

CCETSW, 1989, *Requirements and Regulations for the Diploma in Social Work DipSW*, CCETSW Paper 30, Central Council for Education and Training in Social Work, London.

Centre for Policy on Ageing, 1984, *Home Life: A Code of Practice for Residential Care*, Centre for Policy on Ageing, London.

Cheston, R.I.L., 1988, *Special Education Leavers in Central Scotland: a Socio-psychological Perspective*, Unpublished Ph.D. Thesis, University of Stirling, Stirling.

Chombart de Lauwe, M.J., 1971, *Un Monde Autre: L'Enfance: De ses Représentations à son Mythe*, Payot, Paris.

Christie, N., 1982, *The Limits of Pain*, Robertson, Oxford.

Christie, N., 1989, *Beyond Loneliness and Institutions: Communes for Extraordinary People*, Norwegian University Press, Oslo.

Clark, D.H., 1965, The Therapeutic Community: Concept, Practice and Future, *British Journal of Psychiatry*, 3, 479, pp.947–954.

Cockburn, C., 1977, *The Local State: Management of Cities and People*, Pluto Press, London.

Collis, M. & Whiteley, J.S., 1987, The Therapeutic Factors in Group Psychotherapy allied to the Therapeutic Community, *International Journal of Therapeutic Communities*, 8, 1, pp.21–32.

Cox, H., 1965, *The Secular City*, SCM, London (Pelican 1968).

Dartington, T., Miller, E. & Gwynne, G., 1981, *A Life Together: the Distribution of Attitudes around the Disabled*, Tavistock Publications, London.

Davis, M. & Wallbridge, D., 1981, *Boundary & Space. An Introduction to the Work of D.W. Winnicott*, Karnac, London.

Department of Health, 1989, *Homes Are For Living In*, HMSO, London

DHSS, 1981, *Care in Action: A Handbook of Policies and Priorities for Health and Personal Social Services in England*, HMSO, London.

Dickens, C., 1842, *American Notes for General Circulation*, Chapman and Hall, London.

Dixon, N., 1976, *On the Psychology of Military Incompetence*, Jonathan Cape, London.

Donaldson, C., Atkinson, A., Bond, J., & Wright, K., 1988, Should QALYS be program-specific?, *Journal of Health Economics*, 14, pp.229–256.

Douglas, M., 1966, *Purity and Danger: An Analysis of Concepts of Pollution and Taboo*, Routledge and Kegan Paul, London; Pelican Books, 1970, Harmondsworth.

Duckworth, M., Fraser, W., & Radhakrishnan, G., (in press), *Interviewing Mentally Handicapped People and their Caregivers*.

Dunne, J., 1986, A Radical Philosophy for Mental Handicap Services, in McGinley, P., (ed.) *Research and Practice in the Service of People with Learning Difficulties*, Woodlands Centre, Galway.

Durand, V.M. & Crimmins, D., 1988, Identifying the variables maintaining self-injurious behaviour, *Journal of Autism & Developmental Disorders*, 17, pp.17–28.

Eayrs, C. B. & Ellis, N., 1990, Charity Advertising: For or Against People with a Mental Handicap?, *British Journal of Social Psychology*, 29, pp.349–360.

Edgerton, R.B., 1967, *The Cloak of Competence*, University of California Press, Berkeley.

Edgerton, R.B., 1986, A Case of Delabelling: Some Practical Implications, in Langness L.L. & Levine H.G. (eds.), *Culture and Retardation: Life Histories of Mildly Mentally Retarded Persons in American Society*, D. Reidell Publishing Company, Dordrecht.

Edgerton, R.B. & Berkovici, S.M., 1976, The Cloak of Competence: Years Later, *American Journal of Mental Deficiency*, 80, pp.485–497.

Ellwood, S., 1981, Sex and the Mentally Handicapped, *Bulletin of the British Psychological Society*, 34, pp.169–171.

Erickson, M. & Upsher, C., 1989, Caretaking Burden and Social Support: Comparison of Mothers of Infants with and without Disabilities, *American Journal of Mental Retardation*, 94, pp.250–258.

Evans, G., Beyer, S. & Todd, S., 1987, *Evaluation of the All-Wales Strategy for People with a Mental Handicap: A Report of the Findings of a Preliminary Survey of People with a Mental Handicap in the Ceredigion District*, Mental Handicap in Wales Applied Research Unit, Cardiff.

Evans, G., Beyer, S. & Todd, S., 1988, *Evaluation of the All-Wales Strategy for People with a Mental Handicap: a Report of the Findings of a Preliminary Survey of People with a Mental Handicap in Central Swansea*, Mental Handicap in Wales Applied Research Unit, Cardiff.

Farr, R.M., 1984, Social worlds of childhood, in Greaney V. (ed.), *The Needs and Rights of Children*, Irvington Publications, New York.

Flynn, M., 1989, *Independent Living for Adults with Mental Handicap: "A Place of My Own"*, Cassall Educational, London.

Flynt, S. & Wood, T., 1989, Stress and Coping of Mothers of Children with Moderate Mental Retardation, *American Journal of Mental Retardation*, 94, pp.278–283.

Forder, A., 1971, *Penelope Hall's Social Services of England and Wales*, (8th Edition) Routledge and Kegan Paul, London.

Foucault, M., 1977, *Discipline and Punish: The Birth of the Prison*, Penguin Books, London.

Foulkes, S.H., 1948, *Introduction to Group-Analytic Psychotherapy*, Heinemann, London. (Reprinted 1983, Karnac Books, London)

Foulkes, S.H., 1964, *Therapeutic Group Analysis*, George Allen and Unwin, London.

Foulkes, S.H. & Anthony, E.J., 1957, *Group Psychotherapy: the Psycho-analytic Approach*, Penguin, Harmondsworth.

Frankl, V. E., 1973, *The Doctor and The Soul*, Vintage Books, New York.

Freud, S., 1921, *Group Psychology and the Analysis of the Ego*, translated and edited Strachey, J.1967, Hogarth Press, London.

Frey, K., Greenberg, M. & Fewell, R., 1989, Stress and Coping among Parents of Handicapped Children: a Multidimensional Approach, *American Journal of Mental Retardation*, 94, pp.240–249.

Frith, C.D., 1989, Psychosis, Second Order Representations and the Brain, Abstract in Stefanis, C.N., Soldatos, C.R. & Robavilas, A.D. (eds), VII World Congress of Psychiatry, *Excerpta Medica International Congress Series*, 899, p.330.

Frost, R., 1955, *Selected Poems*, Penguin Books, Harmondsworth.

Gallimore, R., Weisner, T., Kaufman, S. & Bernheimer, L., 1989, The Social Construction of the Ecocultural Niches: Family Accommodation of Developmentally Delayed Children, *American Journal of Mental Retardation*, 94, pp.216–230.

Ganzarain, R., 1977, General Systems and Object Relations Theories, their Usefulness in Group Psychotherapy, *International Journal of Group Psychotherapy*, 27, 4, pp.441–456.

Goffman, E., 1961, *Asylums*, Pelican, London.

Goffman, E., 1963, *Stigma: Notes on the Management of Spoiled Identity*, Prentice-Hall, Englewood Cliffs, N.J.

Gollay, E., 1981, Some Conceptual and Methodological Issues in Studying the Community Adjustment of Deinstitutionalised Mentally Retarded People, in Bruininks, R.H., Meyers, C.E. Sigford, B.B. & Lakin, K.C. (eds.), *Deinstitutionalisation and Community Adjustment of Mentally Retarded People*, American Association on Mental Deficiency, Washington D.C.

Goodyer, I.M., 1990, Family relationships, life events and childhood psychopathology, *Journal of Child Psychology and Psychiatry*, 31, pp.161–192.

Gramsci, A., 1971, *Selections from the Prison Notebooks*, Lawrence & Wishart, London.

Greengross, W., 1976, *Entitled to Love: The Sexual and Emotional Needs of the Handicapped*, Malaby Press, London.

Habermas, J., 1970a, On Systematically Distorted Communication, *Inquiry*, 13.

Habermas, J., 1970b, Towards a Theory of Communicative Competence, *Inquiry*, 13.

Haffter, C., 1968, The Changeling, *Journal of the History of Behavioural Sciences*, 4, pp. 55–61.

Hall, J. N., 1990, Towards a Psychology of Caring, *British Journal of Clinical Psychology*, 29, pp.129–144.

Halsey, A. H., 1973, Government against Poverty in School and Community, in Wedderburn, D (ed.) *Poverty, Inequality and Class Structure*, Cambridge University Press, Cambridge.

Harris, V. & McHale, S., 1989, Family Life Problems, Daily Caregiving Activities, and the Psychological Wellbeing of Mothers of Mentally Retarded Children, *American Journal of Mental Retardation*, 94, pp.231–239.

Hillery, G.A., 1955, Definitions of Community: Areas of Agreement, *Rural Sociology*, 50, pp.20–35.

Hinshelwood, R.D. & Manning, N., 1979, *Therapeutic Communities: Reflections and Progress*, RKP, London.

HMSO, 1986, *Disabled Persons (Services, Consultation and Representation) Act*, HMSO, London.

HMSO, 1989a, *Caring for People: Community Care in the Next Decade and Beyond*, HMSO, London.

HMSO, 1989b, *Working for Patients*, HMSO, London.

Horcones, 1989, Walden Two and Social Change: The Application of Behaviour Analysis to Cultural Design, *Behaviour Analysis and Social Action* 7, 35–41.

Hyman, H. H., 1942, The Psychology of Status, *Archives of Psychology*, 269.

Ineichen, B. & Russell, O., 1980, *Mental Handicap and Community Care: The Viewpoint of the General Practitioner*, Department of Mental Health, Research Report No. 4., University of Bristol, Bristol.

Jacques, E., 1955, Social Systems as a Defence against Persecutory and Depressive Anxiety, in *New Directions in Psychoanalysis*, Tavistock Publications, London.

Jahoda, A., 1988, *Experience of Stigma and the Self-Concept of People with a Mild Mental Handicap*, Unpublished Ph.D. Thesis, University of Stirling, Stirling .

Jahoda, A. & Markova, I., 1990, *Quality of Care for People with Moderate to Severe Mental Handicap in a Long-Stay Hospital and in the Community*, Final Report to the Scottish Home and Health Department, Department of Psychology, University of Stirling.

Jahoda, A., Cattermole, M. & Markova, I., 1989, Day Services for People with a Mental Handicap: a Purpose in Life?, *Mental Handicap*, 17, pp.136–139.

Jahoda, A., Markova, I. & Cattermole, M., 1988, Stigma and Self-Concept of People with a Mild Mental Handicap, *Journal for Mental Deficiency*

Research, 32, pp.102–115, also in *Making Connections*, 1989 Course Reader, The Open University Press, Milton Keynes.

Jones, M., 1953, *The Therapeutic Community: A New Treatment Method in Psychiatry*, Basic Books, New York.

Jones, M., 1956, The Concept of the Therapeutic Community, *American Journal of Psychiatry*, 112, 8, pp.647–650.

Jordan, J., Singh, N. & Repp, A., 1989, An Evaluation of Gentle Teaching and Visual Screening in the Reduction of Stereotypy, *Journal of Applied Behavior Analysis*, 22, pp.9–24.

Kennard, D., 1986, From a Movement to a Method, *International Journal of Therapeutic Communities*, 7, 4, pp.207–209.

Kennard, D., & Roberts, J., 1983, *An Introduction to Therapeutic Communities*, RKP, London.

Kernan, K. & Sabsay, S., 1989, Communication in Social Interactions. Aspects of an Ethnography of Communication of Mildly Mentally Handicapped Adults, in Beveridge, M., Conti-Ramsden, G. & Leudar, I. (eds.), *Language and Communication in Mentally Handicapped People*, Chapman & Hall, London, pp.229–253.

Kernberg, O., 1973, A Systems Approach to Priority Setting of Interpretations in Groups, *International Journal of Group Psychotherapy*, 23, 2.

Kernberg, O., 1975, *Borderline Conditions and Pathological Narcissism*, Jason Aronson, New York.

Kernberg, O., 1980, *Internal World and External Reality – Object Relations Theory Applied*, Jason Aronson, New York.

Kinnell, H.G., 1987, Community Medical Care of People with Mental Handicaps: Room for Improvement, *Mental Handicap*, 15, pp.146–151.

Klein, L., 1989, *Working with Organisations; Papers to Celebrate the 80th Birthday of Harold Bridger*, Tavistock Institute, London.

Klein, M., 1946, Notes on some Schizoid Mechanisms, *International Journal of Psychoanalysis*, 27, pp.99–110.

Kohon, G., 1986, *The British School of Psychoanalysis: The Independent Tradition*, Free Association Books, London.

König, K. 1950, Mignon: An attempt at a History of Curative Education, in *The Contribution of Anthroposophy as an Extension of the Art of Medicine*, School for Spiritual Science, Dornach.

König, K., 1955, *The Superintendent's Report, Camphill Rudolf Steiner Schools 31st January 1952 to 31st January 1955*, Camphill Schools, Aberdeen.

König, K., 1960, The Three Pillars of the Camphill Movement, in K. König, *The Camphill Movement*, Camphill Press, Botton.

König, K., 1965a, Editorial: Three Essentials of Camphill, *The Cresset*, 11, 3 & 4, Michaelmas.

König, K., 1965b, Camphill Brief, Christmas 1965, in Carlo Pietzner (ed.), *Aspects of Curative Education*, Aberdeen University Press, Aberdeen.

Lash, S., & Urry, J., 1987, *The End of Organised Capitalism*, Polity, Cambridge.

Lazerson, M., 1975, Educational Institutions and Mental Subnormality: Notes on Writing a History, in M.J. Begab & S.A. Richardson (eds.), *The Mentally Retarded and Society: A Social Science Perspective*, University Park Press, Baltimore.

Leudar, I., 1981, Strategic Communication in Mental Retardation, in Fraser, W.I. & Grieve, R. (eds.), *Communication with Normal and Retarded Children*, Wright, Bristol.

Leudar, I., 1989, Communicative Environments for Mentally Handicapped People, in Beveridge, M., Conti-Ramsden, G. & Leudar, I. (eds.), *Language and Communication in Mentally Handicapped People*, Chapman & Hall, London, pp.274–300.

Lewin, K., 1947, Frontiers in Group Dynamics, Parts I and II, *Human Relations*, 1, I) pp.5–41, II) pp.143–153.

Lifton, R.J., 1986, *The Nazi Doctors: Medical Killing and the Psychology of Genocide*, Basic Books, New York.

Lowe, K. & De Paiva, S., 1990, *The Evaluation of NIMROD, a Community Based Service for People with Mental Handicap: Client Use of Services*, Mental Handicap in Wales Applied Research Unit, University of Wales College of Medicine, Cardiff.

Lusseyran, J., 1964, *And There was Light*, Heinemann, London.

Machiavelli, N., 1961, *The Prince*, Penguin, Harmondsworth.

Mahony, N., 1979, My Stay and Change at the Henderson Therapeutic Community, in Hinshelwood, R. & Manning, N. (eds), *Therapeutic Communities: Reflections and Progress*, Routledge and Kegan Paul, London.

Main, T.F., 1946, The Hospital as a Therapeutic Institution, *Bulletin of the Menninger Clinic*, 10, pp.66–70.

Main, T.F., 1957, The Ailment, *British Journal of Medical Psychology*, 30, pp.129–145.

Main, T.F., 1975, Some Psychodynamics of Large Groups, in Kreeger, L & de Mare, P. (eds.), *The Large Group*, Constable, London.

Main, T.F., 1983, The Concept of the Therapeutic Community: Variations and Vicissitudes, in Pines, M. (ed.), *The Evolution of Group Analysis*, Routledge and Kegan Paul, London.

Manning, N., 1989, *The Therapeutic Community Movement: Charisma and Routinisation*, Routledge, London.

Manor, O., 1982, The Looking-Glass Effect of Self-Management in a Therapeutic Community, *International Journal of Therapeutic Communities*, 3, 3, pp.138–154.

Marris, P., 1986, *Loss and Change*, Routledge & Kegan Paul, London.

Martin, D. V., 1962, *Adventure in Psychiatry*, Bruno Cassirer, Oxford.

Martin, J. P., 1984, *Hospitals in Trouble*, Blackwell, Oxford.

Matza, D., 1969, *Becoming Deviant*, Prentice Hall, New Jersey.

McGee, J.J., Menolasino, F., Hobbs, D., & Menonsch, P.E., 1987, *Gentle Teaching: a Non-Aversive Approach to Helping Persons with Mental Retardation*, Human Sciences, New York.

Menzies-Lyth, I.E.P., 1970, *The Functioning of Social Systems as a Defence Against Anxiety*, Tavistock Pamphlet No. 3, London.

Menzies-Lyth, I., 1988, *Containing Stress in Institutions*, Free Association Books, London.

Mercer, J.R., 1973, *Labelling the Mentally Retarded*, University of California Press, Berkeley.

Millard, D. W., 1981, Generative Rules and the Therapeutic Community, *British Journal of Medical Psychology*, 54, pp.157–166.

Millard, D. W., 1984, Editorial: Community Care Networks, *International Journal of Therapeutic Communities*, 5, pp.137–139.

Millard, D. W., 1989, Editorial: When is it not a Therapeutic Community?, *International Journal of Therapeutic Communities*, 10, pp.192–194.

Millard, D. W., 1990, *Educated Intuition: Observations on External Staff Consultancy*, Unpublished Lecture, Athens, 8th March, 1990.

Miller, E.J., 1989, *Towards an Organisational Model for Residential Treatment of Adolescents*, (in press).

Miller, E. J. & Gwynne, G. V., 1972, *A Life Apart*, Tavistock, London.

Miller, E.J. & Rice, A.K., 1967, *Systems of Organisation*, Tavistock Publications, London.

Mishra, R., 1984, *The Welfare State in Crisis*, Wheatsheaf, Brighton.

Mittler, P., 1979, *People Not Patients*, Methuen, London.

Moore, B. Jnr., 1970, *Reflections on the Causes of Human Misery and upon Certain Proposals to Eliminate Them*, Allen Lane The Penguin Press, London.

Morgan, G., 1986, *Images of Organisation*, Sage, California.

Moscovici, S., 1984, The Phenomenon of Social Representations, in Farr, R. M. & Moscovici, S. (eds), *Social Representations*, Cambridge University Press, Cambridge; Editions de la Maison des Sciences de l'Homme, Paris.

Muir, E., 1960, *Collected Poems*, Faber & Faber, London.

Murdoch, J. & Anderson, V., 1990, The Management of Down's Syndrome Children and their Families in General Practice, in Fraser, W. (ed.) *Key Issues in Mental Retardation*, Routledge, London.

Niebuhr, R., 1947, *Moral Man and Immoral Society*, Charles Scribners, New York.

Nirje, B., 1969, The Normalisation Principle and its Human Management Implications, in Kugel., R., & Wolfensberger, W., (eds.), *Changing Patterns in Residential Services for the Mentally Retarded*, President's Committee on Mental Retardation, Washington D.C.

Nirje, B., 1970, The Normalisation Principle – Implications and Comments, *Journal of Mental Subnormality*, 16, pp.62–70.

Norris, M., 1983, Changes in Patients during Treatment at the Henderson

Hospital Therapeutic Community during 1977–81, *British Journal of Medical Psychology*, 56, 2, pp.135–147.

Office of Population Censuses and Surveys, 1988, *The Prevalence of Disability among Adults. OPCS Surveys of Disability in Great Britain Report 1*, HMSO, London.

Ogden, T., 1982, *Projective Identification and Psychotherapeutic Technique*, Jason Aronson, New York.

Parker, R., 1981, Tending and Social Policy, in Goldberg, E. M., & Hatch, S. (eds.), *A New Look at the Personal Social Services*, Policy Studies Institute Discussion Paper No.4., London.

Parker, R., 1990, *Safeguarding Standards*, National Institute for Social Work, London.

Parkes, C.M., 1971, Psychosocial Transitions: a Field for Study, *Social Science & Medicine*, pp.101–115.

Piaget, J., 1926, *The Language and Thought of the Child*, Harcourt Brace, New York.

Picture Post, 1949, Edition of 30th April, 1949.

Pietzner, C., 1966, What is Mental Retardation?, in Pietzner, C. (ed.), *Questions of Destiny*, Anthroposophical Press, New York.

Pietzner, C., (Ed.), 1990, *A Candle on the Hill – Images of Camphill Life*, Floris Books, Edinburgh.

Pittock, F., & Potts, M., 1988, Neighbourhood Attitudes to People with a Mental Handicap: a Comparative Study, *British Journal of Mental Subnormality*, 34, 35–46.

Plant, R., 1974, *Community and Ideology*, Routledge & Kegan Paul, London.

Randall, R., 1988, *Action for Carers*, Kings Fund, London.

Rapoport, R., 1960, *Community as Doctor*, Tavistock, London.

Redl, F. & Wineman, D., 1951, *Children Who Hate: The Disorganisation and Breakdown of Behaviour Controls*, Free Press of Glencoe, New York.

Repp, A.C. & Felce, D., 1990, A Micro-Computer System used for Evaluative and Experimental Behavioral Research in Mental Handicap, *Mental Handicap Research*, 3.

Righton, P., 1979, Planned Environment Therapy: A Re-appraisal, *Studies in Environment Therapy*, 3, pp.9–16.

Rose-Ackerman, S., 1982, Mental Retardation and Society: The Ethics and Politics of Normalisation, *Ethics*, 93, 81–101.

Rowitz, L., 1981, Service Paths prior to Clinic Use by Mentally Retarded People: a Retrospective Study, in Bruininks, R.H., Meyers, C.E., Sigford, B.B. & Lakin, K.C., (eds.) *Deinstitutionalisation and Community Adjustment of Mentally Retarded People*, American Association on Mental Deficiency, Washington, D.C.

Royal College of Nursing, 1990, *Prospectus of the RCN/ATC Training Course in Therapeutic Community Practice*, Royal College of Nursing, London.

Royal Commission on Mental Illness and Mental Deficiency (Chairman: Lord Percy), 1957, *Report*, London. HMSO.

Ryan, J. & Thomas, F., 1987, *The Politics of Mental Handicap*, Penguin Books, Harmondsworth.

Scharff, D.E., 1982, *The Sexual Relationship – an Object Relations View of Sex and the Family*, Routledge, London.

Scheidlinger, S., 1968, The Concept of Regression in Group Psychotherapy, *International Journal of Group Psychotherapy*, 18, pp.3–20.

Schein, E., 1969, *Process Consultation*, Addison-Wesley Publishing Co., Reading, Massachusetts.

Schutz, A., 1962, *Collected Papers, Volume 1, The Problem of Social Reality*, Martinus Nijhoff, The Hague.

Scull, A.T., 1977, *Decarceration*, Prentice-Hall, Englewood Cliffs, N.J.

Scull, A.T., 1981, Deinstitutionalisation and the Rights of the Deviant, *Journal of Social Issues*, 37, 3, 6–20.

Serpell, R., 1982, *Intellectual Handicap in a Cross-Cultural Perspective*, Lecture to the 6th International Congress of the International Association for Cross-Cultural Psychology at the University of Aberdeen.

Skinner, B. F., 1948, *Walden Two*, MacMillan, New York.

Sleigh, J., 1987, Community Involvement in the Care and Rehabilitation of the Mentally Retarded, *Journal for Curative Education and Social Therapy*, 6, 3, 1987.

Snare, A. & Christie, N., 1975, Dialogue with Nils Christie, *Issues in Criminology*, 10, 1, Spring, pp.35–47.

Social Services Inspectorate, 1989, *Towards a Climate of Confidence, Report of a National Inspection of Management Arrangements for Public Sector Residential Care for Elderly People*, Department of Health, London.

Sontag, S., 1979, *Illness as Metaphor*, Allen Lane (page references to Penguin edition, 1983), London.

St. Claire, L., 1986, Mental Retardation: Impairment or Handicap? *Disability, Handicap and Society*, 1, pp.233–243.

St. Claire, L., 1989, A Multi-Dimensional Model of Mental Retardation: Impairment, Subnormal Behaviour, Role Failures and Socially Constructed Retardation, *American Journal of Mental Retardation*, 94, 1, pp.88–96.

Steiner, R., 1906, *Lucifer-Gnosis 1905–1906*, translated as *Anthroposophy and the Social Question*, Mercury Press, New York, 1982.

Stockdale, J.E. & Farr, R.M., 1987, *Social Representations of Handicap in Poster Campaigns*, Paper presented at the London conference of the British Psychological Society, December 1987.

Stoneman, Z., Brody, G.H., Davis, C.H. & Crapps, J.M., 1987, Mentally Retarded Children and their Older Same-Sex Siblings: Naturalistic In-Home Observations, *American Journal of Mental Retardation*, 92, pp.290–298.

Sueltze, M. & Keenan, V., 1981, Changes in Family Support Networks over the Life Cycle of Mentally Retarded Persons, *American Journal of Mental Deficiency*, 86, pp.267–274.

Super, C. & Harkness, S., 1986, The Developmental Niche: a Conceptualisation at the Interface of Child and Culture, *International Journal of Behavioral Development*, a, pp.1–25.

Toffler, A., 1970, *Future Shock*, Bodley Head, London.

Tönnies, F., 1955, *Community and Society*, Harper Row, New York.

Twentyman, R., 1989, *The Science and Art of Healing*, Floris Books, Edinburgh.

Vierl, K., 1986, Self-Education and Curative Education, *Journal for Curative Education and Social Therapy*, 5, 3.

Vygotsky, L.S. 1986, *Thought and Language*, M.I.T. Press, Cambridge, Mass.

Weihs, T., 1971, *In Need of Special Care*, Souvenir Press, London.

Weihs, T., 1977, Speech in Acceptance of the Stanley Segal Prize 1977, in C. Hills et al (eds), *Independence and Integration: The School Leaver with Special Needs*, Department of Education, University of Stirling, Stirling.

Whitaker, D.S. & Lieberman, M.A., 1965, *Psychotherapy through the Group Process*, Tavistock, London.

Whiteley, J.S., 1970, The Response of Psychopaths to a Therapeutic Community, *British Journal of Psychiatry*, 116, pp.517–529.

Whiteley, J.S. & Gordon, J., 1979, *Group Approaches in Psychiatry*, Routledge and Kegan Paul, London.

Williams, R., 1975, *The Country and The City*, Paladin, St Albans.

Williams, R., 1976, *Keywords*, Fontana, Glasgow.

Winnicott, D.W., 1965, *The Maturational Processes and the Facilitating Environment – Studies in the Theory of Emotional Development*, Hogarth Press, London.

Winnicott, D.W., 1968, Clinical Regression Compared with Defence Organisation, in Eldred, S. H., & Vanderpol M., (eds.), *Psychotherapy in the Designed Therapeutic Milieu*, International Psychiatry Clinics 5.1, Little and Brown, Boston.

Winnicott, D.W., 1971, *Playing and Reality*, Tavistock Publications, London.

Wolberg, L. R., 1977, *The Technique of Psychotherapy*, (3rd edn.), Grune and Stratton, New York.

Wolfensberger, W., 1972, *Normalisation: The Principle of Normalisation in Human Services*, National Institute on Mental Retardation, Toronto.

Wolfensberger, W., 1980a, A Brief Overview of the Principle of Normalisation, in Flynn, R. & Nitsch, K.E. (eds.), *Normalisation, Social Integration and Community Services*, University Park Press, Baltimore.

Wolfensberger, W., 1980b, The Definition of Normalisation, in Flynn, R. & Nitsch, K.E. (eds.), *Normalisation, Social Integration and Community Services*, University Park Press, Baltimore.

Wolfensberger, W., 1983, Social Role Valorisation: a Proposed New Term for the Principle of Normalisation, *Mental Retardation*, 21, pp.234–239.

Wolfensberger, W. & Thomas, S., 1981, The Principle of Normalisation in Human Services: A Brief Overview, in Lishman, J. (ed.), *Research Highlights Number Two: Normalisation*, Aberdeen People's Press, Aberdeen.

Yeats, W.B., 1924, *The Second Coming: Poetry 1900–1975*, Longman, London.

Name Index

Subject Index

The term 'special needs' and its synoyms are not indexed and all other terms should be read as referring implicitly to 'special needs'.